DATE DUE			
Dec 16 192			

Already published:

THE NEW THEATRE OF EUROPE

Edited by Robert W. Corrigan

Robert Bolt	*A Man For All Seasons*
Alfonso Sastre	*Anna Kleiber*
Notis Peryalis	*Mask of Angels*
Michel de Ghelderode	*Pantagleize*
Ugo Betti	*Corruption in the Palace of Justice*

THE
NEW THEATRE
OF EUROPE
2

Five Contemporary Plays
From the European Stage, Including

MOTHER COURAGE by Bertolt Brecht

THE WICKED COOKS by Günter Grass

VASCO by Georges Schehadé

THE CAGE and **THE SUICIDE** by Mario Fratti

Edited with an Introduction
by
ROBERT W. CORRIGAN

A DELTA BOOK · 1964

A *Delta Book*. Published by Dell Publishing Co., Inc.
750 Third Avenue, New York N.Y. 10017
All rights reserved
Delta (R) TM 755118, Dell Publishing Co., Inc.
Copyright © 1964 by Dell Publishing Co., Inc.

Mother Courage

The Wicked Cooks

Vasco

The Cage

The Suicide

Library of Congress Catalog Card Number: 62-21253
Cover design by Daly Max Std.
First printing—September, 1964
Manufactured in the United States of America

For Norman Rice

TABLE OF CONTENTS

THE DISAVOWAL OF IDENTITY IN THE CONTEMPORARY THEATRE

"We live too variously to live as one."

J. Robert Oppenheimer

No American play in recent years has stirred up quite so much controversy as Arthur Miller's latest work, *After the Fall.* I have no intention of getting embroiled in the argument here, but I believe the situation is worth noting for it is symptomatic of some of the conditions existing in the theatre today. Most of the furor is a reaction to the ways and means that Miller has embodied and developed his hero's attempts to justify his integrity in terms of the search for his own identity. And the play and the author have been either attacked or defended in terms of this search. In fact, if we are to believe Mr. Miller and his critics (and they are certainly not alone in this), the search for identity is the chief preoccupation of the contemporary theatre.

Now, in a way, the theatre has always been centrally concerned with the question of "Who am I?" Beginning with Orestes' mad journey to the Earth's navel in the opening scene of *The Eumenides* in Aeschylus' *Oresteia*, this quest has been a dominant theme in the drama. *Oedipus Rex* is probably the prototype of such a search in the theatre; and just about every great play ever written has touched upon the problem of identity in some way.

At the same time that the theatre has concerned itself with the subject, each of us has had a tendency to talk about the crises involved with the individual's search for his own identity. Each of us desires to know who we really are, as distinct from what others— our parents, siblings, friends, associates, even our enemies—believe or desire us to be. The need to establish a sense of our own identity is a very creative force in our lives (although it is demonstrably destructive, as well), and I am sure that one of the theatre's great appeals is its very concern for identity. In the process of our own search, we are moved by a representation of the search fulfilled. However, when we reflect upon this fulfillment, we discover that the great dramas of identity usually end immediately after the search has been completed; and that ending, though it may be noble and affirming, is more often than not catastrophic. And when we think about it further, we realize that, although the theatre can show the hero discovering his identity, in life this can never happen.

What we call our identity is, in fact, only a convention, a labeling that is descriptive of one or more aspects of our selfhood, but not expressive of our total self. To identify is to fix, or as the dictionary puts it, "to make to be the same; to consider as the same in any relation." Scientists tell us that it is inaccurate for us to think of matter in this way; we know we cannot think of ourselves or others in this way, although at times we may desperately attempt to do so. Personality is always in a state of gradual change. The single being may be compared with other organisms that it resembles; it may be classified, accounted for statistically, subsumed under a type, but its individuality can only be *felt*. Whatever unity, if there is a unity, the human organism maintains at the base of its transformations is something mysterious. To the human being himself, his own coherence is, as Herbert Read once put it, "an organic coherence intuitively based on the real world of sensation."

In life as we experience it, we are conscious of our physical natures, our social situations, and our unique psychic existence; and we live on all three of these levels simultaneously. For this reason it is impossible for us to act or make a choice without some element of human behavior—what we do out of physical necessity or because of social habit—playing a significant role in our decision. At the same time, because of the simultaneity of our being, it is impossible for us to understand completely the individuality of our actions. But in the theatre we see life as pure deed, that is, life in which the arbitrariness of human behavior has been eliminated and in which the mysterious transformations of individuality have been fixed. Thus, in contrast to a person in life, who is recognized by the continuity of his being and finally can only be known through intuition, a character in a play is an "identity" who is defined by the coherence of his acts. The term "identity," then, represents the human individual as an actor, as opposed to the organic concept of personality, which sees a man's actions as only an attribute of, a clue to a being who can be known only through intuition.

All drama of the past is based upon the axiom "By their deeds shall ye know them." The significance of the dramatic hero was revealed by his deeds, and there was a direct relationship between the hero's overt acts and his inner spiritual condition. The significance of Oedipus, for instance, is revealed in his deeds, not by some explanation that he is suffering from an Oedipus complex; and there is a direct relationship between the act of tearing out his own eyes and his solving the riddle of the Sphinx. In most plays, even when a character commits a dissembling deed, it is to deceive the other characters in the play, not the spectators. Certainly one of the chief functions of the soliloquy in Elizabethan drama was to keep the audience continually informed as to what was going on. Hamlet may put an antic disposition on, but not before he tells the audience he is going to do so. For this reason the deeds of a dramatic action were always public, and the characters best suited to drama were men and women who, either by fate or choice, led a public life and whose deeds were of public concern. This explains why traditionally kings, princes, and nobility have been the most suitable subjects for drama.

However, beginning in the nineteenth century the drama began to reflect man's growing distrust in the ability of his senses to comprehend the true nature of reality. Appearances were no longer believed to be direct reflections of ideal reality, like the shadows on the wall of Plato's cave, rather they were thought of as a mask that hides or distorts reality. And as the machine has become an increasingly dominant force in modern life, the direct relation between a man's intention and his deeds has dissolved still further, and public figures have ceased to be our most appropriate heroes because, as W. H. Auden points out in *The Dyer's Hand*, "the good and evil they do depends less upon their characters and intentions than upon the quantity of impersonal force at their disposal."

The growing awareness of this condition has tended to make the modern dramatist, particularly those writing since the Second World War, reject the realm of deeds as the most significant sphere of human action. However, if this is true, and I believe it is, then, no matter what all the critics may say to the contrary, the fact is that the mainstream of the contemporary theatre has not really concerned itself with the search for identity at all. If anything, our playwrights have either underscored the *lack* of modern man's search for identity or they have openly denied the value of such a search. Beginning with the Father's agonizing refusal to be judged by what he had done in the brothel with his stepdaughter in Pirandello's *Six Characters in Search of an Author*, we can trace the modern theatre's increasing tendency to reject the validity of identity. In the most impassioned moment of that play, the Father cries out:

> For the drama lies all in this—in the conscience that I have, that each one of us has. We believe this conscience to be a single thing, but it is many-sided. There is one for this person, and another for that. Diverse consciences. So we have this illusion of being one person for all, of having a personality that is unique in all our acts. But it isn't true. We perceive this when, tragically perhaps, in something we do, we are as it were, suspended, caught up in the air on a kind of hook. Then we perceive that all of us was not in that act, and that it would be an atrocious injustice to judge us by that action alone, as if all our existence were summed up in that one deed.

In short, the Father—like the other characters in the play—does not want to be a character; he does not want to have his personality fixed, and he rebels against the injustice of being identified. Pirandello, like so many modern novelists, and especially Proust, Mann, and Joyce, believed that the traditional concepts of action and character were artificial because they were incapable of expressing the essential flow and change of being. And an increasing number of playwrights have followed suit, so that today most of our serious dramatists seem to sense that Kafka best described modern man's true condition when he wrote in his Notebooks:

> We are in the situation of travelers in a train that has met with an accident in a tunnel, and this at a place where the light of the beginning can no longer be seen, and the light of the end is so very small a glimmer that the gaze must continually search for it and is always losing it again, and, furthermore, both the be-

ginning and the end are not even certainties. Round about us, however, in the confusion of our senses, or in the supersensitiveness of our senses, we have nothing but monstrosities and a kaleidoscopic play of things that is either delightful or exhausting according to the mood and injury of each individual. What shall I do? or: Why should I do it? are not questions to be asked in such places.

One can't ask himself the question, "Who am I?" in such a tunnel, and get a very meaningful or helpful answer.

It is a commonplace that there are no great figures (one can't even think of using the word "hero") in most of the plays of our new writers. But it hasn't been pointed out strongly enough that perhaps the chief reason for this is the fact that these writers are not interested in describing personal histories. The reason there is no Oedipus, Lear, or Macbeth is because, in his concern to show us life as it is, the contemporary playwright has no use for seeing particular men in particular world systems. His only concern is to create in his plays a situation that will reveal the private drama that each man has inside himself and that is enacted every day in the random, apparently meaningless, and undramatic events of our common routine.

"History," said Stephen Daedalus, "is the nightmare from which I must awake." The rapidity of historical change and the apparent powerlessness of the individual to affect collective history has led in the theatre to a retreat from history. Instead of tracing the history of an individual who is born, grows old, and dies—instead of presenting identities—many modern playwrights have devoted their attention to the timeless passionate moments of life, to states of being.

The new playwrights—first in Europe, and now in the United States—are not interested in "imitations of actions"; they want to show "life as it is," and life as it is lacks the direction, the external causality, the cathartic effect of completed events. Like so many painters, composers, poets, and novelists before them, our dramatists are aware that the crises that are so neatly resolved by the linear form of drama are not so neatly resolved in life. To be alive is to be in a continual state of crisis; in life as one crisis is resolved another is always beginning. Today the playwright wants his plays to express the paradox, the contradiction, and the incompleteness of experience; he wants to suggest the raggedness, the confusion, the complexity of motivation, the "discontinuous continuity," and the basic ambiguity of all human behavior. The contemporary playwrights have rejected the traditional concepts of form and character because they are convinced that they are incapable of expressing the "is-ness" of experience. Instead, they have developed a form that might be called, to use the terminology of the new criticism of poetry, "contextual" or "concentric." The structure of these plays, then, is epiphanic; its purpose is to reveal the inner lives of the characters. In such a drama the plot has been twisted into a situation that is to reveal the constantly shifting psychic lives of the characters. Thus, many of the new playwrights, in an attempt to capture "the aimless, unclimactic multiplicity" of their characters' lives, have created a form of drama based on what Marvin Rosenberg has called "the tensions of context, rather than direction, of vertical depth, rather than horizontal movement." In such a form, characters as identities cannot exist.

In rejecting the fixity of identity for the flux of personality, the theatre has followed—as it almost always follows—directions already taken by the other arts. For this reason the innovations in dramatic form that have occurred in recent years were fairly predictable. But since only the dramatist is compelled to deal exclusively with human beings, there is one aspect of the modern theatre's disavowal of identity that is not so readily apparent, but that must be recognized if we are to understand today's drama. Perhaps, the reason that the modern theatre no longer dramatizes the search for identity, in spite of all our talk about modern man's search for it, is because as human beings we have already reversed the process—we have, in fact, tended to become identities in life. Perhaps the dehumanizing forces of industrialized collectivism have shaped our lives in such a way that in our daily existence we have no personality, but have actually become "characters" without our even realizing that such a transformation has occurred.

One of the most difficult roles in the Shakespearean canon to play is Iago. He has baffled actors and critics for better than three hundred years, and he continues to do so. Coleridge attempted to explain him in terms of "motiveless malignancy," and at the other end of the spectrum of *Othello* criticism, E. E. Stoll attempted to resolve the difficulties of the part in terms of the convention of the "calumniator credited." But both of these explanations, and the countless number in between, fail because it is impossible for an actor to play either a "motiveless malignancy" or a convention. However, if the actor tries to find the human wants, aims, and motives of Iago's character that will provide a consistent explanation for his actions, he discovers, if he is honest, that he cannot succeed. And the reason for this is that Iago is not a character in the traditional sense at all; rather, he is a particular kind of personality. A genius like Shakespeare can make him credible, or at least nearly so; but as a type he is difficult, if not impossible, to dramatize adequately. And yet, Iago may well be the prototype of modern man, and if this contention is correct, it may help to explain one of the most difficult problems confronting the contemporary playwright.

In the introduction to the first volume of this series,* I discussed the idea that the central issue facing the theatre of our times is the fact that the traditional drama of the West is based upon the idea of an individual's living in community, and that today such a relationship no longer exists. I pointed out in that book that, since the Renaissance and the Industrial Revolution, we have been moving toward a collective society and that collectivity tends to destroy man's sense of his own individuality. In fact, I went so far as to say that I believed that the average individual of a modern metropolis is no longer an individual at all, but is rather a combination of the various collective interests that meet within him. He was, in short, a collective social personality. I should like to develop this idea further, and particularly as it relates to the plays in this volume.

Many commentators on the contemporary social scene have noted the various ways in which specialization, the cornerstone of all forms of industrialization, has tended to divide the individual. But they usually stop short of pointing out that, once this process has begun, it ultimately invalidates any sense the individual may have of his own identity, for within the collective system only a man's speciality is of value, and his function tends increasingly to be the only source of his identity. (One need only recall the number of times that the first question asked when meeting a stranger is "Who are you with?" Or, how when we introduce even our best of friends, we invariably say "Meet Mr. X, he is a butcher," "a baker," or what have you.) But a sense of identity based on function alone inevitably leads to impersonality. And, in fact, our lives are, for the most part, made up of impersonal relationships of mutual interdependence.

The implications of this shift from a communal to a collective social organization for the institutions of our society are almost frightening in their enormity, but here I am most concerned with the effects that the emergence of the social personality has had upon the theatre.

If it is true that our image of ourselves is to a large degree expressed through our popular heroes, then one of the most significant effects that the emerging social personality has had upon the contemporary imagination is to have changed our popular heroic models. All those heroes of previous ages who supplied us with the images, values, and ethical standards that we sought to emulate and incorporate into our own lives have ceased to have any relevance to the world in which we live today. The Horatio Algers of our grandparents' time are now thought of as slick operators. Similarly the popular imagination has rejected the great work heroes—Franklin, Carnegie, Edison—of the past. In their places, we have substituted (at least currently) Frank Sinatra, Jackie Kennedy, Cary Grant, Colonel Glenn, Willie Mays, or even The Beatles. Specialization has tended to create a new type of hero. Instead of the "whole man" or the rugged individualist, we now have the hero of surfaces, those sandwich-board leaders and celebrities without morality or principle, who are unusually susceptible to corruption, but who are nonetheless fantastically successful in a society where mass communication, audience acceptability, and role-playing skill are the new obligations to greatness.

This shift in heroic types cannot be attributed to a loss of national moral fibre. It is an inevitable consequence of collectivism and a corporateness of specialists. Such a system demands role playing. But it should be pointed out, as many others have already done, that since role playing is not a genuine commitment, it cannot be a strong and durable social bond, however much it looks like one. Nothing characterizes the social personality more accurately than his lack of commitment (even in marriage and friendship); but for the most part we don't notice this shallowness of relationship because of the profusion of superficial feelings, and the ease with which relationships are established in our time.

Modern man has become an expert at generating the appearance of fellowship—even with strangers.

For this reason, I suppose Fred Demara, "The Great Imposter," may well be the perfect symbol of the social personality, and his explanation of his success may well describe the condition that produces the social personality. He remarked: "If you act like you belong somewhere, even people who know you don't belong are hesitant to call you on it. People are so insecure. Deep in their souls they don't feel they belong either." In such a world, success and domination depend upon one's ability to outmanipulate, as it were, others in every situation. And in this sense we are all becoming social personalities. Like Iago, mid-twentieth-century man tends to be an actor whose only reality is the particular role he happens to be playing.

But if this transformation has, in fact, taken place, then the theatre has lost its natural subject. It can no longer celebrate the anguish and the pain, the celebration and the triumph, of a man's search to know who he is and what his place in the universe may be. Rather, our modern playwrights note with increasing horror that modern man has become an actor who is all too willing to have an identity thrust upon him. It is a corporate identity, designed by whatever industrialized collective he happens to be a part of, but it is clearly not his own.

Thus, the central concern of most contemporary dramatists is *not* man's search for his own identity, but rather with the sense of helplessness that the individual must feel if he seeks to face and combat the conflicts of the collective world in which he lives. The great man of our times has ceased to be the doer of heroic deeds, but is the one who is capable of withstanding some of the pressures of a mass society and still manages, somehow, to maintain a face and stance more or less his own.

*   *   *

Probably no character in the contemporary theatre better represents this new kind of heroism than Bertolt Brecht's Mother Courage. Bertolt Brecht (1898–1956) was the prophet for the drama of the collective, and although he never wore his prophet's mantle with ease, he was, nonetheless, the first playwright in the modern theatre to comprehend fully the effects of industrialization and collectivism upon our social structures, and he realized that these forces were creating new kinds of conflicts, which were not being dealt with in the theatre. As early as 1925, he wrote: "When one sees that our world of today no longer fits into the drama, then it is merely that the drama no longer fits into the world." Brecht's epic theatre is an attempt to express the drama of a world that was gradually being transformed from a traditional community into a highly organized collective state. In using the term "epic theatre," Brecht was thinking of the drama as episodic and narrative and, therefore, more like the structure of an epic poem than the well-made play. Like the "Absurdists," but for different reasons, he rejected the traditional Aristotelian idea that a play should have a beginning, middle, and end, because he believed that the dramatic processes of history do not end, but only move on to the next episode. Brecht wanted to translate this episodic nature of history into the theatre, and to this end he took the epic form as it had been developed by his fellow countryman and early collaborator, Erwin Piscator, and shaped it so that it was capable of expressing the dramatic conflicts of our time.

Traditionally, in Western drama, the hero is conceived as a man acting with virtue and courage in the face of powerful opposing forces. Brecht rejected this kind of hero as the necessity of an evil and now outmoded age. ("Unhappy is the land that needs a hero!" —*Galileo*) When viewed in the context of an industrialized collective society, Brecht believed the actions of such "old-fashioned" heroes tend to be little more than the empty posturings of the foolish (Swiss Cheese), the headstrong (The Cook), or the selfish (Eilif). Genuine goodness, such as Kattrin's, is equally irrelevant. While her behavior in the play seems to have a mute nobility about it, Brecht makes it very clear that her dramatic function in the play is to reveal the futility of the instinct to goodness and the impossibility of its surviving in a world in which the ever-growing cult of the celebrity, with its tendency to value charm without character, showmanship without real ability, bodies without minds, and information without wisdom, celebrates the triumph of ordinariness. ("Whenever there are great virtues, it's a sure sign something's wrong. . . . But in a good country the virtues wouldn't be necessary. Everybody could be quite ordinary, middling, and for all of me cowards."—Mother Courage in *Mother*

Courage.) In fact, beginning with A Man's a Man, the idea that the assertion of individuality in the name of virtue is the chief cause of human failure in a collective society is a recurring and dominant theme in almost all of Brecht's plays. It is central to the actions of both The Good Woman of Setzuan and The Caucasian Chalk Circle, and in Mother Courage the idea is more fully developed than in any other play in the modern repertoire. (Although it should be pointed out that here, as elsewhere in Brecht's work, a basic contradiction exists. While it is true that Brecht sees such characters as Bloody Five (A Man's a Man), the Young Comrade (Measures Taken), Joan Dark (St. Joan of the Stockyards), Puntila (Puntila and His Servant Matti), and Kattrin (Mother Courage) as failures because they give in to their human feelings and good instincts, paradoxically, he also believes that to be overwhelmed by the gratuitous impulse to do a good act is the beginning of freedom. These constant contradictions—in language, theme, structure, and characterization—in each of his plays certainly account for the ambiguity of our response to them, as well as for the difficulty most people have in assessing them.)

Mother Courage is a new breed of hero. Like Iago, her actions lack consistency of motivation unless she is viewed as a social personality. But unlike her Shakespearean prototype, she is not a villain, but is presented as a representation of the only positive attitude toward good possible in the modern world. Brecht may use his audiences' habitual responses concerning the nature of heroism as a foil to achieve his effects, but finally, if Mother Courage does achieve a kind of new world heroic stature, it is precisely because she is willing and able to sacrifice her humanity and her individuality to the collective system of which she is a part and which she affirms to the end.

However, Brecht's most daring achievement in this play—one of the great achievements of the contemporary drama, and one that has and will continue to be used by others—is his use of war as an all-encompassing metaphor for the modern world, and his presentation of Mother Courage, who lives off the war and continues to exist because of it, as the symbol of the ordinary human condition. Contrary to what many critics say, Mother Courage is not a pacifistic tract, nor is Brecht the playwright a polemicist. In a recent interview, Jean-Paul Sartre was talking about Brecht, and he made a most significant comment about Brecht's intentions as a playwright. "What Brecht wanted," he said, "was to provoke what Plato called 'the source of all philosophy,' that is wonder, by making the familiar unfamiliar." Seen in this light, *Mother Courage* is not an attack on war, but an attempt to show all aspects of that war which is the central fact of the contemporary human condition. From the ironical speech of the Top Sergeant on the "horrors" of peace in the first scene, it is clear that Brecht is very much aware of the negative and destructive aspects of our warring condition, but other parts of the play make it equally as clear that war does make money, which we hold dear; war does create courage, which we admire; war does support the established institutions of society, which we want to maintain; and war does promote a sense of love and brotherhood, which we find valuable. As the play ends, Mother Courage is seen trudging after another regiment. In her (our) circumstances she cannot do otherwise. The tragedy of the situation, indeed, if it is a tragedy, is that her perception of what is wrong cannot alter her situation as it traditionally does in tragedy. In *Mother Courage* the situation completely dominates the individual. Brecht may not have been happy about this, but he has been one of the few playwrights in our time who was capable of facing up to the realities of life in an industrialized collective society without having to abdicate his responsibility as an artist. *Mother Courage* is an important play in the history of the theatre because it is articulate testimony that to destroy the traditional humanist concept of the individual does not necessarily mean a loss of stature in the theatre, nor the disappearance of dramatic conflict. In his willingness to employ new dramatic forms, a new approach to character, and a different kind of theatrical language, Brecht—unlike so many of his fellow playwrights who seem to have been struck dumb, or at least made inarticulate by the enormities of the modern world—has discovered a way of expressing the complexity, multiplicity, variety, and even the contradiction of a collective world and still maintain that unity of form which is essential for art.

Probably no play written in the past decade is a more perfect complement to *Mother Courage* than *The History of Vasco* by Georges Schehadé (1910—   ). Written in 1956 and first produced in Zurich by Jean-Louis Barrault and Madelaine Renaud in the same year, *Vasco* is similar to Brecht's masterpiece in many significant ways: it, too, has an episodic structure; it is set in the past (a strategy that is increasingly used by our playwrights as a means of coping with the modern world in dramatic terms); and finally, like Brecht, Schehadé uses war as a metaphor for the modern world, and his hero is a wandering "everyman" helplessly caught up in that war at the same time that he is spiritually sustained by it. These similarities are at once superficial and significant—superficial, in that they do not tell us much about the plays themselves, and significant because they indicate an important new trend in the contemporary theatre; for although they are almost diametrically opposed to each other in theme and point of view, Vasco and Mother Courage are nearly identical in dramatic structure and poetic conception.

The most interesting aspect of Schlehadé's work is his conception of the hero. The modern theatre is rapidly learning to live without heroes. The reasons for this are numerous—the loss of belief in permanent and widely accepted values, the inevitable tendency towards leveling in a democratic society, the increase of psychological knowledge, etc.—but very few people seem to have noticed that the disappearance of heroes in our theatre is an inevitable result of industrialized collectivism.

Traditionally, heroes were not necessarily good people; but, whether right or wrong, they always commanded our moral attention. We take them seriously because we believe they have an heroic destiny and because they are struggling with significant issues that are related to the fulfillment of that destiny. Only folk literature, with its iconoclastic wisdom, occasionally protested against the assumption that destiny is determined by the quality of a man's personality. More often than not in folk art, the clown or the nincompoop gets the hero's reward by accident or sheer luck. But an industrialized society, in its open-ended concern for increased expansion, production, and profit, tends to reject the idea of destiny and espouses the belief in progress, and is thus an inhospitable ambience for great men of destiny. This is probably the reason that so many modern dramatists tend to be more interested in man's fate rather than his destiny, why revelation (since fate can only be revealed) has replaced action in the contemporary theatre.

Schehadé's great significance is that he seems to be reversing this trend; in each of his five plays he has attempted to restore the sense of destiny in the theatre, without blinding himself to the realities of our world. Vasco is a hero with a virgin heart, an alien in a disillusioned, war-torn world. He is one of those happy wanderers who embody Yeats' belief that the fool is the paradox of ultimate wisdom. He sees too much, and not enough. Using a structure of mythical embarkment, Schehadé has Vasco journey through the fields of battle, first to find the General to cut his hair and then to find Marguerite. He ultimately fails and is put to death, but in the process of his search Vasco underscores both the fatuity of a world at war and the necessity in such a world for that kind of aspiration which seeks to surpass the boundaries of the spirit's life. Vasco, in his blind naiveté, has a great impact on the lives of all those about him and his death is not in vain, but in the end his innocence is too fragile to survive the war of life.

The play evokes both the myth of the wanderer and an inverted image of history's great explorer of new frontiers, and Schehadé fuses these two elements into a fairy-tale reality that becomes increasingly bizarre as the action unfolds. Vasco is a child of language —his coherence as a character is poetic, not psychological—and he is born not of history but of a verbal design. In the tradition of Giraudoux, Schehadé has created a theatre rich in its metaphoric associations and tough, yet delicate, in texture. He has not abdicated, as so many of his contemporaries in France have done, his responsibility to language in the theatre, but has used all the resources of theatre poetry to create a drama that embraces comedy, fantasy, regret, nostalgia, and a melancholic sadness. The play has no message, for as Schehadé says in his most recent play, *The Voyage*, "Who can tell the story of the wind?" but when one has finished *Vasco* he has the sense that the man who would strive to be himself in this world is a fool and is certain not to survive. However, we know such fools must be suffered gladly, for Schehadé makes us conscious of the worth of a man's search for his destiny no matter how futile the effort may be.

Günter Grass (1927–   ) is best known in this country as a novelist, the author of the highly acclaimed and widely received *The Tin Drum*. However, he began his writing career as a dramatist and wrote five plays before beginning his novel, and the most impressive of these plays is *The Wicked Cooks*, which was written in 1957. *The Tin Drum* is an extremely complex and symbolic book that has a verbal density that is seldom found and rarely equalled in modern fiction. These same qualities are also to be found in *The Wicked Cooks,* which is a complex allegorical drama dealing with the impossibility of maintaining a sense of individuality in a commodity-oriented society. It is an extremely difficult play, and runs the risk of being incomprehensible in the theatre (one cannot help but recall Moss Hart's irreverent references to allegory in the theatre in *Light Up The Sky*); but it does have a zany and wild theatricality about it, and if it were properly produced it might just possibly provide a refreshing (and hopefully, rewarding) change of pace for the contemporary theatre.

The "Cooks" of the title are the promoters and entrepreneurs of a capitalistic society, and Grass tells us that in such a world these cooks are countless in number and are, and always have been, wicked. As the play opens, these purveyors of salvation for profit are trying to force the Count to reveal his secret recipe for "gray soup" (the secret of life) so they can improve their business. Only the Count has the recipe, a sense of what his own life means, and this is what makes him attractive and gives him a vitality that other people lack but desperately want to possess. The Count is, in fact, not a count at all, but a commoner named Herbert Schymanski. It is his recipe that transforms this "everyman" into "someone." Because there is a market for the soup—everyone who has tasted it wants more—the cooks, those panderers of life, want to get it for they cannot let it exist without marketing it.

In the second act we are presented with a series of scenes in which Grass shows what the recipe is not. It is not the church or some form of traditional religion, for the rites of orthodoxy are maimed. It is not art or the life of so-called creativity. And it is not to be found in the usual patterns of family relationship. All the inherited solutions and dependencies are inadequate in the world of the wicked cooks.

In the third and fourth acts we witness the cooks planning their strategies to get the recipe and then going to work on the Count. The tone of these scenes is intentionally ambiguous, and it is difficult to tell whether we are observing the board meeting of a huge industrial empire or a reenactment of the Crime Syndicate's Appalachian meeting. After the Count has been brought by force to the meeting, the cooks first try to cajole and persuade him to tell his secret; then they try to bargain and buy it; and finally they resort to "the one and only truth," force (the spoon). All these

attempts fail, and it is only when the cook Vasco discovers the
Count's Achilles' heel—his feelings for Martha—that he willingly
capitulates:

> VASCO: You are silent, Count. But you are not silent because I am
> wrong, but because I am right and I have touched you on a
> sore spot! So—let people talk, I said. Let them say that the
> Count has no heart. But now I know you have and that I have
> touched it! Right? Have I?
> THE COUNT: Yes, Vasco, you have. You are a great discoverer,
> after all.

And so for love, the Count is willing to give up the recipe if only
the cooks will give him a chance to enjoy it first with Martha
alone. The cooks agree and a contract is signed.

The last act opens with the Count and Martha happily together
at an idyllic country house. Soon the cooks come to claim the recipe
and the Count discovers that, in living his love, he has lost the
recipe. More accurately, he rediscovers that the recipe is not a
recipe at all, but a way of life. In an attempt to explain this to the
cooks, he says:

> I have told you over and over again, it's not a recipe—it's an
> experience, a living knowledge, a way of life. You must know
> that no cook has ever succeeded in making this soup twice.

Vasco alone understands this, but the rest of the cooks, knowing
that their consumers want a recipe and that it is their business to
provide one, insist on having one even if the Count has none
to reveal. Since he can tell them nothing, he must be exterminated
and the Count and Martha are killed.

Such an account of the play—and this is about the only strategy
a critic can employ—is bound to be inadequate. And Grass, himself,
indicates the danger of too much symbolism when he has the
Count remark in the third act: "For a while there I almost had
the feeling that I was being confronted with a symbol, or—worse
yet—that I was going to have to spend the rest of this night under
the burden of symbolism." I feel certain that many readers and
audiences will think they have spent the whole evening under such
a burden after they have experienced Grass' play. However, through
all the symbolism there emerges the unforgettable character of the
Count, a man who has achieved nobility because he has a stance of

his own. The wicked cooks of our world will market this kind of individuality if they can; but if it exists of itself and not as a product, it is dangerous and must be destroyed. Such acts of destruction do not bother the cooks; rather than bemoan the loss, they go off immediately to begin the search for a new recipe.

Unlike the other plays in this volume, the dramas of the Italian playwright, Mario Fratti (1927–   ), are more traditional in form, theme, and character. This is not to imply that Fratti is not a powerful writer, but we are not conscious of that sense of rebellion which characterizes so much of the serious contemporary theatre when we read his work. He is not even characteristically Italian; there is none of the tortured intellectuality that we associate with Pirandello, nor that quality of metaphoric explosiveness which informs Ugo Betti's plays. Fratti's plays are tight, safe, sure; they have a directness of style that precludes ambiguity and insures theatrical effectiveness. In a time when the theatre seems to be celebrating obscurity, Fratti stands firm for simplicity and the importance of immediate communication in the theatre. In a note on his work, he wrote: "I am aware. I believe in the possibility of man becoming aware. By writing plays I hope to communicate my awareness. Because I believe in man, man notwithstanding."

The Cage is Fratti's most recent play (although he is presently completing one to be entitled *The Refrigerator*), and it is both a melodramatic story of a triangle that ends in a bizarre murder, and a serious investigation of a man's inability to cope with the horrors of life. The play's two central characters are Cristiano, who is afraid of and disgusted by life that he has literally locked himself in a cage, and Chiara, his unhappy sister-in-law, who is seeking a way to escape from her miserable marriage without dishonor. Fratti's greatest accomplishment in the play, apart from the overriding metaphor of the cage itself, is his use of Chekhov's writings as a means of dramatizing Cristiano's attempts to escape from all human contact. It is well known that many of Chekhov's characters, in the awareness of their own inadequacy and in their failure to relate to others, seek comfort in words—their own, and more significantly, those of great writers. In their attempts to identify with the more perfect worlds of art, they vainly hope to compensate for their own botched existence; while, in fact, the very need to aestheticize life is a sure sign of their failure. Fratti uses the same device—it is the central conceit of the play—and underscores it by having Cristiano quote Chekhov continually and exclusively: he lives all experience, his own and that of others, through the words of Chekhov. Cristiano thinks the world is a jungle (which it well may be) and cannot cope with life; he is desirous but afraid of sex; he abhors all thought of work; and he cannot stand contact in any form with others. He has locked himself in the cage to protect himself from the world, and he spends all of his time reading and memorizing the works of Chekhov.

He is befriended by his voluptuous sister-in-law, Chiara, who, as much out of unhappiness as anything else, begins to talk with him. Gradually, feelings of love and desire begin to stir in Cristiano—he, significantly, quotes Chekhov less and less—and he wants to come out of the cage only to discover that it is as much a trap as it is a refuge. It suddenly dawns on Chiara that she can use Cristiano as a means of getting rid of her brutal husband, and the last half of the play is a fascinating *malentendu* in which Chiara prepares for Pietro's death. Frankly, the murder and Chiara's betrayal of Cristiano are not completely convincing. There are two reasons for this, one cultural and the other dramaturgic: Given the *mores* of Catholic Italy, Chiara cannot leave her husband, no matter how unpleasant he may be, for her lover without being considered a whore. Since she is a typically middle-class matron she could not stand this, so she must plot to get rid of Pietro within the bounds of propriety. When we understand this, her desire to have him killed is sufficiently motivated. The dramaturgic flaw, however, is more telling. The ending lacks believability because Fratti has not, to my mind, established clearly enough early in the play that Chiara has a lover and that she is using (perhaps unconsciously) Cristiano as a tool to achieve her release. Her part in the relationship with Cristiano, if not misleading, is certainly not clear. But Fratti does make it quite clear that there are no villiains in his plays, and in his already-mentioned notes he explains why we should not fault the ending of the play on moral grounds:

> In *The Suicide* the husband appears to be a monster of cruelty. He is not. In *The Cage*, Chiara appears to be a monster of cruelty. She is not. They are not responsible for what is happening around them. They only struggle to survive, which is

human and justifiable. They do not *see* that they are the cause of grief; they do not see that their victims are their friends.

Finally, however, it is the character of the tortured Cristiano that haunts us. He is the little man, who is sensitive and not without talent, who lives lonely and afraid in a world that is already too large and brutal for him. He is not an everyman, but he is certainly symbolic of that fear in each of us which drives us—at least occasionally—to those cages from which we seek to escape the seemingly unconquerable pressures of everyday reality. Fratti is not afraid of facing this reality and he believes that one of the chief functions of the theatre is to provide a direct confrontation with it. He writes:

> If the characters in my plays do not see, do not realize the harm they do, all the more reason why the average man does not comprehend this struggle to survive when he witnesses it in the streets around him. Cruelty and the victims of cruelty do not move him. He can turn his back on them whenever they demand too much. But for the spectator in the theatre there is no escape. He cannot turn away. He must be aware.

All of the plays in this volume force us to such an awareness, and for this reason I believe they will take their place in the tradition of important theatre. The theatre must, and always has at its greatest moments, expressed what men have felt, and I am convinced that people will not go much longer to a theatre that does not deal with those conflicts which are central to the lives of its audience, nor will they be content to listen to representations of their own inarticulacy. We come to the theatre to hear what we cannot express for ourselves; to have crystallized for us emotions that we bear within us in solution. Sometimes we come to the theatre to escape out of ourselves; but we also come to escape into ourselves by sharing emotionally in the life of the characters on the stage. The dilemma confronting the contemporary theatre is to make this possible, and I believe the five plays in this volume have in large measure succeeded.

—*Robert W. Corrigan*

Pittsburgh
Spring, 1964

MOTHER COURAGE
and her Children

A Chronicle of the Thirty Years' War

Bertolt Brecht

English version by Eric Bentley

CHARACTERS

MOTHER COURAGE
KATTRIN, her dumb daughter
EILIF, her elder son
SWISS CHEESE, her younger son
RECRUITING OFFICER
SERGEANT
COOK
SWEDISH COMMANDER
CHAPLAIN
ORDNANCE OFFICER
YVETTE POTTIER
MAN WITH THE BANDAGE
ANOTHER SERGEANT
OLD COLONEL
CLERK
YOUNG SOLDIER
OLDER SOLDIER
PEASANT
PEASANT WOMAN
YOUNG MAN
OLD WOMAN
ANOTHER PEASANT
ANOTHER PEASANT WOMAN
YOUNG PEASANT
LIEUTENANT
VOICE

ACKNOWLEDGEMENT

I have been at work on the translating of *Mother Courage* since 1950. I have acknowledged the help I received in making the first two versions of it that I brought out. For this, the complete text just published by the Grove Press in 1963, I received further help and counsel from Dr. Hugo Schmidt.

E.B.
1963

Scene One

Spring, 1624. In Dalarna, the SWEDISH COMMANDER Oxenstierna is recruiting for the campaign in Poland. The canteen woman Anna Fierling, commonly known as MOTHER COURAGE, loses a son.

Highway outside a town. A SERGEANT *and a* RECRUITING OFFICER *stand shivering.*

THE RECRUITING OFFICER: How the hell can you line up a squadron in a place like this? You know what I keep thinking about, Sergeant? Suicide. I'm supposed to knock four platoons together by the twelfth—four platoons the Chief's asking for! And they're so friendly around here, I'm scared to go to sleep at night. Suppose I do get my hands on some character and squint at him so I don't notice he's pigeon-chested and has varicose veins. I get him drunk and relaxed, he signs on the dotted line. I pay for the drinks, he steps outside for a minute. I have a hunch I should follow him to the door, and am I right? Away he's gone like a louse from a scratch. You can't take a man's word any more, Sergeant. There's no loyalty left in the world, no trust, no faith, no sense of honor. I'm losing my confidence in mankind, Sergeant.

THE SERGEANT: What they could use around here is a good war. What else can you expect with peace running wild all over the place? You know what the trouble with peace is? No organization. And when do you get organization? In a war. Peace is one big waste of equipment. Anything goes, no one gives a damn. See the way they eat? Cheese on pumpernickel, bacon on the cheese? Disgusting! How many horses have they got in this town? How many young men? Nobody knows! They haven't bothered to count 'em! That's peace for you! I've been in places where they haven't had a war for seventy years and you know what? The people haven't even been given names! They don't know who they are! It takes a war to fix that. In a war, everyone registers, everyone's name's on a list. Their shoes are stacked, their corn's in the bag, you count it all up—cattle, men, *et cetera*—and you take it away! That's the story: no organization, no war!

THE RECRUITING OFFICER: It's the God's truth.

THE SERGEANT: Of course, a war's like any good deal: hard to get going. But when it does get moving, it's a pisser, and they're all scared of peace, like a dice player who can't stop—'cause when peace comes they have to pay up. Of course, *until* it gets going, they're just as scared of war, it's such a novelty!

THE RECRUITING OFFICER: Hey, look, here's a canteen wagon. Two women and a couple of fellows. Stop the old lady, Sergeant. And if there's nothing doing this time, you won't catch me freezing my ass in the April wind any longer.

[*A harmonica is heard. A canteen wagon rolls on, drawn by two young fellows.* MOTHER COURAGE *is sitting on it with her dumb daughter,* KATTRIN.]

MOTHER COURAGE: A good day to you, Sergeant!

THE SERGEANT [*Barring the way.*]: Good day to *you*! Who d'you think *you* are?

MOTHER COURAGE: Tradespeople.

[*She sings*]

> Stop all the troops: here's Mother Courage!
> Hey, Captain, let them come and buy!
> For they can get from Mother Courage
> Boots they will march in till they die!
> Your marching men do not adore you
> (Packs on their backs, lice in their hair)
> But it's to death they're marching for you
> And so they need good boots to wear!
> > Christians, awake! Winter is gone!
> > The snows depart! Dead men sleep on!
> > Let all of you who still survive
> > Get out of bed and look alive!
>
> You men will walk till they are dead, sir,

But cannot fight, sir, unless they eat.
The blood they spill for you is red, sir,
What fires that blood, sir, is my red meat.
Cannon is rough on empty bellies:
First with my meat they should be crammed.
Then let them go and find where hell is
And give my greetings to the damned!
    Christians, awake! Winter is gone!
    The snows depart! Dead men sleep on!
    Let all of you who still survive
    Get out of bed and look alive!

THE SERGEANT: Halt! Where are you from, riffraff?

EILIF: Second Finnish Regiment!

THE SERGEANT: Where are your papers?

MOTHER COURAGE: Papers?

SWISS CHEESE: But this is Mother Courage!

THE SERGEANT: Never heard of her. Where'd she get a name like that?

MOTHER COURAGE: They call me Mother Courage 'cause I was afraid I'd be ruined, so I drove through the bombardment of Riga like a madwoman, with fifty loaves of bread in my cart. They were going moldy, what else could I do?

THE SERGEANT: No funny business! Where are your papers?

MOTHER COURAGE [Rummaging among papers in a tin box and clambering down from her wagon.]: Here, Sergeant! Here's a missal—I got it in Altötting to wrap my cucumbers in. Here's a map of Moravia—God knows if I'll ever get there—the birds can have it if I don't. And here's a document saying my horse hasn't got hoof and mouth disease—pity he died on us, he cost fifteen guilders, thank God I didn't pay it. Is that enough paper?

THE SERGEANT: Are you pulling my leg? Well, you've got another guess coming. You need a license and you know it.

MOTHER COURAGE: Show a little respect for a lady and don't go telling these grown children of mine I'm pulling anything of yours. What would I want with you? My license in the Second Protestant Regiment is an honest face. If you wouldn't know how to read it, that's not my fault, I want no rubber stamp on it anyhow.

THE RECRUITING OFFICER: Sergeant, we have a case of insubordination on our hands. Do you know what we need in the army?—Discipline!

MOTHER COURAGE: I was going to say sausages.

THE SERGEANT: Name?

MOTHER COURAGE: Anna Fierling.

THE SERGEANT: So you're all Fierlings.

MOTHER COURAGE: I was talking about me.

THE SERGEANT: And I was talking about your children.

MOTHER COURAGE: Must they all have the same name? [*Pointing to the elder son.*] This fellow, for instance, I call him Eilif Noyocki. Why? He got the name from his father who told me he was called Koyocki. Or was it Moyocki? Anyhow, the lad remembers him to this day. Only the man he remembers is someone else, a Frenchman with a pointed beard. But he certainly has his father's brains—that man could whip the breeches off a farmer's backside before he could turn around. So we all have our own names.

THE SERGEANT: You're all called something different?

MOTHER COURAGE: Are you pretending you don't understand?

THE SERGEANT [*Pointing at the younger son.*]: He's Chinese, I suppose.

MOTHER COURAGE: Wrong again. Swiss.

THE SERGEANT: After the Frenchman?

MOTHER COURAGE: Frenchman? What Frenchman? Don't confuse the issue, Sergeant, or we'll be here all day. He's Swiss, but he happens to be called Feyos, a name that has nothing to do with his father, who was called something else—a military engineer, if you please, and a drunkard.

[SWISS CHEESE *nods, beaming; even* KATTRIN *smiles.*]

THE SERGEANT: Then how come his name's Feyos?

MOTHER COURAGE: Oh, Sergeant, you have no imagination. Of *course* he's called Feyos: when he came, I was with a Hungarian. He didn't mind. He had a floating kidney, though he never touched a drop. He was a very *honest* man. The boy takes after him.

THE SERGEANT: But that wasn't his father!

MOTHER COURAGE: I said: he took after him. I call him Swiss Cheese. Why? Because he's good at pulling wagons. [*Pointing to her daughter.*] And that is Kattrin Haupt, she's half German.

THE SERGEANT: A nice family, I must say!

MOTHER COURAGE: And we've seen the whole wide world together
—this wagonload and me.

THE SERGEANT: We'll need all that in writing. [*He writes.*] You're
from Bamberg in Bavaria. What are you doing *here*?

MOTHER COURAGE: I can't wait till the war is good enough to
come to Bamberg.

THE RECRUITING OFFICER: And you two oxen pull the cart. Jacob
Ox and Esau Ox! D'you ever get out of harness?

EILIF: Mother! May I smack him in the puss? I'd like to.

MOTHER COURAGE: I'd like *you* to stay where you are. And now,
gentlemen, what about a brace of pistols? Or a belt? Sergeant?
Yours is worn clean through.

THE SERGEANT: It's something else *I'm* looking for. These lads of
yours are straight as birch trees, strong limbs, massive chests. . . .
What are such fine specimens doing out of the army?

MOTHER COURAGE [*Quickly.*]: A soldier's life is not for sons of
mine!

THE RECRUITING OFFICER: Why not? It means money. It means
fame. Peddling shoes is woman's work. [*To* EILIF.] Step this
way and let's see if that's muscle or chicken fat.

MOTHER COURAGE: It's chicken fat. Give him a good hard look,
and he'll fall right over.

THE RECRUITING OFFICER: Yes, and kill a calf in the falling!
[*He tries to hustle* EILIF *away.*]

MOTHER COURAGE: Let him alone! He's not for you!

THE RECRUITING OFFICER: He called my face a puss. That is an
insult. The two of us will now go and settle the affair on the
field of honor.

EILIF: Don't worry, Mother, I can handle him.

MOTHER COURAGE: Stay here. You're never happy till you're in a
fight. He has a knife in his boot and he knows how to use it.

THE RECRUITING OFFICER: I'll draw it out of him like a milk tooth.
Come on, young fellow!

MOTHER COURAGE: Officer, I'll report you to the Colonel, and he'll
throw you in jail. His lieutenant is courting my daughter.

THE SERGEANT: Go easy. [*To* MOTHER COURAGE.] What have you
got against the service, wasn't his own father a soldier? Didn't
you say he died a soldier's death?

MOTHER COURAGE: This one's just a baby. You'll lead him like a lamb to the slaughter. I know you, you'll get five guilders for him.

THE RECRUITING OFFICER [To EILIF.]: First thing you know, you'll have a lovely cap and high boots, how about it?

EILIF: Not from you.

MOTHER COURAGE: "Let's you and me go fishing," said the angler to the worm. [To SWISS CHEESE.] Run and tell everybody they're trying to steal your brother! [She draws a knife.] Yes, just you try, and I'll cut you down like dogs! We sell cloth, we sell ham, we are peaceful people!

THE SERGEANT: You're peaceful all right: your knife proves that. Why, you should be ashamed of yourself. Give me that knife, you hag! You admit you live off the war, what else could you live off? Now tell me, how can we have a war without soldiers?

MOTHER COURAGE: Do they have to be mine?

THE SERGEANT: So that's the trouble. The war should swallow the peach stone and spit out the peach, hm? Your brood should get fat off the war, but the poor war must ask nothing in return, it can look after itself, can it? Call yourself Mother Courage and then get scared of the war, your breadwinner? Your sons aren't scared, I know that much.

EILIF: Takes more than a war to scare me.

THE SERGEANT: Correct! Take me. The soldier's life hasn't done me any harm, has it? I enlisted at seventeen.

MOTHER COURAGE: You haven't reached seventy.

THE SERGEANT: I will, though.

MOTHER COURAGE: Above ground?

THE SERGEANT: Are you trying to rile me, telling me I'll die?

MOTHER COURAGE: Suppose it's the truth? Suppose I see it's your fate? Suppose I know you're just a corpse on furlough?

SWISS CHEESE: She can look into the future. Everyone says so.

THE RECRUITING OFFICER: Then by all means look into the sergeant's future. It might amuse him.

THE SERGEANT: I don't believe in that stuff.

MOTHER COURAGE: Helmet!

[The SERGEANT gives her his helmet.]

THE SERGEANT: It means less than a crap in the grass. Anything for a laugh.

MOTHER COURAGE [Taking a sheet of parchment and tearing it in two.]: Eilif, Swiss Cheese, Kattrin! So shall we all be torn in two if we let ourselves get too deep into this war! [*To the* SERGEANT.] I'll give you the bargain rate, and do it free. Watch! Death is black, so I draw a black cross.

SWISS CHEESE: And the other she leaves blank, see?

MOTHER COURAGE: I fold them, put them in the helmet, and mix 'em up together, the way we're all mixed up together from our mother's womb on. Now draw!

[*The* SERGEANT *hesitates.*]

THE RECRUITING OFFICER [*To* EILIF.]: I don't take just anybody. I'm choosy. And you've got guts, I like that.

THE SERGEANT [*Fishing around in the helmet.*]: It's silly. Means as much as blowing your nose.

SWISS CHEESE: The black cross! Oh, his number's up!

THE RECRUITING OFFICER: Don't let them get under your skin. There aren't enough bullets to go around.

THE SERGEANT [*Hoarsely.*]: You cheated me!

MOTHER COURAGE: You cheated yourself the day you enlisted. And now we must drive on. There isn't a war every day in the week, we must get to work.

THE SERGEANT: Hell, you're not getting away with this! We're taking that bastard of yours with *us!*

EILIF: I'd like that, Mother.

MOTHER COURAGE: Quiet—you Finnish devil, you!

EILIF: And Swiss Cheese wants to be a soldier, too.

MOTHER COURAGE: That's news to me. I see I'll have to draw lots for all three of you. [*She goes to the back to draw the crosses on bits of paper.*]

THE RECRUITING OFFICER [*To* EILIF.]: People've been saying the Swedish soldier is religious. That kind of loose talk has hurt us a lot. One verse of a hymn every Sunday—and then only if you have a voice. . . .

MOTHER COURAGE [*Returning with the slips and putting them in the* SERGEANT'*s helmet.*]: So they'd desert their old mother, would they, the scoundrels? They take to war like a cat to cream. But I'll consult these slips, and they'll see the world's no promised land, with a "Join up, son, you're officer material!" Sergeant, I'm afraid for them, very afraid they won't get through this war. They have terrible qualities, all three. [*She holds the helmet out to* EILIF.] There. Draw your lot. [EILIF *fishes in the helmet, unfolds a slip. She snatches it from him.*] There you have it: a cross. Unhappy mother that I am, rich only in a mother's sorrows! He dies. In the springtime of his life, he must go. If he's a soldier, he must bite the dust, that's clear. He's too brave, like his father. And if he doesn't use his head, he'll go the way of all flesh, the slips prove it. [*Hectoring him.*] Will you use your head?

EILIF: Why not?

MOTHER COURAGE: It's using your head to stay with your mother. And when they make fun of you and call you a chicken, just laugh.

THE RECRUITING OFFICER: If you're going to wet your pants, I'll try your brother.

MOTHER COURAGE: I told you to laugh! Laugh! Now it's your turn, Swiss Cheese. You should be a better bet, you're honest. [*He fishes in the helmet.*] Why are you giving that slip such a funny look? You've drawn a blank for sure. It can't be there's a cross on it. It can't be I'm going to lose *you*. [*She takes the slip.*] A cross? Him too! Could it be 'cause he's so simple? Oh, Swiss Cheese, you'll be a goner too, if you aren't honest, honest, honest the whole time, the way I always brought you up to be, the way you always bring me all the change when you buy me a loaf. It's the only way you can save yourself. Look, Sergeant, if it isn't a black cross!

THE SERGEANT: It's a cross! I don't understand how *I* got one. I always stay well in the rear. [*To the* OFFICER.] But it can't be a trick: it gets *her* children too.

SWISS CHEESE: It gets me too. But I don't accept it!

MOTHER COURAGE [*To* KATTRIN.]: And now all I have left for certain is you, you're a cross in yourself, you have a good heart. [*She holds the helmet up high toward the wagon but takes the slip out herself.*] Oh, I could give up in despair! There must be some mistake, I didn't mix them right. Don't be too kind, Kattrin, just don't, there's a cross in your path too. Always be very quiet, it can't be hard, you can't speak. Well, so now you know, all of you: be careful, you'll need to be. Now let's climb on the wagon and move on. [*She returns the helmet to the* SERGEANT *and climbs on the wagon.*]

THE RECRUITING OFFICER [*To the* SERGEANT.]: Do something!

THE SERGEANT: I don't feel very well.

THE RECRUITING OFFICER: Maybe you caught a chill when you handed over your helmet in this wind. Get her involved in a business transaction! [*Aloud.*] That belt, Sergeant, you could at least take a look at it. These good people live by trade, don't they? Hey, all of you, the sergeant wants to buy the belt!

MOTHER COURAGE: Half a guilder. A belt like that is worth two guilders. [*She clambers down again from the wagon.*]

THE SERGEANT: It isn't new. But there's too much wind here. I'll go and look at it behind the wagon. [*He does so.*]

MOTHER COURAGE: I don't find it windy.

THE SERGEANT: Maybe it's worth half a guilder at that. There's silver on it.

MOTHER COURAGE [*Following him behind the wagon.*]: A solid six ounces worth!

THE RECRUITING OFFICER [*To* EILIF.]: And we can have a drink, just us men. I'll advance you some money to cover it. Let's go.

[EILIF *stands undecided.*]

MOTHER COURAGE: Half a guilder, then.

THE SERGEANT: I don't understand it. I always stay in the rear. There's no safer spot for a sergeant to be. You can send the others on ahead in quest of fame. My appetite is ruined. I can tell you right now: I won't be able to get anything down.

MOTHER COURAGE: You shouldn't take on so, just because you can't eat. Just stay in the rear. Here, take a slug of brandy, man. [*She gives him brandy.*]

THE RECRUITING OFFICER [*Taking* EILIF *by the arm and making off toward the back.*]: Ten guilders in advance and you're a soldier of the king and a stout fellow and the women will be mad about you. And you can give me a smack in the puss for insulting you.

[*Both leave.*]

[*Dumb* KATTRIN *jumps down from the wagon and lets out harsh cries.*]

MOTHER COURAGE: Coming, Kattrin, coming! The sergeant's just paying up. [*She bites the half guilder.*] I'm suspicious of all money, I've been badly burned, Sergeant. But this money's good. And now we'll be going. Where's Eilif?

SWISS CHEESE: Gone with the recruiting officer.

MOTHER COURAGE [*Standing quite still, then.*]: Oh, you simpleton! [*To* KATTRIN.] You *can't* speak, I know. You are innocent.

THE SERGEANT: That's life. Take a slug yourself, Mother. Being a soldier isn't the worst that could happen. You want to live off war and keep you and yours out of it, do you?

MOTHER COURAGE: You must help your brother now, Kattrin.

[*Brother and sister get into harness together and pull the wagon.* MOTHER COURAGE *walks at their side. The wagon gets under way.*]

THE SERGEANT [*Looking after them.*]:

> When a war gives you all you earn
> One day it may claim something in return!

Scene Two

In the years 1625 and 1626 MOTHER COURAGE journeys through Poland in the baggage train of the Swedish army. She meets her son again before the fortified town of Wallhof.—Of the successful sale of a capon and great days for the brave son.

[*Tent of the Swedish Commander. Kitchen next to it. Thunder of cannon. The* COOK *is quarreling with* MOTHER COURAGE, *who is trying to sell him a capon.*]

THE COOK: Sixty hellers for that miserable bird?

MOTHER COURAGE: Miserable bird? This fat fowl? Your Commander is a glutton. Woe betide you if you've nothing for him to eat. This capon is worth sixty hellers to you.

THE COOK: They're ten hellers a dozen on every corner.

MOTHER COURAGE: A capon like this on every corner! With a siege going on and people all skin and bones? Maybe you can get a field rat! I said maybe. Because we're all out of *them* too. Don't you see the soldiers running five deep after one hungry little field rat? All right then, in a siege, my price for a giant capon is fifty hellers.

THE COOK: But we're not "in a siege," we're doing the besieging, it's the other side that's "in a siege," when will you get this into your head?

MOTHER COURAGE: A fat lot of difference that makes, *we* haven't got a thing to eat either. They took everything into the town with them before all this started, and now they've nothing to do but eat and drink, I hear. It's us I'm worried about. Look at the farmers around here, they haven't a thing.

THE COOK: Certainly they have. They hide it.

MOTHER COURAGE [*Triumphant*.]: They have not, they're ruined, that's what. They're so hungry I've seen 'em digging up roots to eat. I could boil your leather belt and make their mouths water with it. That's how things are around here. And I'm expected to let a capon go for forty hellers!

THE COOK: Thirty. Not forty. I said thirty hellers.

MOTHER COURAGE: I say this is no ordinary capon. It was a talented animal, so I hear. It would only feed to music—one march in particular was its favorite. It was so intelligent it could count. Forty hellers is too much for all this? I know *your* problem: if you don't find something to eat and quick, the Chief will—cut—your—fat—head—off!

THE COOK: All right, just watch. [*He takes a piece of beef and lays his knife on it.*] Here's a piece of beef, I'm going to roast it. I give you one more chance.

MOTHER COURAGE: Roast it, go ahead, it's only one year old.

THE COOK: One *day* old! Yesterday it was a cow. I saw it running around.

MOTHER COURAGE: In that case it must have started stinking before it died.

THE COOK: I don't care if I have to cook it for five hours. We'll see if it's still hard after that. [*He cuts into it.*]

MOTHER COURAGE: Put plenty of pepper in, so the Commander won't smell the smell.

[*The* SWEDISH COMMANDER, *a* CHAPLAIN, *and* EILIF *enter the tent.*]

THE COMMANDER [*Clapping* EILIF *on the shoulder*.]: In the Commander's tent with you, my son! Sit at my right hand, you happy warrior! You've played a hero's part, you've served the Lord in his own Holy War, *that's* the thing! And you'll get a gold brace-let out of it when we take the town if *I* have any say in the mat-ter! We come to save their souls and what do they do, the filthy, shameless peasant pigs? Drive their cattle away from *us*, while they stuff their priests with beef at both ends! But you showed 'em. So here's a can of red wine for you, we'll drink together! [*They do so.*] The chaplain gets the dregs, he's pious. Now what would you like for dinner, my hearty?

EILIF: How about a slice of meat?

THE COMMANDER: Cook, meat!

THE COOK: Nothing to eat, so he brings company to eat it!

[MOTHER COURAGE *makes him stop talking; she wants to listen.*]

EILIF: Tires you out, skinning peasants. Gives you an appetite.

MOTHER COURAGE: Dear God, it's my Eilif!

THE COOK: Who?

MOTHER COURAGE: My eldest. It's two years since I saw him, he was stolen from me in the street. He must be in high favor if the Commander's invited him to dinner. And what do you have to eat? Nothing. You hear what the Commander's guest wants? Meat! Better take my advice, buy the capon. The price is one guilder.

[*The* COMMANDER *has sat down with* EILIF *and the* CHAPLAIN.]

THE COMMANDER [*Roaring.*]: Cook! Dinner, you pig, or I'll have your head!

THE COOK: This is blackmail. Give me the damn thing!

MOTHER COURAGE: A miserable bird like this?

THE COOK: You were right. Give it here. It's highway robbery, fifty hellers.

MOTHER COURAGE: I said one guilder. Nothing's too high for my eldest, the Commander's guest of honor.

THE COOK [*Giving her the money.*]: Well, you might at least pluck it till I have a fire going.

MOTHER COURAGE [*Sitting down to pluck the capon.*]: I can't wait to see his face when he sees me. This is my brave and clever son. I have a stupid one as well but he's honest. The daughter is nothing. At least, she doesn't talk: we must be thankful for small mercies.

THE COMMANDER: Have another glass, my son, it's my favorite
Falernian. There's only one cask left—two at the most—but it's
worth it to meet a soldier that still believes in God! The shepherd
of our flock here just looks on, he only preaches, he hasn't a clue
how anything gets done. So now, Eilif, my son, give us the details: tell us how you fixed the peasants and grabbed the twenty
bullocks. And let's hope they'll soon be here.

EILIF: In one day's time. Two at the most.

MOTHER COURAGE: Now that's considerate of Eilif—to bring the
oxen tomorrow—otherwise my capon wouldn't have been so
welcome today.

EILIF: Well, it was like this. I found out that the peasants had
hidden their oxen and—on the sly and chiefly at night—had
driven them into a certain wood. The people from the town
were to pick them up there. I let them get their oxen in peace—
they ought to know better than me where they are, I said to myself. Meanwhile I made my men crazy for meat. Their rations
were short and I made sure they got shorter. Their mouths'd
water at the sound of any word beginning with MEA . . . , like
measles.

THE COMMANDER: Smart fella.

EILIF: Not bad. The rest was a snap. Only the peasants had clubs
and outnumbered us three to one and made a murderous attack
on us. Four of them drove me into a clump of trees, knocked
my good sword from my hand, and yelled, "Surrender!" What
now, I said to myself, they'll make mincemeat of me.

THE COMMANDER: What did you do?

EILIF: I laughed.

THE COMMANDER: You what?

EILIF: I laughed. And so we got to talking. I came right down to
business and said: "Twenty guilders an ox is too much, I bid
fifteen." Like I wanted to buy. That foxed 'em. So while they
were scratching their heads, I reached for my good sword and
cut 'em to pieces. Necessity knows no law, huh?

THE COMMANDER: What do *you* say, shepherd of the flock?

THE CHAPLAIN: Strictly speaking, that saying is not in the Bible.
Our Lord made five hundred loaves out of five so that no such
necessity would arise. When he told men to love their neighbors,
their bellies were full. Things have changed since his day.

THE COMMANDER [*Laughing.*]: Things have changed! A swallow

of wine for those wise words, you pharisee! [*To* EILIF.] You cut
'em to pieces in a good cause, our fellows were hungry and you
gave 'em to eat. Doesn't it say in the Bible "Whatsoever thou
doest to the least of these my children, thou doest unto me?"
And what *did* you do for 'em? You got 'em the best steak dinner they ever tasted. Moldy bread is not what they're used to.
They always ate white bread, and drank wine in their helmets,
before going out to fight for God.

EILIF: I reached for my good sword and cut 'em to pieces.

THE COMMANDER: You have the makings of a Julius Caesar, why,
you should be presented to the King!

EILIF: I've seen him—from a distance of course. He seemed to
shed a light all around. I must try to be like him!

THE COMMANDER: I think you're succeeding, my boy! Oh, Eilif,
you don't know how I value a brave soldier like you! I treat
such a chap as my very own son. [*He takes him to the map.*]
Take a look at our position, Eilif, it isn't all it might be, is it?

[MOTHER COURAGE *has been listening and is now plucking angrily
at her capon.*]

MOTHER COURAGE: He must be a very bad Commander.

THE COOK: Just a gluttonous one. Why bad?

MOTHER COURAGE: Because he needs *brave* soldiers, that's why.
If his plan of campaign was any good, why would he need *brave*
soldiers, wouldn't plain, ordinary soldiers do? Whenever there
are great virtues, it's a sure sign something's wrong.

THE COOK: You mean, it's a sure sign something's right.

MOTHER COURAGE: I mean what I say. Why? When a general or
a king is stupid and leads his soldiers into a trap, they need this
virtue of courage. When he's tightfisted and hasn't enough soldiers, the few he does have need the heroism of Hercules—another virtue. And if he's slovenly and doesn't give a damn about
anything, they have to be as wise as serpents or they're finished.
Loyalty's another virtue and you need plenty of it if the king's
always asking too much of you. All virtues which a well-regu-
lated country with a good king or a good general wouldn't need.
In a good country virtues wouldn't be necessary. Everybody
could be quite ordinary, middling, and, for all I care, cowards.

THE COMMANDER: I bet your father was a soldier.

EILIF: I've heard he was a great soldier. My mother warned me.
  I know a song about that.
THE COMMANDER: Sing it to us. [*Roaring.*] Bring that meat.
EILIF: It's called The Song of the Wise Woman and the Soldier.

[*He sings and at the same time does a war dance with his saber.*]

A shotgun will shoot and a jackknife will knife,
If you wade in the water, it will drown you,
Keep away from the ice, if you want my advice,
Said the wise woman to the soldier.

But that young soldier, he loaded his gun,
And he reached for his knife, and he started to run:
For marching never could hurt him!
From the north to the south he will march through the land
With his knife at his side and his gun in his hand:
That's what the soldiers told the wise woman.

Woe to him who defies the advice of the wise!
If you wade in the water, it will drown you!
Don't ignore what I say or you'll rue it one day,
Said the wise woman to the soldier.

But that young soldier, his knife at his side
And his gun in his hand, he steps into the tide:
For water never could hurt him!
When the new moon is shining on yonder church tower
We are all coming back: go and pray for that hour:
That's what the soldiers told the wise woman.

[MOTHER COURAGE *continues the song from her kitchen, beating on a pan with a spoon.*]

Then the wise woman spoke: you will vanish like smoke
Leaving nothing but cold air behind you!
Just watch the smoke fly! Oh God, don't let him die!
Said the wise woman to the soldier.

EILIF: What's that?

[MOTHER COURAGE, *singing on.*]

And the lad who defied the wise woman's advice,
When the new moon shone, floated down with the ice:
He waded in the water and it drowned him.

The wise woman spoke, and they vanished like smoke,
And their glorious deeds did not warm us.
Your glorious deeds do not warm us!

THE COMMANDER: What a kitchen I've got! There's no end to the
liberties they take!

[EILIF *has entered the kitchen and embraced his mother.*]

EILIF: To see you again! Where are the others?
MOTHER COURAGE [*In his arms.*]: Happy as ducks in a pond. Swiss
Cheese is paymaster with the Second Regiment, so at least he
isn't in the fighting. I couldn't keep him out altogether.
EILIF: Are your feet holding up?
MOTHER COURAGE: I've a bit of trouble getting my shoes on in the
morning.

[*The* COMMANDER *has come over.*]

THE COMMANDER: So you're his mother! I hope you have more
sons for me like this fellow.
EILIF: If I'm not the lucky one: to be feasted by the Commander
while you sit listening in the kitchen!
MOTHER COURAGE: Yes. I heard all right. [*She gives him a box on
the ear.*]
EILIF [*His hand to his cheek.*]: Because I took the oxen?
MOTHER COURAGE: No. Because you didn't surrender when the
four peasants let fly at you and tried to make mincemeat of you!
Didn't I teach you to take care of yourself? You Finnish devil,
you!

[*The* COMMANDER *and the* CHAPLAIN *stand laughing in the doorway.*]

Scene Three

Three years pass and MOTHER COURAGE, with parts of a Finnish regiment, is taken prisoner. Her daughter is saved, her wagon likewise, but her honest son dies.

A camp. The regimental flag is flying from a pole. Afternoon. All sorts of wares hanging on the wagon. MOTHER COURAGE'S clothesline is tied to the wagon at one end, to a cannon at the other. She and KATTRIN are folding the washing on the cannon. At the same time she is bargaining with an ORDNANCE OFFICER over a bag of bullets. SWISS CHEESE, in paymaster's uniform now, looks on. YVETTE POTTIER, a very good-looking young person, is sewing at a colored hat, a glass of brandy before her. She is in stocking feet. Her red boots are nearby.

THE OFFICER: I'm letting you have the bullets for two guilders. Dirt cheap. 'Cause I need the money. The Colonel's been drinking with the officers for three days and we're out of liquor.

MOTHER COURAGE: They're army property. If they find 'em on me, I'll be court-martialed. You sell your bullets, you bastards, and send your men out to fight with nothing to shoot with.

THE OFFICER: Oh, come on, you scratch my back, and I'll scratch yours.

MOTHER COURAGE: I won't take army stuff. Not at *that* price.

THE OFFICER: You can resell 'em for five guilders, maybe eight, to the Ordnance Officer of the Fourth Regiment. All you have to do is to give him a receipt for twelve. He hasn't a bullet left.

MOTHER COURAGE: Why don't you do it yourself?

THE OFFICER: I don't trust him. We're friends.

MOTHER COURAGE [Taking the bag.]: Give it here. [To KATTRIN.] Take it around to the back and pay him a guilder and a half. [As the OFFICER protests.] I said a guilder and a half! [KATTRIN drags the bag away. The OFFICER follows. MOTHER COURAGE speaks

to SWISS CHEESE.] Here's your underwear back, take care of it;
it's October now, autumn may come at any time; I purposely
don't say it must come, I've learned from experience there's
nothing that must come, not even the seasons. But your books
must balance now you're the regimental paymaster. *Do* they
balance?

SWISS CHEESE: Yes, Mother.

MOTHER COURAGE: Don't forget they made you paymaster because
you're honest and so simple you'd never think of running off
with the cash. Don't lose that underwear.

SWISS CHEESE: No, Mother. I'll put it under the mattress. [*He
starts to go.*]

THE OFFICER: I'll go with you, paymaster.

MOTHER COURAGE: Don't teach him any monkey business.

[*Without a good-by the* OFFICER *leaves with* SWISS CHEESE.]

YVETTE [*Waving to him.*]: You might at least say good-by!

MOTHER COURAGE [*To* YVETTE.]: I don't like that. *He's* no sort of
company for my Swiss Cheese. But the war's not making a bad
start. Before all the different countries get into it, four or five
years'll have gone by like nothing. If I look ahead and make no
mistakes, business will be good. Don't you know you shouldn't
drink in the morning with your illness?

YVETTE: Who says I'm ill? That's libel!

MOTHER COURAGE: They all say so.

YVETTE: They're all liars. I'm desperate, Mother Courage. They
all avoid me like a stinking fish. Because of those lies. So what
am I arranging my hat for? [*She throws it down.*] That's why
I drink in the morning. I never used to, it gives you crow's feet.
But what's the difference? Every man in the regiment knows
me. I should have stayed at home when my first was unfaithful.
But pride isn't for the likes of us, you eat dirt or down you go.

MOTHER COURAGE: Now don't you start again with your friend
Peter and how it all happened—in front of my innocent daughter.

YVETTE: She's the one that should hear it. So she'll get hardened
against love.

MOTHER COURAGE: That's something no one ever gets hardened
against.

YVETTE: I'll tell you about it, and get it off my chest. I grew up in

Flanders' fields, that's where it starts, or I'd never even have caught sight of him and I wouldn't be here in Poland today. He was an army cook, blond, a Dutchman, but thin. Kattrin, beware of thin men! I didn't. I didn't even know he'd had another girl before me and she called him Peter Piper because he never took his pipe out of his mouth the whole time, it meant so little to him.

[*She sings "The Fraternization Song."*]

> When I was almost seventeen
> The foe came to our land
> And laying aside his saber
> He took me gently by the hand.
>
> > First came the May Day Rite
> > Then came the May Day night.
> > The pipes played and the drums did beat.
> > The foe paraded down the street.
> > And then with us they took their ease
> > And fraternized behind the trees.
>
> Our foes they came in plenty.
> A cook was my own foe.
> I hated him by daylight
> But in the dark I loved him so.
>
> > First comes the May Day Rite
> > Then comes the May Day night.
> > The pipes play and the drums do beat.
> > The foe parades down every street.
> > And then with us they take their ease
> > And fraternize behind the trees.
>
> The heavens seemed to open
> Such passion did I feel.
> But my people never understood
> The love I felt was real.
>
> > One day the sun rose slow
> > On all my pain and woe.
> > My loved one, with the other men,
> > Presented arms and stood at ease

Yvette's lover =
Peter Piper

Then marched away past all those trees
And never did come back again.

I made the mistake of running after him, I never found him.
It's five years ago now. [*With swaying gait she goes behind the
wagon.*]

MOTHER COURAGE: You've left your hat.
YVETTE: For the birds.
MOTHER COURAGE: Let this be a lesson to you Kattrin, never start
anything with a soldier. The heavens do seem to open, so watch
out! Even with men who're not in the army life's no honeypot.
He tells you he'd like to kiss the ground under your feet—did
you wash 'em yesterday, while we're on the subject?—and then if
you don't look out, your number's up, you're his slave for life.
Be glad you're dumb, Kattrin: you'll never contradict yourself,
you'll never want to bite your tongue off because you spoke out
of turn. Dumbness is a gift from God. Here comes the Commander's cook, what's bothering *him?*

[*Enter the* COOK *and the* CHAPLAIN.]

THE CHAPLAIN: I bring a message from your son Eilif. The cook
came with me. You've made, ahem, an impression on him.
THE COOK: I thought I'd get a little whiff of the balmy breeze.
MOTHER COURAGE: You're welcome to that if you behave yourself,
and even if you don't I think I can handle you. But what does
Eilif want? I don't have any money.
THE CHAPLAIN: Actually, I have something to tell his brother, the
paymaster.
MOTHER COURAGE: He isn't here. And he isn't anywhere else either.
He's not his brother's paymaster, and I won't have him led into
temptation. Let Eilif try it on with someone else! [*She takes
money from the purse at her belt.*] Give him this. It's a sin.
He's speculating in mother love, he ought to be ashamed of
himself.
THE COOK: Not for long. He has to go with his regiment now—to
his death maybe. Send some more money, or you'll be sorry.
You women are hard—and sorry afterward. A glass of brandy
wouldn't cost very much, but you refuse to provide it, and six
feet under goes your man and you can't dig him up again.

THE CHAPLAIN: All very touching, my dear cook, but to fall in this war is not a misfortune, it's a blessing. This is a war of religion. Not just any old war but a special one, a religious one, and therefore pleasing unto God.

THE COOK: Correct. In one sense it's a war because there's fleecing, bribing, plundering, not to mention a little raping, but it's different from all other wars because it's a war of religion. That's clear. All the same, it makes you thirsty.

THE CHAPLAIN [To MOTHER COURAGE, pointing at the COOK.]: I tried to hold him off but he said you'd bewitched him. He dreams about you.

THE COOK [Lighting a clay pipe.]: Brandy from the fair hand of a lady, that's for me. And don't embarrass me any more: the stories the chaplain was telling me on the way over still have me blushing.

MOTHER COURAGE: A man of his cloth! I must get you both something to drink or you'll be making improper advances out of sheer boredom.

THE CHAPLAIN: That is indeed a temptation, said the court chaplain, and gave way to it. [Turning toward KATTRIN as he walks.] And who is this captivating young person?

MOTHER COURAGE: She's not a captivating young person, she's a respectable young person.

[The CHAPLAIN and the COOK go with MOTHER COURAGE behind the cart, and one hears them talk politics.]

MOTHER COURAGE: The trouble here in Poland is that the Poles would keep meddling. It's true our King moved in on them with man, beast, and wagon, but instead of keeping the peace the Poles attacked the Swedish King when he was in the act of peacefully withdrawing. So they were guilty of a breach of the peace and their blood is on their own heads.

THE CHAPLAIN: Anyway, our King was thinking of nothing but freedom. The Kaiser enslaved them all, Poles and Germans alike, so our King had to liberate them.

THE COOK: Just what I think. Your health! Your brandy is firstrate, I'm never mistaken in a face.

[KATTRIN looks after them, leaves the washing, goes to the hat, picks it up, sits down, and takes up the red boots.]

And the war is a war of religion. [*Singing while* KATTRIN *puts the boots on.*] "A mighty fortress is our God . . ." [*He sings a verse or so of Luther's hymn.*] And talking of King Gustavus, this freedom he tried to bring to Germany cost him a pretty penny. Back in Sweden he had to levy a salt tax, the poorer folks didn't like it a bit. Then, too, he had to lock up the Germans and even cut their heads off, they clung so to slavery and their Kaiser. Of course, if no one had *wanted* to be free, the King wouldn't have had any fun. First it was just Poland he tried to protect from bad men, especially the Kaiser, then his appetite grew with eating, and he ended up protecting Germany too. Now Germany put up a pretty decent fight. So the good King had nothing but worries in return for his outlay and his goodness, and of course he had to get his money back with taxes, which made bad blood, but he didn't shrink even from that. For he had one thing in his favor anyway, God's Holy Word, which was all to the good, because otherwise they could have said he did it for profit. That's how he kept his conscience clear. He always put conscience first.

MOTHER COURAGE: It's plain you're no Swede, or you'd speak differently of the Hero King.

THE CHAPLAIN: What's more, you eat his bread.

THE COOK: I don't eat his bread. I bake his bread.

MOTHER COURAGE: He's unbeatable. Why? His men believe in him. [*Earnestly.*] To hear the big fellows talk, they wage war from fear of God and for all things bright and beautiful, but just look into it, and you'll see they're not so silly: they want a good profit out of it, or else the little fellows like you and me wouldn't back 'em up.

THE COOK: That's right.

THE CHAPLAIN: And as a Dutchman you'd do well to see which flag's flying here before you express an opinion!

MOTHER COURAGE: All good Protestants forever!

THE COOK: A health!

[KATTRIN *has begun to strut about with* YVETTE's *hat on, copying* YVETTE's *sexy walk. Suddenly cannon and shots. Drums.* MOTHER COURAGE, *the* COOK, *and the* CHAPLAIN *rush around to the front of the cart, the last two with glasses in their hands.*

The ORDNANCE OFFICER *and a* SOLDIER *come running to the cannon and try to push it along.*]

MOTHER COURAGE: What's the matter? Let me get my washing off that gun, you slobs! [*She tries to do so.*]

THE OFFICER: The Catholics! Surprise attack! We don't know if we can get away! [*To the* SOLDIER.] Get that gun! [*He runs off.*]

THE COOK: For heaven's sake! I must go to the Commander. Mother Courage, I'll be back in a day or two—for a short conversation. [*He rushes off.*]

MOTHER COURAGE: Hey, you've left your pipe!

THE COOK [*Off.*]: Keep it for me, I'll need it!

MOTHER COURAGE: This *would* happen just when we were making money.

THE CHAPLAIN: Well, I must be going too. Yes, if the enemy's so close, it can be dangerous. "Blessed are the peace-makers," a good slogan in war time! If only I had a cloak.

MOTHER COURAGE: I'm lending no cloaks. Not even to save a life, I'm not. I've had experience in that line.

THE CHAPLAIN: But I'm in special danger. Because of my religion.

MOTHER COURAGE [*Bringing him a cloak.*]: It's against my better judgment. Now run!

THE CHAPLAIN: I thank you, you're very generous, but maybe I'd better stay and sit here. If I run, I might attract the enemy's attention, I might arouse suspicion.

MOTHER COURAGE [*To the* SOLDIER.]: Let it alone, you dolt, who's going to pay you for this? It'll cost you your life, let me hold it for you.

THE SOLDIER [*Running away.*]: You're my witness: I tried!

MOTHER COURAGE: I'll swear to it! [*Seeing* KATTRIN *with the hat.*] What on earth are you up to—with a whore's hat! Take it off this minute! Are you mad? With the enemy coming? [*She tears the hat off her head.*] Do you want them to find you and make a whore of you? And she has the boots on too, straight from Babylon. I'll soon settle that. [*She tries to get them off.*] Oh God, Chaplain, help me with these boots, I'll be right back. [*She runs to the wagon.*]

YVETTE [*Entering and powdering her face.*]: What's that you say: the Catholics are coming? Where's my hat? Who's been trampling on it? I can't run around in that, what will they think of me? And I don't even have a mirror. [*To the* CHAPLAIN.] How do I look—too much powder?

THE CHAPLAIN: Just, er, right.

YVETTE: And where are my red boots? [*She can't find them because* KATTRIN *is hiding her feet under her skirt.*] I left them here! Now I've got to go barefoot to my tent, it's a scandal! [*Exit.*]

[SWISS CHEESE *comes running in carrying a cash box.*]

[MOTHER COURAGE *enters with her hands covered with ashes.*]

MOTHER COURAGE [*To* KATTRIN.]: Ashes! [*To* SWISS CHEESE.] What have you got there?

SWISS CHEESE: The regimental cash box.

MOTHER COURAGE: Throw it away! Your paymastering days are over!

SWISS CHEESE: It's a trust! [*He goes to the back.*]

MOTHER COURAGE [*To the* CHAPLAIN.]: Off with your pastor's coat, Chaplain, or they'll recognize you, cloak or no cloak. [*She is rubbing ashes into* KATTRIN'S *face.*] Keep still. A little dirt, and you're safe. A calamity! The sentries were drunk. Well, one must hide one's light under a bushel, as they say. When a soldier sees a clean face, there's one more whore in the world. Especially a Catholic soldier. For weeks on end, no grub. Then, when the plundering starts and they steal some, they jump on top of the womenfolk. That should do. Let me look at you. Not bad. Looks like you've been rolling in muck. Don't tremble. Nothing can happen to you now. [*To* SWISS CHEESE.] Where've you left the cash box?

SWISS CHEESE: I thought I'd just put it in the wagon.

MOTHER COURAGE [*Horrified.*]: What! In my wagon? God punish you for a prize idiot! If I just look away for a moment! They'll hang all three of us!

SWISS CHEESE: Then I'll put it somewhere else. Or escape with it.

MOTHER COURAGE: You'll stay where you are. It's too late.

THE CHAPLAIN [*Still changing his clothes.*]: For heaven's sake: the flag!

MOTHER COURAGE [*Taking down the flag.*]: God in heaven! I don't notice it any more. I've had it twenty-five years.

[*The thunder of cannon grows.*]

[*Three days later. Morning. The cannon is gone.* MOTHER COURAGE, KATTRIN, *the* CHAPLAIN, *and* SWISS CHEESE *sit anxiously eating.*]

SWISS CHEESE: This is the third day I've been sitting here doing nothing, and the Sergeant, who's always been patient with me, may be slowly beginning to ask, "Where on earth is Swiss Cheese with that cash box?"

MOTHER COURAGE: Be glad they're not on the trail.

THE CHAPLAIN: What about me? I can't hold a service here or I'll be in hot water. It is written, "Out of the abundance of the heart, the tongue speaketh." But woe is me if *my* tongue speaketh!

MOTHER COURAGE: That's how it is. Here you sit—one with his religion, the other with his cash box, I don't know which is more dangerous.

THE CHAPLAIN: We're in God's hands now!

MOTHER COURAGE: I hope we're not *that* desperate, but it *is* hard to sleep nights. 'Course it'd be easier if *you* weren't here, Swiss Cheese, all the same I've not done badly. I told them I was against the Antichrist, who's a Swede with horns on his head. I told them I noticed his left horn's a bit threadbare. When they cross-examined me, I always asked where I could buy holy candles a bit cheaper. I know these things because Swiss Cheese's father was a Catholic and made jokes about it. They didn't quite believe me but they needed a canteen, so they turned a blind eye. Maybe it's all for the best. We're prisoners. But so are lice in fur.

THE CHAPLAIN: The milk is good. As far as quantity goes, we may have to reduce our Swedish appetites somewhat. We are defeated.

MOTHER COURAGE: Who's defeated? The defeats and victories of the fellows at the top aren't always defeats and victories for the fellows at the bottom. Not at all. There've been cases where a defeat is a victory for the fellows at the bottom, it's only their honor that's lost, nothing serious. In Livonia once, our Chief took such a knock from the enemy, in the confusion I got a fine gray mare out of the baggage train, it pulled my wagon seven months—till we won and there was an inventory. But in general both defeat and victory are a costly business for us that haven't got much. The best thing is for politics to get stuck in the mud. [*To* swiss cheese.] Eat!

Swiss Cheese: I don't like it. How will the sergeant pay his men?

Mother Courage: Soldiers in flight don't get paid.

Swiss Cheese: Well, they could claim to be. No pay, no flight. They can refuse to budge.

Mother Courage: Swiss Cheese, your sense of duty worries me. I've brought you up to be honest because you're not very bright. But don't overdo it. And now I'm going with the chaplain to buy a Catholic flag and some meat. There's no one can hunt out meat like him, sure as a sleepwalker. He can tell a good piece of meat from the way his mouth waters. A good thing they let me stay in the business. In business you ask what price, not what religion. And Protestant trousers keep you just as warm.

The Chaplain: As the mendicant monk said when there was talk of the Lutherans turning the whole world upside down: Beggars will *always* be needed. [mother courage *disappears into the wagon.*] She's worried about the cash box. Up to now they've ignored us—as if we were part of the wagon—but can it last?

Swiss Cheese: I can get rid of it.

The Chaplain: That's almost *more* dangerous. Suppose you're seen. They have spies. Yesterday morning one jumped out of the very hole I was relieving myself in. I was so scared I almost broke out in prayer—*that* would have given me away all right! I believe their favorite way of finding a Protestant is smelling his excrement. The spy was a little brute with a bandage over one eye.

Mother Courage [*Clambering out of the wagon with a basket.*]: I've found you out, you shameless hussy! [*She holds up* yvette's *red boots in triumph.*] Yvette's red boots! She just swiped them— because you went and told her she was a captivating person. [*She lays them in the basket.*] Stealing Yvette's boots! But *she* disgraces herself for money, *you* do it for nothing—for pleasure! I told you, you must wait for the peace. No soldiers! Save your proud peacock ways for peacetime!

The Chaplain: I don't find her proud.

Mother Courage: Prouder than she can afford to be. I like her when people say "I never noticed the poor thing." I like her when she's a stone in Dalarna, where there's nothing but stones. [*To* swiss cheese.] Leave the cash box where it is, do you hear? And pay attention to your sister, she needs it. Between the two of you, you'll be the death of me yet. I'd rather take care of a bag of fleas.

[*She leaves with the* CHAPLAIN. KATTRIN *clears the dishes away.*]

SWISS CHEESE: Not many days more when you can sit in the sun in your shirtsleeves. [KATTRIN *points to a tree.*] Yes, the leaves are yellow already. [*With gestures,* KATTRIN *asks if he wants a drink.*] I'm not drinking, I'm thinking. [*Pause.*] She says she can't sleep. So I *should* take the cash box away. I've found a place for it. I'll keep it in the mole hole by the river till the time comes. I might get it tonight before sunrise and take it to the regiment. How far can they have fled in three days? The Sergeant's eyes'll pop out of his head. "You've disappointed me most pleasantly, Swiss Cheese," he'll say, "*I* let you have the cash box and *you* bring it back!" Yes, Kattrin, I *will* have a glass now!

[*When* KATTRIN *reappears behind the wagon two men confront her. One of them is a* SERGEANT. *The other doffs his hat and flourishes it in a showy greeting. He has a bandage over one eye.*]

THE MAN WITH THE BANDAGE: Good morning, young lady. Have you seen a man from the Second Protestant Regiment?

[*Terrified,* KATTRIN *runs away, spilling her brandy. The two men look at each other and then withdraw after seeing* SWISS CHEESE.]

SWISS CHEESE [*Starting up from his reflection*]: You're spilling it! What's the matter with you, have you hurt your eye? I don't understand. Yes, and I must be going, too. I've decided it's the thing to do. [*He stands up. She does all she can to make him aware of the danger he is in. He only pushes her away.*] I'd like to know what you mean. I know you mean well, poor thing, you just can't get it out. And don't trouble yourself about the brandy, I'll live to drink so much of it, what's one glass? [*He takes the cash box out of the wagon and puts it under his coat.*] I'll be back right away. But don't hold me up or I'll have to scold you. Yes, I know you mean well. If you could only speak!

[*When she tries to hold him back he kisses her and pulls himself free. Exit. She is desperate and runs up and down, emitting little sounds.* MOTHER COURAGE *and the* CHAPLAIN *return.* KATTRIN *rushes at her mother.*]

MOTHER COURAGE: What *is* it, what *is* it, Kattrin? Control yourself! Has someone done something to you? Where is Swiss Cheese? [*To the* CHAPLAIN.] Don't stand around, get that Catholic flag up! [*She takes a Catholic flag out of her basket and the* CHAPLAIN *runs it up the pole.*]

THE CHAPLAIN [*Bitterly.*]: All good Catholics forever!

MOTHER COURAGE: Now, Kattrin, calm down and tell all about it, your mother understands you. What, that little bastard of mine's taken the cash box away? I'll box his ears for him, the rascal! Now take your time and don't try to talk, use your hands. I don't like it when you howl like a dog, what'll the chaplain think of you? You're giving him the creeps. A man with one eye was here?

THE CHAPLAIN: That fellow with one eye is an informer! Have they caught Swiss Cheese? [KATTRIN *shakes her head, shrugs her shoulders.*] This is the end.

[*Voices off. The two men bring in* SWISS CHEESE.]

SWISS CHEESE: Let me go. I've nothing on me. You're breaking my shoulder! I am innocent.

THE SERGEANT: This is where he comes from. There are his friends.

MOTHER COURAGE: Us? Since when?

SWISS CHEESE: I don't even know 'em. I was just getting my lunch here. Ten hellers it cost me. Maybe you saw me sitting on that bench. It was too salty.

THE SERGEANT: Who *are* you people, anyway?

MOTHER COURAGE: Law-abiding citizens! It's true what he says. He bought his lunch here. And it was too salty.

THE SERGEANT: Are you pretending you don't know him?

MOTHER COURAGE: I can't know all of them, can I? *I* don't ask, "What's your name and are you a heathen?" If they pay up, they're not heathens to me. Are you a heathen?

SWISS CHEESE: Oh, no!

THE CHAPLAIN: He sat there like a law-abiding fellow and never once opened his mouth. Except to eat. Which is necessary.

THE SERGEANT: Who do you think *you* are?

MOTHER COURAGE: Oh, he's my barman. And you're thirsty, I'll bring you a glass of brandy. You must be footsore and weary!

THE SERGEANT: No brandy on duty. [*To* SWISS CHEESE.] You were carrying something. You must have hidden it by the river. We saw the bulge in your shirt.

MOTHER COURAGE: Sure it was him?

SWISS CHEESE: I think you mean another fellow. There *was* a fellow with something under his shirt, I saw him. I'm the wrong man.

MOTHER COURAGE: I think so too. It's a misunderstanding. Could happen to anyone. Oh, I know what people are like, I'm Mother Courage, you've heard of me, everyone knows about me, and I can tell you this: he looks honest.

THE SERGEANT: We're after the regimental cash box. And we know what the man looks like who's been keeping it. We've been looking for him two days. It's you.

SWISS CHEESE: No, it's not!

THE SERGEANT: And if you don't shell out, you're dead, see? Where is it?

MOTHER COURAGE [*Urgently.*]: 'Course he'd give it to you to save his life. He'd up and say, *I've* got it, here it is, you're stronger than me. He's not *that* stupid. Speak, little stupid, the sergeant's giving you a chance!

SWISS CHEESE: What if I *haven't* got it?

THE SERGEANT: Come with us. We'll get it out of you. [*They take him off.*]

MOTHER COURAGE [*Shouting after them.*]: He'd tell you! He's not *that* stupid! And don't you break his shoulder! [*She runs after them.*]

[*The same evening. The* CHAPLAIN *and* KATTRIN *are rinsing glasses and polishing knives.*]

THE CHAPLAIN: Cases of people getting caught like this are by no means unknown in the history of religion. I am reminded of the Passion of Our Lord and Savior. There's an old song about it.

[*He sings "The Song of the Hours."*]

> In the first hour of the day
> Simple Jesus Christ was
> Presented as a murderer
> To the heathen Pilate.

Pilate found no fault in him
No cause to condemn him
So he sent the Lord away.
Let King Herod see him!

Hour the third: the Son of God
Was with scourges beaten
And they set a crown of thorns
On the head of Jesus.

And they dressed him as a king
Joked and jested at him
And the cross to die upon
He himself must carry.

Six: they stripped Lord Jesus bare.
To the cross they nailed him.
When the blood came gushing, he
Prayed and loud lamented.

Each upon his cross, two thieves
Mocked him like the others.
And the bright sun crept away
Not to see such doings.

Nine: Lord Jesus cried aloud
That he was forsaken!
In a sponge upon a pole
Vinegar was fed him.

Then the Lord gave up the ghost
And the earth did tremble.
Temple curtain split in twain.
Cliffs fell in the ocean.

Evening: they broke the bones
Of the malefactors.
Then they took a spear and pierced
The side of gentle Jesus.

And the blood and water ran
And they laughed at Jesus.
Of this simple son of man
Such and more they tell us.

Mother Courage [*Entering, excited.*]: It's life and death. But
the Sergeant will still listen to us. The only thing is, he mustn't
know it's our Swiss Cheese, or they'll say we helped him. It's
only a matter of money, but where can *we* get money? Isn't
Yvette here yet? I talked to her on the way over. She's picked up
a Colonel who may be willing to buy her a canteen business.

The Chaplain: You'd sell the wagon, everything?

Mother Courage: Where else would I get the money for the
Sergeant?

The Chaplain: What are you to live off?

Mother Courage: That's just it.

[*Enter* yvette *with a hoary old* colonel.]

Yvette [*Embracing* mother courage.]: *Dear* Mistress Courage,
we meet again. [*Whispering.*] He didn't say no. [*Aloud.*] This
is my friend, my, um, business adviser. I happened to hear you
might sell your wagon. Due to special circumstances, I'd like
to think about it.

Mother Courage: I want to pawn it, not sell it. And nothing
hasty. In war time you don't find another wagon like that so easy.

Yvette [*Disappointed.*]: Only pawn it? I thought you wanted to
sell. I don't know if I'm interested. [*To the* colonel.] What do
you think, my dear?

The Colonel: I quite agree with you, bunny.

Mother Courage: It's only for pawn.

Yvette: I thought you *had* to have the money.

Mother Courage [*Firmly.*]: I do have to have it. But I'd rather
wear my feet off looking for an offer than just sell. Why? We
live off the wagon. It's an opportunity for you, Yvette. Who
knows when you'll have another such? Who knows when you'll
find another business adviser?

The Colonel: Take it, take it!

Yvette: My friend thinks I should go ahead, but I'm not sure,
if it's only for pawn. You think we should buy it outright,
don't you?

The Colonel: I do, bunny, I do!

Mother Courage: Then you must go and find something that's
for sale. Maybe you'll find it—if you have the time, and your
friend goes with you, let's say in about a week, or two weeks,
you may find the right thing.

YVETTE: Yes, we can certainly look around for something. I love going around looking, I love going around with you, Poldy. . . .

THE COLONEL: Really? Do you?

YVETTE: Oh, it's lovely! I could take two weeks of it!

THE COLONEL: Really, could you?

YVETTE: If you get the money, when are you thinking of paying it back?

MOTHER COURAGE: In two weeks. Maybe one.

YVETTE: I can't make up my mind, Poldy, advise me, *chéri [She takes the* COLONEL *to one side.*] She'll *have* to sell, don't worry. That Lieutenant—the blond one, you know the one I mean— he'll lend me the money. He's *mad* about me, he says I remind him of someone. What do you advise?

THE COLONEL: Oh, I have to warn you against *him.* He's no good. He'll exploit the situation. I told you, bunny, I told you *I'd* buy you something, didn't I tell you that?

YVETTE: I simply can't let you!

THE COLONEL: Oh, please, please!

YVETTE: Well, if you think the Lieutenant might exploit the situation I *will* let you!

THE COLONEL: I do think so.

YVETTE: So you advise me to?

THE COLONEL: I do, bunny, I do!

YVETTE [*Returning to* MOTHER COURAGE.]: My friend says all right. Write me out a receipt saying the wagon's mine when the two weeks are up—with everything in it. I'll just run through it all now, the two hundred guilders can wait. [*To the* COLONEL.] You go ahead to the camp, I'll follow, I must go over all this so nothing'll be missing later from *my* wagon!

THE COLONEL: Wait, I'll help you up! [*He does so.*] Come soon, honey bun! [*Exit.*]

MOTHER COURAGE: Yvette, Yvette!

YVETTE: There aren't many boots left!

MOTHER COURAGE: Yvette, this is no time to go through the wagon, yours or not yours. You promised you'd talk to the Sergeant about Swiss Cheese. There isn't a minute to lose. He's up before the court-martial one hour from now.

YVETTE: I just want to count these shirts again.

MOTHER COURAGE [*Dragging her down the steps by the skirt.*]: You hyena, Swiss Cheese's life's at stake! And don't say who the money comes from. Pretend he's your sweetheart, for heaven's sake, or we'll all get it for helping him.

YVETTE: I've arranged to meet One Eye in the bushes. He must be there by now.

THE CHAPLAIN: And don't hand over all two hundred, a hundred and fifty's sure to be enough.

MOTHER COURAGE: Is it your money? I'll thank you to keep your nose out of this, I'm not doing *you* out of your porridge. Now run, and no haggling, remember his life's at stake. [*She pushes* YVETTE *off.*]

THE CHAPLAIN: I didn't want to talk you into anything, but what are we going to live on? You have an unemployable daughter around your neck.

MOTHER COURAGE: I'm counting on that cash box, smart aleck. They'll pay his expenses out of it.

THE CHAPLAIN: You think she can work it?

MOTHER COURAGE: It's in her own interest: I pay the two hundred and she gets the wagon. She knows what she's doing, she won't have her Colonel on the string forever. Kattrin, go and clean the knives, use pumice stone. And don't *you* stand around like Jesus in Gethsemane. Get a move on, wash those glasses. There'll be over fifty cavalrymen here tonight, and you'll be saying you're not used to being on your feet. "Oh my poor feet, in church I never had to run around like this!" I think they'll let us have him. Thanks be to God they're corruptible. They're not wolves, they're human and after money. God is merciful, and men are bribable, that's how His will is done on earth as it is in Heaven. Corruption is our only hope. As long as there's corruption, there'll be merciful judges and even the innocent may get off.

[YVETTE *comes in panting.*]

YVETTE: They'll do it for two hundred if you make it snappy—these things change from one minute to the next. I'd better take One Eye to my Colonel at once. He confessed he had the cash box, they put the thumbscrews on him. But he threw it in the river when he noticed them coming up behind him. So it's gone. Shall I run and get the money from my Colonel?

MOTHER COURAGE: The cash box gone? How'll I ever get my two hundred back?

YVETTE: So you thought you could get it from the cash box? I *would* have been sunk. Not a hope, Mother Courage. If you want your Swiss Cheese, you'll have to pay. Or should I let the whole thing drop, so you can keep your wagon?

MOTHER COURAGE: I wasn't figuring on this. But you needn't hound me, you'll get the wagon, it's yours already, and it's been mine seventeen years. I need a minute to think it over, it's all so sudden. What can I do? I *can't* pay two hundred. You *should* have haggled with them. I must hold on to something, or any passer-by can kick me in the ditch. Go and say I'll pay a hundred and twenty or the deal's off. Even then I lose the wagon.

YVETTE: They won't do it. And anyway, One Eye's in a hurry. He keeps looking over his shoulder all the time, he's so worked up. Hadn't I better give them the whole two hundred?

MOTHER COURAGE [*Desperate.*]: I can't pay it! I've been working thirty years. She's twenty-five and still no husband. I have her to think of. So leave me alone. I know what I'm doing. A hundred and twenty or no deal.

YVETTE: You know best. [*She runs off.*]

MOTHER COURAGE *turns away and slowly walks a few paces to the rear. Then she turns around, looks neither at the* CHAPLAIN *nor her daughter, and sits down to help* KATTRIN *polish the knives.*

MOTHER COURAGE: Don't break the glasses, they're not ours. Watch what you're doing, you're cutting yourself. Swiss Cheese will be back. I'll give two hundred, if I have to. You'll get your brother back. With eighty guilders we could pack a hamper with goods and begin again. It wouldn't be the end of the world.

THE CHAPLAIN: The Bible says: the Lord will provide.

MOTHER COURAGE: Rub them dry, I said.

[*They clean the knives in silence.*]

They say the war will stop soon. How would it? I ask. And no one can answer me. [*Slowly.*] The King and the Pope are mortal enemies, their Faith is different. They must go for each other till one of them drops dead, neither of them can relax till then. Even so they can't get on with it. Why not? The Emperor is in the way, and they both have something against him. They're not going to fight each other to the death with the Emperor lurking about till they're half dead so he can fall on both of 'em! No, they're banding together against the Emperor so he'll drop dead first and they can go for each other.

[*Suddenly* KATTRIN *runs sobbing behind the wagon.*]

Someone once offered me five hundred guilders for the wagon. I didn't take it. My Eilif, wherever he may be, thought I'd taken it and cried all night.

[YVETTE *comes running in.*]

YVETTE: They won't do it. I warned you. One Eye was going to drop it then and there. There's no point, he said. He said the drums would roll any second now and that's the sign a verdict has been reached. I offered a hundred and fifty, he didn't even shrug. I could hardly get him to stay there while I came here.
MOTHER COURAGE: Tell him I'll pay two hundred. Run!

[YVETTE *runs.* MOTHER COURAGE *sits, silent. The* CHAPLAIN *has stopped doing the glasses.*]

I believe—I've haggled too long.

[*In the distance, a roll of drums. The* CHAPLAIN *stands up and walks toward the rear.* MOTHER COURAGE *remains seated. It grows dark. It gets light again.* MOTHER COURAGE *has not moved.* YVETTE *appears, pale.*]

YVETTE: Now you've done it—with your haggling. You can keep the wagon now. He got eleven bullets in him. I don't know why I still bother about you, you don't deserve it, but I just happened to learn they don't think the cash box is really in the river. They suspect it's here, they think you're connected with him. I think they're going to bring him here to see if you'll give yourself away when you see him. You'd better not know him or we're in for it. And I'd better tell you straight, they're just behind me. Shall I keep Kattrin away? [MOTHER COURAGE *shakes her head.*] Does she know? Maybe she never heard the drums or didn't understand.
MOTHER COURAGE: She knows. Bring her.

[YVETTE *brings* KATTRIN, *who walks over to her mother and stands by her.* MOTHER COURAGE *takes her hand. Two men come on with a stretcher; there is a sheet on it and something underneath. Beside them, the* SERGEANT. *They put the stretcher down.*]

THE SERGEANT: Here's a man we can't identify. But he has to be registered to keep the records straight. He bought a meal from you. Look at him, see if you know him. [*He pulls back the sheet.*] Do you know him? [MOTHER COURAGE *shakes her head.*] What? You never saw him before he took that meal? [MOTHER COURAGE *shakes her head.*] Lift him up. Throw him in the carrion pit. He has no one that knows him.

[*They carry him off.*]

Scene Four

MOTHER COURAGE *sings The Song of the Great Capitulation.*

Outside an officer's tent. MOTHER COURAGE *waits.* A CLERK *looks out of the tent.*

THE CLERK: I know you. You had a Protestant paymaster with you, he was hiding out with you. Better make no complaint.

MOTHER COURAGE: But I'm innocent and if I give up it'll look as if I have a bad conscience. They cut everything in my wagon to ribbons with their sabers and then claimed a fine of five thalers for nothing and less than nothing.

THE CLERK: For your own good, keep your trap shut. We haven't many canteens, so we let you stay in business, especially if you've a bad conscience and have to pay a fine now and then.

MOTHER COURAGE: I'm going to file a complaint.

THE CLERK: As you wish. Wait here till the Captain has time.

[*He withdraws into the tent.*]

[A YOUNG SOLDIER *comes storming in.*]

THE YOUNG SOLDIER: Screw the Captain! Where *is* the son of a bitch? Swiping my reward, spending it on brandy for his whores, I'll rip his belly open!

AN OLDER SOLDIER [*Coming after him.*]: Shut your hole, you'll wind up in the stocks.

THE YOUNG SOLDIER: Come out, you thief, I'll make lamb chops out of you! I was the only one in the squad who swam the river and *he* grabs my money, I can't even buy myself a beer. Come on out! And let me slice you up!

THE OLDER SOLDIER: Holy Christ, he'll destroy himself!

THE YOUNG SOLDIER: Let me go or I'll run *you* down too. This has got to be settled!

THE OLDER SOLDIER: Saved the Colonel's horse and didn't get the reward. He's young, he hasn't been at it long.

MOTHER COURAGE: Let him go. He doesn't have to be chained, he's not a dog. Very reasonable to want a reward. Why else should he want to shine?

THE YOUNG SOLDIER: He's in there pouring it down! You're all nice. I've done something special, I want the reward!

MOTHER COURAGE: Young man, don't scream at *me*, I have my own troubles. And go easy with your voice, you may need it when the Captain comes. The Captain'll come and you'll be hoarse and can't make a sound, so he'll have to deny himself the pleasure of sticking you in the stocks till you pass out. The screamers don't scream long, only half an hour, after which they have to be sung to sleep, they're all in.

THE YOUNG SOLDIER: I'm not all in, and sleep's out of the question. I'm hungry. They're making their bread out of acorns and hempseed, and not even much of that. He's whoring on my money, and I'm hungry. I'll murder him!

MOTHER COURAGE: I understand: you're hungry. Last year your Commander ordered you people out of the streets and into the fields. So the crops got trampled down. I could have got ten guilders for boots, if anyone'd had ten guilders, and if I'd had any boots. He didn't expect to be around this year, but he is, and there's famine. I understand: you're angry.

THE YOUNG SOLDIER: It's no use your talking. I won't stand for injustice!

MOTHER COURAGE: You're quite right. But how long? How long won't you stand for injustice? One hour? Or two? you haven't asked yourself that, have you? And yet it's the main thing. It's pure misery to sit in the stocks. Especially if you leave it till then to decide you do stand for injustice.

THE YOUNG SOLDIER: I don't know why I listen to you. Screw that Captain! Where is he?

MOTHER COURAGE: You listen because you know I'm right. Your rage has calmed down already. It was a short one and you'd need a long one. But where would you find it?

THE YOUNG SOLDIER: Are you trying to say it's not right to ask for the money?

MOTHER COURAGE: Just the opposite. I only say, your rage won't last. You'll get nowhere with it, it's a pity. If your rage was a long one, I'd urge you on. Slice him up, I'd advise you. But what's the use if you *don't* slice him up because you *can* feel your tail between your legs? You stand there and the Captain lets you have it.

THE OLDER SOLDIER: You're quite right, he's crazy.

THE YOUNG SOLDIER: All right, we'll see whether I slice him up or not. [*He draws his sword.*] When he comes out, I slice him up!

THE CLERK [*Looking out.*]: The Captain will be out in a minute. [*In the tone of military command.*] Be seated!

[*The* YOUNG SOLDIER *sits.*]

MOTHER COURAGE: And he *is* seated. What did I tell you? You are seated. They know us through and through. They know how they must work it. Be seated! And we sit. And in sitting there's no revolt. Better not stand up again—not the way you did before —don't stand up again. And don't be embarrassed in front of me, I'm no better, not a scrap. They've drawn our teeth, haven't they? If we say boo, it's bad for business. Let me tell you about the great capitulation.

[*She sings "The Song of the Great Capitulation."*]

> Long ago when I was a green beginner
> I believed I was a special case.

(None of your ordinary run of the mill girls, with my looks and talent, and my love of the higher things in life!)

> And if I picked a hair out of my dinner
> I would put the cook right in his place.

(All or nothing. Anyhow, never the second best. I am the master of my Fate. I'll take no orders from no one.)

> Then a little bird whispered in my ear:
> "That's all very well, but wait a year
> And you will join the big brass band
> And with your trumpet in your hand
> You'll march in lockstep with the rest.
> Then one day, look! The battalions wheel!
> The whole thing swings from east to west!
> And falling on your knees, you'll squeal:
> The Lord God, He knows best!
> (But don't give *me* that!)"

> And a month or two before that year was over
> I had learned to drink their cup of tea.

(Two children round your neck, and the price of bread and what all!)

> And the day soon came when I was to discover
> They had me just where they wanted me.

(You must get in good with people. If you scratch my back, I'll scratch yours. Don't stick your neck out.)

> And that little bird whispered in my ear:
> "You didn't even take a year!
> And you have joined the big brass band
> And with your trumpet in your hand
> You marched in lockstep with the rest.
> But one day, look! The battalions wheeled!
> The whole thing swung from east to west!
> And falling on your knees, you squealed:
> The Lord God, He knows best!
> (But don't give *me* that!)"

> Yes, our hopes are high, our plans colossal!
> And we hitch our wagon to a star!

(Where there's a will there's a way. One can't hold a good man down.)

We can move mountains, says St. Paul the great
      Apostle
And yet: how heavy one cigar!

(We must cut our coat according to our cloth.)

> For that little bird whispers in your ear:
> "That's all very well but wait a year
> And we will join the big brass band
> And with our trumpet in our hand
> We march in lockstep with the rest.
> But one day, look! The battalions wheel!
> The whole thing swings from east to west!
> And falling on our knees, we squeal:
> The Lord God, He knows best!
> (But don't give *me* that!)"

And so I think you should stay here with your sword drawn if
you're set on it and your anger is big enough. You have good
cause, I admit. But if your anger is a short one, you'd better go.

THE YOUNG SOLDIER: Kiss my ass. [*He stumbles off, the other*
SOLDIER *following him.*]

THE CLERK [*Sticking his head out.*]: The Captain is ready now.
You can file your complaint.

MOTHER COURAGE: I've thought better of it. I'm not complaining.
[*Exit.*]

[*The* CLERK *looks after her, shaking his head.*]

Scene Five

*Two years have passed. The war covers wider and wider
territory. Forever on the move, the little wagon crosses Poland,
Moravia, Bavaria, Italy, and again Bavaria. 1631. Tilly's victory
at Magdeburg costs* MOTHER COURAGE *four officers' shirts.*

The wagon stands in a war-ravaged village. Faint military music from the distance. Two SOLDIERS *are being served at a counter by* KATTRIN *and* MOTHER COURAGE. *One of them has a woman's fur coat about his soulders.*

MOTHER COURAGE: What, you can't pay? No money, no brandy! They can play victory marches, they should pay their men.

THE FIRST SOLDIER: I want my brandy! I arrived too late for plunder. The Chief allowed one hour to plunder the town, it's a swindle. He's not inhuman, he says. So I suppose they bought him off.

THE CHAPLAIN [*Staggering in.*]: There are more in the farmhouse. A family of peasants. Help me someone. I need linen!

[*The* SECOND SOLDIER *goes with him.* KATTRIN *is getting very excited. She tries to get her mother to bring linen out.*]

MOTHER COURAGE: I have none. I sold all my bandages to the regiment. I'm not tearing up my officers' shirts for these people.

THE CHAPLAIN [*Calling over his shoulder.*]: I said I need linen!

MOTHER COURAGE [*Stopping* KATTRIN *from entering the wagon.*]: Not a thing! They can't pay, and why? They have nothing and they pay nothing!

THE CHAPLAIN [*To a* WOMAN *he is carrying in.*]: Why did you stay out there in the line of fire?

THE WOMAN: Our farm—

MOTHER COURAGE: Think they'd ever let go of *anything*? And now I'm supposed to pay. Well, I won't!

THE FIRST SOLDIER: They're Protestants, why should they be Protestants?

MOTHER COURAGE: Protestant, Catholic, what do *they* care? Their farm's gone, that's what.

THE SECOND SOLDIER: They're not Protestants anyway, they're Catholics.

THE FIRST SOLDIER: In a bombardment we can't pick and choose.

A PEASANT [*Brought on by the* CHAPLAIN.]: My arm's gone.

THE CHAPLAIN: Where's that linen?

[*All look at* MOTHER COURAGE, *who does not budge.*]

MOTHER COURAGE: I can't give you any. With all I have to pay out—taxes, duties, bribes. . . . [KATTRIN *takes up a board and threatens her mother with it, emitting gurgling sounds.*] Are you out of your mind? Put that board down or I'll let you have one, you lunatic! I'm giving nothing, I don't dare, I have myself to think of. [*The* CHAPLAIN *lifts her bodily off the steps of the wagon and sets her down on the ground. He takes out shirts from the wagon and tears them in strips.*] My shirts, my officers' shirts!

[*From the house comes the cry of a child in pain.*]

THE PEASANT: The child's still in there.

[KATTRIN *runs in.*]

THE CHAPLAIN [*To the* WOMAN.]: Stay where you are. She's getting it for you.

MOTHER COURAGE: Hold her back, the roof may fall in!

THE CHAPLAIN: I'm not going back in there!

MOTHER COURAGE [*Pulled in both directions.*]: Go easy on my expensive linen.

[*The* SECOND SOLDIER *holds her back.* KATTRIN *brings a baby out of the ruins.*]

MOTHER COURAGE: Another baby to drag around, you must be pleased with yourself. Give it to its mother this minute! Or do I have to fight you again for hours till I get it from you? Are you deaf? [*To the* SECOND SOLDIER.] Don't stand about gawking, go back there and tell 'em to stop that music, I can see their victory without it. I have nothing but losses from your victory!

THE CHAPLAIN [*Bandaging.*]: The blood's coming through.

[KATTRIN *is rocking the child and half humming a lullaby.*]

MOTHER COURAGE: There she sits, happy as a lark in all this misery. Give the baby back, the mother is coming to! [*She sees the* FIRST SOLDIER. *He had been handling the drinks, and is now trying to make off with the bottle.*] God's truth! You beast! You want another victory, do you? Then pay for it!

THE FIRST SOLDIER: I have nothing.

MOTHER COURAGE [*Snatching the fur coat back.*]: Then leave this coat, it's stolen goods anyhow.

THE CHAPLAIN: There's still someone in there.

Scene Six

Before the city of Ingolstadt in Bavaria MOTHER COURAGE is present at the funeral of the fallen commander, Tilly. Conversations take place about war heroes and the duration of the war. The chaplain complains that his talents are lying fallow and KATTRIN gets the red boots. The year is 1632.

The inside of a canteen tent. The inner side of a counter at the rear. Rain. In the distance, drums and funeral music. The CHAPLAIN *and the regimental* CLERK *are playing draughts.* MOTHER COURAGE *and her daughter are taking an inventory.*

THE CHAPLAIN: The funeral procession is just starting out.

MOTHER COURAGE: Pity about the Chief—twenty-two pairs of socks—getting killed that way. They say it was an accident. There was a fog over the fields that morning, and the fog was to blame. The Chief called up another regiment, told 'em to fight to the death, rode back again, missed his way in the fog, went forward instead of back, and ran smack into a bullet in the thick of the battle—only four lanterns left. [*A whistle from the rear. She goes to the counter. To a* SOLDIER.] It's a disgrace the way you're all skipping your Commander's funeral! [*She pours a drink.*]

THE CLERK: They shouldn't have handed the money out before the funeral. Now the men are all getting drunk instead of going to it.

THE CHAPLAIN [*To the* CLERK]: Don't you have to be there?

THE CLERK: I stayed away because of the rain.

MOTHER COURAGE: It's different for you, the rain might spoil your uniform. I hear they wanted to ring the bells for his funeral, which is natural, but it came out that the churches had been shot up by his orders, so the poor Commander won't be hearing any bells when they lower him in his grave. Instead, they'll fire off three shots so the occasion won't be *too* sober—sixteen leather belts.

A VOICE FROM THE COUNTER: Service! One brandy!

MOTHER COURAGE: Your money first. No, you *can't* come inside the tent, not with those boots on. You can drink outside, rain or no rain. I only let officers in here. [*To the* CLERK.] The Chief had his troubles lately, I hear. There was unrest in the Second Regiment because he didn't pay 'em but he said it was a war of religion and they must fight it free of charge.

[*Funeral march. All look toward the rear.*]

THE CHAPLAIN: Now they're filing past the body.

MOTHER COURAGE: I feel sorry for a Commander or an Emperor like that—when he might have had something special in mind, something they'd talk about in times to come, something they'd raise a statue to him for. The conquest of the world now, *that's* a goal for a Commander, he wouldn't know any better.... Lord, worms have got into the biscuits.... In short, he works his hands to the bone and then it's all spoiled by the common riffraff that only wants a jug of beer or a bit of company, not the higher things in life. The finest plans have always been spoiled by the littleness of them that should carry them out. Even Emperors can't do it all by themselves. They count on support from their soldiers and the people round about. Am I right?

THE CHAPLAIN [*Laughing.*]: You're right, Mother Courage, till you come to the soldiers. They do what they can. Those fellows outside, for example, drinking their brandy in the rain, I'd trust 'em to fight a hundred years, one war after another, two at a time if necessary. And I wasn't trained as a commander.

MOTHER COURAGE: ... Seventeen leather belts.... Then you don't think the war might end?

THE CHAPLAIN: Because a commander's dead? Don't be childish, they're a dime a dozen. There are always heroes.

MOTHER COURAGE: Well, I wasn't asking for the sake of argument. I was wondering if I should buy up a lot of supplies. They happen to be cheap just now. But if the war ended, I might just as well throw them away.

THE CHAPLAIN: I realize you are serious, Mother Courage. Well, there've always been people going around saying some day the war will end. I say, you can't be sure the war will *ever* end. Of

course it may have to pause occasionally—for breath, as it were—
it can even meet with an accident—nothing on this earth is
perfect—a war of which we could say it left nothing to be desired
will probably never exist. A war can come to a sudden halt—from
unforeseen causes—you can't think of everything—a little over-
sight, and the war's in the hole, and someone's got to pull it out
again! The someone is the Emperor or the King or the Pope.
They're such friends in need, the war has really nothing to worry
about, it can look forward to a prosperous future.

A SOLDIER [*Singing at the counter.*]:

> One schnapps, mine host, make haste!
> For we have no time to waste:
> We must be shooting, shooting, shooting
> Our Emperor's enemies uprooting!

Make it a double. This is a holiday.

MOTHER COURAGE: If I was sure you're right. . . .

THE CHAPLAIN: Think it out for yourself: how *could* the war end?

THE SOLDIER [*Off-stage.*]:

> Two breasts, mine host, make haste!
> For we have no time to waste:
> We must be hating, hating, hating
> We cannot keep our Emperor waiting!

THE CLERK [*Suddenly.*]: What about peace? Yes, peace. I'm from
Bohemia. I'd like to get home once in a while.

THE CHAPLAIN: Oh, you would, would you? Dear old peace! What
happens to the hole when the cheese is gone?

THE SOLDIER [*Off-stage.*]:

> Your blessing, priest, make haste!
> For we have no time to waste:
> We must be dying, dying, dying
> Our Emperor's greatness glorifying!

THE CLERK: In the long run you can't live without peace!

THE CHAPLAIN: Well, I'd say there's peace even in war, war has
its islands of peace. For war satisfies *all* needs, even those of

peace, yes, they're provided for, or the war couldn't keep going. In war—as in the very thick of peace—you can take a crap, and between one battle and the next there's always a beer, and even on the march you can snatch a nap—on your elbow maybe, in a gutter—something can always be managed. Of course you can't play cards during an attack, but neither can you while ploughing the fields in peace time: it's when the victory's won that there are possibilities. You have your leg shot off, and at first you raise quite an outcry as if it *was* something, but soon you calm down or take a swig of brandy, and you end up hopping about, and the war is none the worse for your little misadventure. And can't you be fruitful and multiply in the thick of slaughter—behind a barn or somewhere? Nothing can keep you from it very long in any event. And so the war has your offspring and can carry on. War is like love, it always finds a way. Why *should* it end?

[KATTRIN *has stopped working. She stares at the* CHAPLAIN.]

MOTHER COURAGE: Then I *will* buy those supplies, I'll rely on you. [KATTRIN *suddenly bangs a basket of glasses down on the ground and runs out.* MOTHER COURAGE *laughs.*] Kattrin! Lord, Kattrin's still going to wait for peace. I promised her she'll get a husband—when it's peace. [*She runs after her.*]

THE CLERK [*Standing up.*]: I win. You were talking. You pay.

MOTHER COURAGE [*Returning with* KATTRIN.]: Be sensible, the war'll go on a bit longer, and we'll make a bit more money, then peace'll be all the nicer. Now you go into the town, it's not ten minutes walk, and bring the things from the Golden Lion, just the more expensive ones, we can get the rest later in the wagon. It's all arranged, the clerk will go with you, most of the soldiers are at the Commander's funeral, nothing can happen to you. Do a good job, don't lose anything, Kattrin, think of your trousseau!

[KATTRIN *ties a cloth around her head and leaves with the* CLERK.]

THE CHAPLAIN: You don't mind her going with the clerk?

MOTHER COURAGE: She's not so pretty anyone would want to ruin her.

THE CHAPLAIN: The way you run your business and always come through is highly commendable, Mother Courage—I see how you got your name.

MOTHER COURAGE: The poor need courage. Why? They're lost. That they even get up in the morning is something—in *their* plight. Or that they plough a field—in war time. Even their bringing children into the world shows they have courage, for they have no prospects. They have to hang each other one by one and slaughter each other in the lump, so if they want to look each other in the face once in a while, well, it takes courage. That they put up with an Emperor and a Pope, that takes an unnatural amount of courage, for *they* cost you your life. [*She sits, takes a small pipe from her pocket and smokes it.*] You might chop me a bit of firewood.

THE CHAPLAIN [*Reluctantly taking his coat off and preparing to chop wood.*]: Properly speaking, I'm a pastor of souls, not a woodcutter.

MOTHER COURAGE: But I don't have a soul. And I do need wood.

THE CHAPLAIN: What's that little pipe you've got there?

MOTHER COURAGE: Just a pipe.

THE CHAPLAIN: I think it's a very particular pipe.

MOTHER COURAGE: Oh?

THE CHAPLAIN: The cook's pipe in fact. The cook from the Oxenstierna Regiment.

MOTHER COURAGE: If you know, why beat about the bush?

THE CHAPLAIN: Because I don't know if you've been *aware* that's what you've been smoking. It was possible you just rummaged among your belongings and your fingers just lit on a pipe and you just took it. In pure absent-mindedness.

MOTHER COURAGE: How do you know that's not it?

THE CHAPLAIN: It isn't. You *are* aware of it. [*He brings the ax down on the block with a crash.*]

MOTHER COURAGE: What if I was?

THE CHAPLAIN: I must give you a warning, Mother Courage, it's my duty. You are unlikely to see the gentleman again but that's no pity, you're in luck. Mother Courage, he did not impress me as trustworthy. On the contrary.

MOTHER COURAGE: Really? He was such a nice man.

THE CHAPLAIN: Well! So that's what you call a nice man. I do not. [*The ax falls again.*] Far be it from me to wish him ill, but I cannot—cannot—describe him as nice. No, no, he's a Don Juan, a cunning Don Juan. Just look at that pipe if you don't believe me. You must admit it tells all.

MOTHER COURAGE: I see nothing special in it. It's been used, of course.

THE CHAPLAIN: It's bitten halfway through! He's a man of great violence! It is the pipe of a man of great violence, you can see *that* if you've any judgment left! [*He deals the block a tremendous blow.*]

MOTHER COURAGE: Don't bite my chopping block halfway through!

THE CHAPLAIN: I told you I had no training as a woodcutter. The care of souls was my field. Around here my gifts and capabilities are grossly misused. In physical labor my God-given talents find no—um—adequate expression—which is a sin. You haven't heard me preach. Why, I can put such spirit into a regiment with a single sermon that the enemy's a mere flock of sheep to them and their own lives no more than smelly old shoes to be thrown away at the thought of final victory! God has given me the gift of tongues. I can preach you out of your senses!

MOTHER COURAGE: I need my senses. What would I do without them?

THE CHAPLAIN: Mother Courage, I have often thought that—under a veil of plain speech—you conceal a heart. You are human, you need warmth.

MOTHER COURAGE: The best way of warming this tent is to chop plenty of firewood.

THE CHAPLAIN: You're changing the subject. Seriously, my dear Courage, I sometimes ask myself how it would be if our relationship should be somewhat more firmly cemented. I mean, now the wild wind of war has whirled us so strangely together.

MOTHER COURAGE: The cement's pretty firm already. I cook your meals. And you lend a hand—at chopping firewood, for instance.

THE CHAPLAIN: [*Going over to her, gesturing with the ax*]: You know what I mean by a close relationship. It has nothing to do with eating and woodcutting and such base necessities. Let your heart speak!

MOTHER COURAGE: Don't come at me like that with your ax, that'd be *too* close a relationship!

THE CHAPLAIN: This is no laughing matter, I am in earnest. I've thought it all over.

MOTHER COURAGE: Dear Chaplain, be a sensible fellow. I like

you, and I don't want to heap coals of fire on your head. All I want is to bring me and my children through in that wagon. It isn't just mine, the wagon, and anyway I've no mind to start any adventures. At the moment I'm taking quite a risk buying these things when the Commander's fallen and there's all this talk of peace. Where would you go, if I was ruined? See? You don't even know. Now chop some firewood and it'll be warm of an evening, which is quite a lot in times like these. What was that? [*She stands up.* KATTRIN *enters, breathless, with a wound across the eye and forehead. She is dragging all sorts of articles, parcels, leather goods, a drum, etc.*] What is it, were you attacked? On the way back? She was attacked on the way back! I'll bet it was that soldier who got drunk on my liquor. I should never have let you go. Dump all that stuff! It's not bad, the wound is only a flesh wound. I'll bandage it for you, it'll all be healed in a week. They're worse than animals. [*She bandages the wound.*]

THE CHAPLAIN: I reproach them with nothing. At home they never did these shameful things. The men who start the wars are responsible, they bring out the worst in people.

MOTHER COURAGE: Didn't the clerk walk you back home? That's because you're a respectable girl, he thought they'd leave you alone. The wound's not at all deep, it will never show. There: all bandaged up. Now, I've got something for you, rest easy. I've been keeping them secret. [*She digs* YVETTE's *red boots out of a bag.*] Well, what do you see? You always wanted them. Now you have them. [*She helps her to put the boots on.*] Put them on quick, before I change my mind. It will never show, though it wouldn't bother *me* if it did. The ones they like fare worst. They drag them around till they're finished. Those they don't care for they leave alone. I've seen so many girls, pretty as they come in the beginning, then all of a sudden they're so ugly they'd scare a wolf. They can't even go behind a tree on the street without having something to fear from it. They lead a frightful life. Like with trees: the tall, straight ones are cut down for roof timber, and the crooked ones can enjoy life. So this wound here is really a piece of luck. The boots have kept well. I gave them a good cleaning before I put them away.

[KATTRIN *leaves the boots and creeps into the wagon.*]

THE CHAPLAIN [*When she's gone.*]: I hope she won't be dis-
figured?

MOTHER COURAGE: There'll be a scar. She needn't wait for peace
now.

THE CHAPLAIN: She didn't let them get any of the stuff.

MOTHER COURAGE: Maybe I shouldn't have made such a point
of it. If only I ever knew what went on inside her head. Once
she stayed out all night, once in all the years. Afterward she
seemed much the same, except that she worked harder. I could
never get out of her what happened. I worried about it for quite
a while. [*She picks up the things* KATTRIN *spilled and sorts them
angrily.*] This is war. A nice source of income, I must say!

[*Cannon shots.*]

THE CHAPLAIN: Now they're lowering the Commander into his
grave! A historic moment.

MOTHER COURAGE: It's a historic moment to me when they hit
my daughter over the eye. She's all but finished now, she'll never
get a husband, and she's so mad about children! Even her
dumbness comes from the war. A soldier stuck something in her
mouth when she was little. I'll never see Swiss Cheese again,
and where my Eilif is the Good Lord knows. Curse the war!

Scene Seven

MOTHER COURAGE *at the height of her business career.*

A highway. The CHAPLAIN, MOTHER COURAGE, *and her daughter* KATTRIN *pull the wagon, and new wares are hanging from
it.* MOTHER COURAGE *wears a necklace of silver coins.*

MOTHER COURAGE: I won't let you spoil my war for me. Destroys
the weak, does it? Well, what does peace do for 'em, huh? War
feeds its people better.

[*She sings.*]

> If war don't suit your disposition
> When victory comes, you will be dead.
> War is a business proposition:
> But not with cheese, with steel instead!
>> Christians, awake! Winter is gone!
>> The snows depart! Dead men sleep on!
>> Let all of you who still survive
>> Get out of bed and look alive!

And staying in one place won't help either. Those who stay at home are the first to go.

[*She sings.*]

> Too many seek a bed to sleep in:
> Each ditch is taken, and each cave
> And he who digs a hole to creep in
> Finds he has dug an early grave.
> And many a man spends many a minute
> In hurrying toward some resting place.
> You wonder, when at last he's in it
> Just why the fellow forced the pace.

[*The wagon proceeds.*]

Scene Eight

1632. In this same year Gustavus Adolphus fell in the battle of Lützen. The peace threatens MOTHER COURAGE *with ruin. Her brave son performs one heroic deed too many and comes to a shameful end.*

[*A camp. A summer morning. In front of the wagon, an* OLD WOMAN *and her son. The son is dragging a large bag of bedding.*]

MOTHER COURAGE [*From inside the wagon.*]: Must you come at the crack of dawn?

THE YOUNG MAN: We've been walking all night, twenty miles it was, we have to be back today.

MOTHER COURAGE [*Still inside.*]: What do I want with bed feathers? People don't even have houses.

THE YOUNG MAN: At least wait till you see 'em.

THE OLD WOMAN: Nothing doing here either, let's go.

THE YOUNG MAN: And let 'em sign away the roof over our heads for taxes? Maybe she'll pay three guilders if you throw in that bracelet. [*Bells start ringing.*] You hear, mother?

VOICES [*From the rear.*]: It's peace! The King of Sweden's been killed!

[MOTHER COURAGE *sticks her head out of the wagon. She hasn't done her hair yet.*]

MOTHER COURAGE: Bells! What are the bells for, middle of the week?

THE CHAPLAIN [*Crawling out from under the wagon.*]: What's that they're shouting?

THE YOUNG MAN: It's peace.

THE CHAPLAIN: Peace!

MOTHER COURAGE: Don't tell me peace has broken out—when I've just gone and bought all these supplies!

THE CHAPLAIN [*Calling, toward the rear.*]: Is it peace?

VOICE [*From a distance.*]: They say the war stopped three weeks ago. I've only just heard.

THE CHAPLAIN [*To* MOTHER COURAGE.]: Or why would they ring the bells?

VOICE: A great crowd of Lutherans have just arrived with wagons —they brought the news.

THE YOUNG MAN: It's peace, mother. [*The* OLD WOMAN *collapses.*] What's the matter?

MOTHER COURAGE [*Back in the wagon.*]: Kattrin, it's peace! Put on your black dress, we're going to church, we owe it to Swiss Cheese! Can it be true?

THE YOUNG MAN: The people here say so too, the war's over. Can you stand up? [*The* OLD WOMAN *stands up, dazed.*] I'll get the harness shop going again now, I promise you. Everything'll be all right, father will get his bed back. . . . Can you walk? [*To the* CHAPLAIN.] She felt ill, it was the news. She didn't believe there'd ever be peace again. Father always said there would. We're going home. [*They leave.*]

MOTHER COURAGE [*Off.*]: Give her some brandy.

THE CHAPLAIN: They've left already.

MOTHER COURAGE [*Still off.*]: What's going on in the camp over there?

THE CHAPLAIN: They're all getting together. I think I'll go over. Shall I put my pastor's coat on again?

MOTHER COURAGE: Better get the exact news first, and not risk being taken for the Antichrist. I'm glad about the peace even though I'm ruined. At least I've got two of my children through the war. Now I'll see my Eilif again.

THE CHAPLAIN: And who may this be coming down from the camp? Well, if it isn't our Swedish Commander's cook!

THE COOK [*Somewhat bedraggled, carrying a bundle.*]: Who's here? The chaplain!

THE CHAPLAIN: Mother Courage, a visitor!

[MOTHER COURAGE *clambers out.*]

THE COOK: Well, I promised I'd come over for a brief conversation as soon as I had time. I didn't forget your brandy, Mrs. Fierling.

MOTHER COURAGE: Jesus, the Commander's cook! After all these years! Where is Eilif, my eldest?

THE COOK: Isn't he here yet? He went on ahead yesterday, he was on his way over.

THE CHAPLAIN: I *will* put my pastor's coat on. I'll be back. [*He goes behind the wagon.*]

MOTHER COURAGE: He may be here any minute then. [*She calls toward the wagon.*] Kattrin, Eilif's coming! Bring a glass of brandy for the cook, Kattrin! [KATTRIN *doesn't come.*] Just pull your hair over it. Mr. Lamb is no stranger. [*She gets the brandy herself.*] She won't come out. Peace is nothing to her, it was too long coming. They hit her right over the eye. You can hardly see it now. But she thinks people stare at her.

THE COOK: Ah yes, war! [*He and* MOTHER COURAGE *sit.*]

MOTHER COURAGE: Cook, you come at a bad time: I'm ruined.

THE COOK: What? That's terrible!

MOTHER COURAGE: The peace has broken my neck. On the chaplain's advice I've gone and bought a lot of supplies. Now everybody's leaving and I'm holding the baby.

THE COOK: How could you listen to the chaplain? If I'd had time—but the Catholics were too quick for me—I'd have warned you against him. He's a windbag. Well, so now he's the big man round here!

MOTHER COURAGE: He's been doing the dishes for me and helping with the wagon.

THE COOK: With the wagon—him! And I'll bet he's told you a few of his jokes. He has a most unhealthy attitude to women. I tried to influence him but it was no good. He isn't sound.

MOTHER COURAGE: Are you sound?

THE COOK: If I'm nothing else, I'm sound. Your health!

MOTHER COURAGE: Sound! Only one person around here was ever sound, and I never had to slave as I did then. He sold the blankets off the children's beds in the spring, and he called my harmonica unchristian. You aren't recommending yourself if you *admit* you're sound.

THE COOK: You fight tooth and nail, don't you? I like that.

MOTHER COURAGE: Don't tell me you've been dreaming of my teeth and nails.

THE COOK: Well, here we sit, while the bells of peace do ring, and you pouring your famous brandy as only you know how!

MOTHER COURAGE: I don't think much of the bells of peace at the moment. I don't see how they can hand out all this pay that's in arrears. And then where shall I be with my famous brandy? Have you all been paid?

THE COOK [*Hesitating.*]: Not exactly. That's why we disbanded. In the circumstances, I thought, why stay? For the time being, I'll look up a couple of friends. So here I sit—with you.

MOTHER COURAGE: In other words, you're broke.

THE COOK [*Annoyed by the bells.*]: It's about time they stopped that racket! I'd like to set myself up in some business. I'm fed up with being their cook. I'm supposed to make do with tree roots and shoe leather, and then they throw my hot soup in my face! Being a cook nowadays is a dog's life. I'd sooner be a soldier, but of course, it's peace now. [*As the* CHAPLAIN *turns up, wearing his old coat.*] We'll talk it over later.

THE CHAPLAIN: The coat's pretty good. Just a few moth holes.

THE COOK: I don't know why you take the trouble. You won't find another pulpit. Who could you incite now to earn an honest living or risk his life for a cause? Besides, I have a bone to pick with you.

THE CHAPLAIN: Have you?

THE COOK: I have. You advised a lady to buy superfluous goods on the pretext that the war would never end.

THE CHAPLAIN [*Hotly.*]: I'd like to know what business it is of yours?

THE COOK: It's unprincipled behavior! How can you give unwanted advice? And interfere with the conduct of other people's business?

THE CHAPLAIN: Who's interfering now, I'd like to know? [*To* MOTHER COURAGE.] I had no idea you were such a close friend of this gentleman and had to account to *him* for everything.

MOTHER COURAGE: Now don't get excited. The cook's giving his personal opinion. You can't deny your war was a flop.

THE CHAPLAIN: You have no respect for peace, Courage. You're a hyena of the battlefield!

MOTHER COURAGE: A what?

THE COOK: Who insults my girl friend insults me!

THE CHAPLAIN: I am *not* speaking to you, your intentions are only too transparent! [*To* MOTHER COURAGE.] But when I see *you* take peace between finger and thumb like a snotty old hanky, my humanity rebels! It shows that you want war, not peace, for what you get out of it. But don't forget the proverb: he who sups with the devil must use a long spoon!

MOTHER COURAGE: Remember what one fox said to another that was caught in a trap? "If you stay there, you're just asking for trouble!" There isn't much love lost between me and the war. And when it comes to calling me a hyena, you and I part company.

THE CHAPLAIN: Then why all this grumbling about the peace just as everyone's heaving a sigh of relief? Is it for the junk in your wagon?

MOTHER COURAGE: My goods are not junk. I live off them. *You've* been living off them.

THE CHAPLAIN: You live off war. Exactly.

THE COOK [*To the* CHAPLAIN.]: As a grown man, you should know better than to go around advising people. [*To* MOTHER COURAGE.] Now, in your situation you'd be smart to get rid of certain goods at once—before the prices sink to nothing. Get ready and get going, there isn't a moment to lose!

MOTHER COURAGE: That's sensible advice, I think I'll take it.

THE CHAPLAIN: Because the cook says so.

MOTHER COURAGE: Why didn't *you* say so? He's right, I must get to the market. [*She climbs into the wagon.*]

THE COOK: One up for me, Chaplain. You have no presence of mind. You should have said, "I gave you advice? Why, I was just talking politics!" And you shouldn't take me on as a rival. Cockfights are not becoming to your cloth.

THE CHAPLAIN: If you don't shut your trap, I'll murder you, cloth or no cloth!

THE COOK [*Taking his boots off and unwinding the wrappings on his feet.*]: If you hadn't degenerated into a godless tramp, you could easily get yourself a parsonage, now it's peace. Cooks won't be needed, there's nothing to cook, but there's still plenty to believe, and people will go right on believing it.

THE CHAPLAIN: Mr. Lamb, please don't drive me out! Since I became a tramp, I'm a somewhat better man. I couldn't preach to 'em any more.

[YVETTE POTTIER *enters, decked out in black, with a stick. She is much older, fatter, and heavily powdered. Behind her, a* SERVANT.]

YVETTE: Hello, everybody! Is this Mother Courage's establishment?

THE CHAPLAIN: Quite right. And with whom have we the pleasure?

YVETTE: I am Madame Colonel Starhemberg, good people. Where's Mother Courage?

THE CHAPLAIN [*Calling to the wagon.*]: Madame Colonel Starhemberg wants to speak to you!

MOTHER COURAGE [*From inside.*]: Coming!

YVETTE [*Calling.*]: It's Yvette!

MOTHER COURAGE [*Inside.*]: Yvette!

YVETTE: Just to see how you're getting on! [*As the* COOK *turns around in horror.*] Peter!

THE COOK: Yvette!

YVETTE: Of all things! How did *you* get here?

THE COOK: On a cart.

THE CHAPLAIN: Well! You know each other? Intimately?

YVETTE: I'll say. [*Scrutinizing the* COOK.] You're fat.

THE COOK: For that matter, *you're* no beanpole.

YVETTE: Anyway, nice meeting you, tramp. Now I can tell you what I think of you.

THE CHAPLAIN: Do so, tell him all, but wait till Mother Courage comes out.

THE COOK: Now don't make a scene . . .

MOTHER COURAGE [*Coming out, laden with goods.*]: Yvette! [*They embrace.*] But why are you in mourning?

YVETTE: Doesn't it suit me? My husband, the colonel, died several years ago.

MOTHER COURAGE: The old fellow that nearly bought my wagon?

YVETTE: His elder brother.

MOTHER COURAGE: So you're not doing badly. Good to see one person who got somewhere in the war.

YVETTE: I've had my ups and downs.

MOTHER COURAGE: Don't let's speak ill of colonels. They make money like hay.

THE CHAPLAIN [*To the* COOK.]: If I were you, I'd put my shoes on again. [*To* YVETTE.] You promised to give us your opinion of this gentleman.

THE COOK: Now, Yvette, don't make a stink!

MOTHER COURAGE: He's a friend of mine, Yvette.

YVETTE: He's—Peter Piper, that's who.

MOTHER COURAGE: What!

THE COOK: Cut the nicknames. My name's Lamb.

MOTHER COURAGE [*Laughing.*]: Peter Piper? Who turned the women's heads? And I've been keeping your pipe for you.

THE CHAPLAIN: And smoking it.

YVETTE: Lucky I can warn you against him. He's a bad lot. You won't find worse on the whole coast of Flanders. He got more girls in trouble than . . . .

THE COOK: That's a long time ago, it isn't true any more.

YVETTE: Stand up when you talk to a lady! Oh, how I loved that man; and all the time he was having a little bow-legged brunette. He got *her* into trouble too, of course.

THE COOK: I seem to have brought *you* luck!

YVETTE: Shut your trap, you hoary ruin! And you take care, Mother Courage, this type is still dangerous even in decay!

MOTHER COURAGE [*To* YVETTE.]: Come with me, I must get rid of this stuff before the prices fall.

YVETTE [*Concentrating on the* COOK.]: Miserable cur!

MOTHER COURAGE: Maybe you can help me at army headquarters, you have contacts.

YVETTE: Seducer!

MOTHER COURAGE [*Shouting into the wagon.*]: Kattrin, church is all off, I'm going to market!

YVETTE: Whore hunter!

MOTHER COURAGE [*Still to* KATTRIN.]: When Eilif comes, give him something to drink!

YVETTE: That a man like him should have been able to turn me from the straight and narrow! I have my own star to thank that I rose none the less to the heights! But I've put an end to your tricks, Peter Piper, and one day—in a better life than this—the Lord God will reward me! Come, Mother Courage! [*She leaves with* MOTHER COURAGE.]

THE CHAPLAIN: As our text this morning let us take the saying: the mills of God grind slowly. And you complain of my jokes!

THE COOK: I never have any luck. I'll be frank, I was hoping for a good hot dinner, I'm starving. And now they'll be talking about me, and she'll get a completely wrong picture. I think I should go before she comes back.

THE CHAPLAIN: I think so too.

THE COOK: Chaplain, peace makes me sick. Mankind must perish by fire and sword, we're born and bred in sin! Oh, how I wish I was roasting a great fat capon for the Commander—God knows where *he's* got to—with mustard sauce and those little yellow carrots. . . .

THE CHAPLAIN: Red cabbage—with capon, red cabbage.

THE COOK: You're right. But he always wanted yellow carrots.

THE CHAPLAIN: He never understood a thing.

THE COOK: You always put plenty away.

THE CHAPLAIN: Under protest.

THE COOK: Anyway, you must admit, those were the days.

THE CHAPLAIN: Yes, that I might admit.

THE COOK: Now you've called her a hyena, there's not much future for you here either. What are you staring at?

THE CHAPLAIN: It's Eilif!

[*Followed by two soldiers with halberds,* EILIF *enters. His hands are fettered. He is white as chalk.*]

THE CHAPLAIN: What's happened to you?
EILIF: Where's mother?
THE CHAPLAIN: Gone to town.
EILIF: They said she was here. I was allowed a last visit.
THE COOK [*To the* SOLDIERS.]: Where are you taking him?
A SOLDIER: For a ride.

[*The other* SOLDIER *makes the gesture of throat cutting.*]

THE CHAPLAIN: What has he done?
THE SOLDIER: He broke in on a peasant. The wife is dead.
THE CHAPLAIN: Eilif, how could you?
EILIF: It's no different. It's what I did before.
THE COOK: That was in war time.
EILIF: Shut your hole. Can I sit down till she comes?
THE SOLDIER: No.
THE CHAPLAIN: It's true. In war time they honored him for it.
    He sat at the Commander's right hand. It was bravery. Couldn't
    we speak with the military police?
THE SOLDIER: What's the use? Stealing cattle from a peasant,
    what's brave about that?
THE COOK: It was just stupid.
EILIF: If I'd been stupid, I'd have starved, smarty.
THE COOK: So you were bright and paid for it.
THE CHAPLAIN: At least we must bring Kattrin out.
EILIF: Let her alone. Just give me some brandy.
THE SOLDIER: No.
THE CHAPLAIN: What shall we tell your mother?
EILIF: Tell her it was no different. Tell her it was the same. Oh,
    tell her nothing.

[*The* SOLDIERS *take him away.*]

THE CHAPLAIN: I'll come with you, I'll . . . .
EILIF: I don't need a priest!
THE CHAPLAIN: You don't know—yet. [*He follows him.*]
THE COOK [*Calling after him.*]: I'll have to tell her, she'll want to
    see him!

THE CHAPLAIN: Better tell her nothing. Or maybe just that he was here, and he'll return, maybe tomorrow. Meantime I'll be back and can break the news. [*He leaves quickly.*]

[*The* COOK *looks after him, shakes his head, then walks about uneasily. Finally, he approaches the wagon.*]

THE COOK: Hello! Won't you come out? You want to sneak away from the peace, don't you? Well, so do I! I'm the Swedish Commander's cook, remember me? I was wondering if you've got anything to eat in there—while we're waiting for your mother. I wouldn't mind a bit of bacon—or even bread—just to pass the time. [*He looks in.*] She's got a blanket over her head.

[*The thunder of cannon.*]

[MOTHER COURAGE *runs in, out of breath, still carrying the goods.*]

MOTHER COURAGE: Cook, the peace is over, the war's on again, has been for three days! I didn't get rid of this stuff after all, thank God! There's a shooting match in the town already—with the Lutherans. We must get away with the wagon. Pack, Kattrin! What's on *your* mind? Something the matter?

THE COOK: Nothing.

MOTHER COURAGE: But there is. I see it in your face.

THE COOK: Because the war's on again, most likely. May it last till tomorrow evening, so I can get something in my belly!

MOTHER COURAGE: You're not telling me.

THE COOK: Eilif was here. Only he had to go away again.

MOTHER COURAGE: He was here? Then we'll see him on the march. I'll be with our side this time. How'd he look?

THE COOK: The same.

MOTHER COURAGE: He'll *never* change. And the war couldn't get *him*, he's bright. Help me with the packing. [*She starts it.*] Did he tell you anything? Is he well in with the Captain? Did he tell you about his heroic deeds?

THE COOK [*Darkly.*]: He's done one of them again.

MOTHER COURAGE: Tell me about it later. [KATTRIN *appears.*] Kattrin, the peace is over, we're on the move again. [*To the* COOK.]: What *is* the matter with you?

THE COOK: I'll enlist.

MOTHER COURAGE: A good idea. Where's the Chaplain?

THE COOK: In the town. With Eilif.

MOTHER COURAGE: Stay with us a while, Lamb, I need a bit of help.

THE COOK: This matter of Yvette . . . .

MOTHER COURAGE: Hasn't done you any harm at all in my eyes. Just the opposite. Where there's smoke, there's fire, they say. You'll come?

THE COOK: I may as well.

MOTHER COURAGE: The Twelfth Regiment's under way. Into harness with you! Maybe I'll see Eilif before the day is out, just think! That's what I like best. Well, it wasn't such a long peace, we can't grumble. Let's go!

[*The* COOK *and* KATTRIN *are in harness.*]

MOTHER COURAGE *sings:*

> From Ulm to Metz, past dome and steeple
> My wagon always moves ahead.
> The war can care for all its people
> So long as there is steel and lead.
> Though steel and lead are stout supporters
> A war needs human beings too.
> Report today to your headquarters!
> If it's to last, this war needs you!

Scene Nine

The great war of religion has lasted sixteen years and Germany has lost half its inhabitants. Those who are spared in battle die by plague. Over once blooming countryside hunger rages. Towns are burned down. Wolves prowl the empty streets. In the autumn of 1634 we find MOTHER COURAGE in the Fichtelgebirge not far from the road the Swedish army is taking. Winter has come early and is hard. Business is bad.

Only begging remains. The cook *receives a letter from Utrecht and is sent packing.*

In front of a half-ruined parsonage. Early winter. A gray morning. Gusts of wind. mother courage *and the cook at the wagon in shabby clothes.*

The Cook: There are no lights on. No one's up.

Mother Courage: But it's a parsonage. The parson'll have to leave his feather bed and ring the bells. Then he'll have some hot soup.

The Cook: Where'll he get it from? The whole village is starving.

Mother Courage: The house is lived in. There was a dog barking.

The Cook: If the parson has anything, he'll hang on to it.

Mother Courage: Maybe if we sang him something . . . .

The Cook: I've had enough. [*Suddenly.*] I didn't tell you, a letter came from Utrecht. My mother's died of cholera, the inn is mine. There's the letter, if you don't believe me. I'll show it to you, though my aunt's railing about me and my ups and downs is none of your business.

Mother Courage [*Reading.*]: Lamb, I'm tired of wandering, too. I feel like a butcher's dog taking meat to my customers and getting none myself. I've nothing more to sell and people have nothing to pay with. In Saxony someone tried to force a chestful of books on me in return for two eggs. And in Württemberg they would have let me have their plough for a bag of salt. Nothing grows any more, only thorn bushes. In Pomerania I hear the villagers have been eating their younger children. Nuns have been caught committing robbery.

The Cook: The world's dying out.

Mother Courage: Sometimes I see myself driving through hell with this wagon and selling brimstone. And sometimes I'm driving through heaven handing our provisions to wandering souls! If only we could find a place where there's no shooting, me and my children—what's left of 'em—we might rest a while.

The Cook: We could open this inn together. Think about it, Courage. *My* mind's made up. With or without you, I'm leaving for Utrecht. And today too.

Mother Courage: I must talk to Kattrin, it's a bit sudden, and I don't like to make my decisions in the cold on an empty stomach. [kattrin *emerges from the wagon.*] Kattrin, I've something to tell you. The cook and I want to go to Utrecht, he's been left an inn. You'd be able to stay put and get to know some people. Many a man'd be prepared to take on a girl with a position. Looks aren't everything. I like the idea. I get on well with the cook. I'll say this for him: he has a head for business. We'd be sure of our dinner, that would be all right, wouldn't it? You'd have your own bed, what do you think of *that*? In the long run, this is no life, on the road. You might be killed any time. You're eaten up with lice as it is. And we must decide now, because otherwise we go north with the Swedes. They must be over there somewhere. [*She points left.*] I think we'll decide to go, Kattrin.

THE COOK: Anna, I must have a word with you alone.

MOTHER COURAGE: Go back inside, Kattrin.

[KATTRIN *does so.*]

THE COOK: I'm interrupting because there's a misunderstanding, Anna. I thought I wouldn't have to say it right out, but I see I must. If you're bringing *her*, it's all off. Do we understand each other?

[KATTRIN *has her head out of the back of the wagon and is listening.*]

MOTHER COURAGE: You mean I leave Kattrin behind?

THE COOK: What do you think? There's no room in the inn, it isn't one of those places with three counters. If the two of us look lively we can earn a living, but three's too many. Let Kattrin keep your wagon.

MOTHER COURAGE: I was thinking we might find her a husband in Utrecht.

THE COOK: Don't make me laugh. With that scar? And old as she is? And dumb?

MOTHER COURAGE: Not so loud!

THE COOK: Loud or soft, what is, is. That's another reason I can't have her in the inn. Customers don't like having something like that always before their eyes. You can't blame them.

MOTHER COURAGE: Shut up. I told you not to talk so loud.

THE COOK: There's a light in the parsonage, we can sing now!

MOTHER COURAGE: Cook, how could she pull the wagon by herself? The war frightens her. She can't bear it. She has terrible dreams. I hear her groan at night, especially after battles. What she sees in her dreams I don't know. She suffers from sheer pity. The other day I found her with a hedgehog that we'd run over.

THE COOK: The inn's too small. [*Calling.*] Worthy Sir, menials, and all within! We now present the song of Solomon, Julius Caesar, and other great souls who came to no good, so you can see we're law-abiding folk too, and have a hard time getting by, especially in winter.

[*He sings "The Song of the Great Souls on this Earth."*]

King Solomon was very wise,
So what's his history?
He came to view this life with scorn,
Yes, he came to regret he ever had been born
Declaring: all is vanity.
King Solomon was very wise,
But long before the day was out
The consequence was clear, alas:
His wisdom 'twas that brought him to this pass.
A man is better off without.

For the virtues are dangerous in this world, as our fine song tells. You're better off without, you have a nice life, breakfast included —some good hot soup maybe . . . . I'm an example of a man who's not had any, and I'd like some, I'm a soldier, but what good did my bravery do me in all those battles? None at all. I might just as well have wet my pants like a poltroon and stayed at home. For why?

Old Julius Caesar, he was brave.
His fame shall never cease.
He sat like a god on an altar piece.
Yet they tore brave old Julius limb from valiant limb
And Brutus helped to slaughter him.
Old Julius was very brave
But long before the day was out
The consequence was clear, alas:
His bravery 'twas that brought him to this pass.
A man is better off without.

[*Under his breath.*] They don't even look out. [*Aloud.*] Worthy Sir, menials, and all within! You could say, no, courage isn't the thing to fill a man's belly, try honesty, that should be worth a dinner, at any rate it must have *some* effect. Let's see.

You all know honest Socrates
Who always spoke the truth.
They owed him thanks for that, you'd think,
But what happened? Why, they put hemlock in his drink
And swore that he misled the youth.
How honest was this Socrates!
Yet long before the day was out
The consequence was clear, alas:
His honesty had brought him to this pass.
A man is better off without.

Yes, we're told to be unselfish and share what we have, but what if we have nothing? And those who do share it don't have an easy time either, for what's left when you're through sharing? Unselfishness is a very rare virtue—it doesn't pay.

Unselfish Martin could not bear
His fellow creatures' woes.
He met a poor man in the snows
And he gave this poor fellow half his cloak to wear:
So both of them fell down and froze.
His brothers' woes he could not bear,
So long before the day was out
The consequence was clear, alas:
Unselfishness had brought him to this pass.
A man is better off without.

That's how it is with us. We're law-abiding folk, we keep to ourselves, don't steal, don't kill, don't burn the place down. And in this way we sink lower and lower and the song proves true and there's no soup going. And if we were different, if we were thieves and killers, maybe we could eat our fill! For virtues bring no reward, only vices. Such is the world, need it be so?

God's ten commandments we have kept
And acted as we should.

It has not done us any good.
All you people who sit beside a roaring fire
O help us in our need so dire!
The ten commandments we have kept
And long before the day was out
The consequence was clear, alas:
Our godliness has brought us to this pass.
A man is better off without.

VOICE [*From above.*]: You there! Come up! There's some soup here for you!

MOTHER COURAGE: Lamb, I couldn't swallow a thing. I don't say what you said is unreasonable, but was it your last word? We've always understood each other.

THE COOK: Yes, Anna. Think it over.

MOTHER COURAGE: There's nothing to think over. I'm not leaving her here.

THE COOK: You're going to be silly, but what can I do? I'm not inhuman, it's just that the inn's a small one. And now we must go up, or there'll be nothing doing here too, and we've been singing in the cold for nothing.

MOTHER COURAGE: I'll fetch Kattrin.

THE COOK: Better stick something in your pocket for her. If there are three of us, they'll get a shock.

[*Exeunt.*]

[KATTRIN *clambers out of the wagon with a bundle. She makes sure they are both gone. Then, on a wagon wheel, she lays out a skirt of her mother's and a pair of the cook's trousers side by side and easy to see. She has just finished, and has picked up her bundle, when* MOTHER COURAGE *returns.*]

MOTHER COURAGE [*With a plate of soup.*]: Kattrin! Stay where you are, Kattrin! Where do you think you're going with that bundle? [*She examines the bundle.*] She's packed her things. Were you listening? I told him there was nothing doing, he can *have* Utrecht and his lousy inn, what would we want with a lousy inn? [*She sees the skirt and trousers.*] Oh, you're a stupid girl, Kattrin, what if I'd seen that and you gone? [*She takes hold of* KATTRIN *who is trying to leave.*] And don't think I've sent him packing on your account. It was the wagon. You can't part us, I'm too used to it, *you* didn't come into it, it was the wagon. Now we're leaving, and we'll put the cook's things here where he'll find 'em, the stupid man. [*She clambers up and throws a couple of things down to go with the trousers.*] There! He's fired. The last man I'll take into *this* business! Now let's be going, you and me. This winter'll pass, like all the others. Get into harness, it looks like snow.

[*They harness themselves to the wagon, turn it around, and start out. A gust of wind. Enter the* COOK, *still chewing. He sees his things.*]

Scene Ten

During the whole of 1635 MOTHER COURAGE and KATTRIN pull the wagon along the roads of central Germany in the wake of the ever more tattered armies.

[*On the highway.* MOTHER COURAGE *and* KATTRIN *are pulling the wagon. They come to a prosperous farmhouse. Someone inside is singing.*]

THE VOICE:

> In March a bush we planted
> To make the garden gay.
> In June we were enchanted:
> A lovely rose was blooming
> The balmy air perfuming!
> Blest are they
> Who have gardens gay!
> In June we were enchanted.
>
> When snow falls helter-skelter
> And loudly blows the storm

Our farmhouse gives us shelter.
The winter's in a hurry
But we've no cause to worry.
We are warm
In the midst of the storm!
Our farmhouse gives us shelter.

[MOTHER COURAGE *and* KATTRIN *have stopped to listen. Then they start out again.*]

Scene Eleven

January, 1636. Catholic troops threaten the Protestant town of Halle. The stone begins to speak. MOTHER COURAGE *loses her daughter and journeys onward alone. The war is not yet near its end.*

The wagon, very far gone now, stands near a farmhouse with a straw roof. It is night. Out of the woods come a LIEUTENANT *and three* SOLDIERS *in full armor.*

THE LIEUTENANT: And there mustn't be a sound. If anyone yells, cut him down.

THE FIRST SOLDIER: But we'll have to knock—if we want a guide.

THE LIEUTENANT: Knocking's a natural noise, it's all right, could be a cow hitting the wall of the cowshed.

[*The* SOLDIERS *knock at the farmhouse door. An* OLD PEASANT WOMAN *opens. A hand is clapped over her mouth. Two* SOLDIERS *enter.*]

A MAN'S VOICE: What is it?

[*The* SOLDIERS *bring out an* OLD PEASANT *and his son.*]

THE LIEUTENANT [*Pointing to the wagon on which* KATTRIN *has appeared.*]: There's one. [A SOLDIER *pulls her out.*] Is this every-body that lives here?

THE PEASANTS [*Alternating.*]: That's our son. And that's a girl that can't talk. Her mother's in town buying up stocks because the shopkeepers are running away and selling cheap. They're canteen people.

THE LIEUTENANT: I'm warning you. Keep quiet. One sound and we'll crack you over the head with a pike. And I need someone to show us the path to the town. [*He points to the* YOUNG PEASANT.] You! Come here!

THE YOUNG PEASANT: I don't know any path!

THE SECOND SOLDEIR [*Grinning.*]: He don't know any path!

THE YOUNG PEASANT: I don't help Catholics.

THE LIEUTENANT [*To the* SECOND SOLDIER.]: Let him feel your pike in his side.

THE YOUNG PEASANT [*Forced to his knees, the pike at his throat.*]: I'd rather die!

THE SECOND SOLDIER [*Again mimicking.*]: He'd rather die!

THE FIRST SOLDIER: I know how to change his mind. [*He walks over to the cowshed.*] Two cows and a bull. Listen, you. If you aren't going to be reasonable, I'll saber your cattle.

THE YOUNG PEASANT: Not the cattle!

THE PEASANT WOMAN [*Weeping.*]: Spare the cattle, Captain, or we'll starve!

THE LIEUTENANT: If he must be pigheaded!

THE FIRST SOLDIER: I think I'll start with the bull.

THE YOUNG PEASANT [*To the old one.*]: Do I have to? [*The older one nods.*] I'll do it.

THE PEASANT WOMAN: Thank you, thank you, Captain, for sparing us, for ever and ever, Amen.

[*The* OLD MAN *stops her going on thanking him.*]

THE FIRST SOLDIER: I knew the bull came first all right!

[*Led by the* YOUNG PEASANT, *the* LIEUTENANT *and the* SOLDIERS *go on their way.*]

THE OLD PEASANT: I wish we knew what it was. Nothing good, I suppose.

THE PEASANT WOMAN: Maybe they're just scouts. What are you doing?

THE OLD PEASANT [*Setting a ladder against the roof and climbing up.*]: I'm seeing if they're alone. [*On the roof.*] Things are moving—all over. I can see armor. And a cannon. There must be more than a regiment. God have mercy on the town and all within!

THE PEASANT WOMAN: Are there lights in the town?

THE OLD PEASANT: No, they're all asleep. [*He climbs down.*] There'll be an attack, and they'll all be slaughtered in their beds.

THE PEASANT WOMAN: The watchman'll give warning.

THE OLD PEASANT: They must have killed the watchman in the tower on the hill or he'd have sounded his horn before this.

THE PEASANT WOMAN: If there were more of us . . . .

THE OLD PEASANT: But being that we're alone with that cripple . . . .

THE PEASANT WOMAN: There's nothing we can do, is there?

THE OLD PEASANT: Nothing.

THE PEASANT WOMAN: We can't get down there. In the dark.

THE OLD PEASANT: The whole hillside's swarming with 'em.

THE PEASANT WOMAN: We could give a sign?

THE OLD PEASANT: And be cut down for it?

THE PEASANT WOMAN: No, there's nothing we can do. [*To* KATTRIN.] Pray, poor thing, pray! There's nothing we can do to stop this bloodshed, so even if you can't talk, at least pray! He hears, if no one else does. I'll help you. [*All kneel,* KATTRIN *behind.*] Our Father, which art in Heaven, hear our prayer, let not the town perish with all that lie therein asleep and fearing nothing. Wake them, that they rise and go to the walls and see the foe that comes with fire and sword in the night down the hill and across the fields. [*Back to* KATTRIN.] God protect our mother and make the watchman not sleep but wake ere it's too late. And save our son-in-law too, O God, he's there with his four children, let them not perish, they're innocent, they know nothing— [*To* KATTRIN, *who groans.*]—one of them's not two years old, the eldest is seven. [KATTRIN *rises, troubled.*] Heavenly Father, hear us, only Thou canst help us or we die, for we are weak and have no sword nor nothing; we cannot trust our own strength but only Thine, O Lord; we are in Thy hands, our cattle, our farm, and the town too, we're all in Thy hands, and the foe is nigh unto the walls with all his power.

[KATTRIN, *unperceived, has crept off to the wagon, has taken*

*something out of it, put it under her apron, and has climbed
up the ladder to the roof.*]

Be mindful of the children in danger, especially the little ones,
be mindful of the old folk who cannot move, and of all Christian souls, O Lord.

THE OLD PEASANT: And forgive us our trespasses as we forgive
them that trespass against us. Amen.

[*Sitting on the roof,* KATTRIN *takes a drum from under her apron
and starts to beat it.*]

THE PEASANT WOMAN: Heavens, what's she doing?
THE OLD PEASANT: She's out of her mind!
THE PEASANT WOMAN: Get her down, quick.

[*The* OLD PEASANT *runs to the ladder but* KATTRIN *pulls it up
on the roof.*]

She'll get us in trouble.
THE OLD PEASANT: Stop it this minute, you silly cripple!
THE PEASANT WOMAN: The soldiers'll come!
THE OLD PEASANT [*Looking for stones.*]: I'll stone you!
THE PEASANT WOMAN: Have you no pity, have you no heart? We
have relations there too, four grandchildren, but there's nothing
we can do. If they find us now, it's the end, they'll stab us to
death!

[KATTRIN *is staring into the far distance, toward the town. She
goes on drumming.*]

THE PEASANT WOMAN [*To the* PEASANT.]: I told you not to let
that riffraff in your farm. What do *they* care if we lose our cattle?
THE LIEUTENANT [*Running back with* SOLDIERS *and the* YOUNG
PEASANT.] I'll cut you all to bits!
THE PEASANT WOMAN: We're innocent, sir, there's nothing we
can do. She did it, a stranger!
THE LIEUTENANT: Where's the ladder?
THE OLD PEASANT: On the roof.
THE LIEUTENANT [*Calling.*]: Throw down the drum. I order you!
[KATTRIN *goes on drumming.*] You're all in this, but you won't
live to tell the tale.
THE OLD PEASANT: They've been cutting down fir trees around

here. If we bring a tall enough trunk we can knock her off the roof . . .

THE FIRST SOLDIER [*To the* LIEUTENANT.]: I beg leave to make a suggestion. [*He whispers something to the* LIEUTENANT, *who nods.*] Listen, you! We have an idea—for your own good. Come down and go with us to the town. Show us your mother and we'll spare her.

[KATTRIN *goes on drumming.*]

THE LIEUTENANT [*Pushing him away.*]: She doesn't trust you, no wonder with your face. [*He calls up to* KATTRIN.] Hey, you! Suppose I give you my word? I'm an officer, my word's my bond!

[KATTRIN *drums harder.*]

Nothing is sacred to her.

THE YOUNG PEASANT: Sir, it's not just because of her mother!

THE FIRST SOLDIER: This can't go on, they'll hear it in the town as sure as hell.

THE LIEUTENANT: We must make another noise with something. Louder than that drum. What can we make a noise with?

THE FIRST SOLDIER: But we mustn't make a noise!

THE LIEUTENANT: A harmless noise, fool, a peacetime noise!

THE OLD PEASANT: I could start chopping wood.

THE LIEUTENANT: That's it! [*The* PEASANT *brings his ax and chops away.*] Chop! Chop harder! Chop for your life!

[KATTRIN *has been listening, beating the drum less hard. Very upset, and peering around, she now goes on drumming.*]

It's not enough. [*To the* FIRST SOLDIER.] You chop too!

THE OLD PEASANT: I've only one ax. [*He stops chopping.*]

THE LIEUTENANT: We must set fire to the farm. Smoke her out.

THE OLD PEASANT: That's no good, Captain. When they see fire from the town, they'll know everything.

[*During the drumming* KATTRIN *has been listening again. Now she laughs.*]

THE LIEUTENANT: She's laughing at us, that's too much, I'll have her guts if it's the last thing I do. Bring a musket!

[*Two* SOLDIERS *off.* KATTRIN *goes on drumming.*]

THE PEASANT WOMAN: I have it, Captain. That's their wagon over there, Captain. If we smash that, she'll stop. It's all they have, Captain.

THE LIEUTENANT [*To the* YOUNG PEASANT.]: Smash it! [*Calling.*] If you don't stop that noise, we'll smash your wagon!

[*The* YOUNG PEASANT *deals the wagon a couple of feeble blows with a board.*]

THE PEASANT WOMAN [*To* KATTRIN.]: Stop, you little beast!

[KATTRIN *stares at the wagon and pauses. Noises of distress come out of her. But she goes on drumming.*]

THE LIEUTENANT: Where are those sons of bitches with that gun?

THE FIRST SOLDIER: They can't have heard anything in the town or we'd hear their cannon.

THE LIEUTENANT [*Calling.*]: They don't hear you. And now we're going to shoot you. I'll give you one more chance: throw down that drum!

THE YOUNG PEASANT [*Dropping the board, screaming to* KAT-TRIN.]: Don't stop now! Or they're all done for. Go on, go on, go on . . . .

[*The* SOLDIER *knocks him down and beats him with his pike.* KATTRIN *starts crying but goes on drumming.*]

THE PEASANT WOMAN: Not in the back, you're killing him!

[*The* SOLDIERS *arrive with the musket.*]

THE SECOND SOLDIER: The Colonel's foaming at the mouth. We'll be court-martialed.

THE LIEUTENANT: Set it up! Set it up! [*Calling while the musket is set up on forks.*] Once and for all: stop that drumming!

[*Still crying,* KATTRIN *is drumming as hard as she can.*]

Fire!

[*The* SOLDIERS *fire.* KATTRIN *is hit. She gives the drum another feeble beat or two, then slowly collapses.*]

THE LIEUTENANT: That's an end to the noise.

[*But the last beats of the drum are lost in the din of cannon from the town. Mingled with the thunder of cannon, alarm bells are heard in the distance.]*

THE FIRST SOLDIER: She made it.

Scene Twelve

Toward morning. The drums and pipes of troops on the march, receding. In front of the wagon MOTHER COURAGE *sits by* KATTRIN's *body. The* PEASANTS *of the last scene are standing near.*

THE PEASANTS: You must leave, woman. There's only one regiment to go. You can never get away by yourself.
MOTHER COURAGE: Maybe she's fallen asleep.

[*She sings.*]

> Lullaby, baby, what's that in the hay?
> The neighbor's kids cry but mine are gay.
> The neighbor's kids are dressed in dirt:
> Your silks are cut from an angel's skirt.
> They are all starving: you have a pie.
> If it's too stale, you need only cry.
> Lullaby, baby, what's rustling there?
> One lad fell in Poland. The other is—where?

You shouldn't have told her about the children.
THE PEASANTS: If you hadn't gone off to the town to get your cut, maybe it wouldn't have happened.
MOTHER COURAGE: She's asleep now.
THE PEASANTS: She's not asleep, it's time you realized. She's gone. You must get away. There are wolves in these parts. And the bandits are worse.
MOTHER COURAGE: That's right.

[*She goes and fetches a cloth from the wagon to cover up the body.*]

THE PEASANT WOMAN: Have you no one now? Someone you can go to?

MOTHER COURAGE: There's one. My Eilif.

THE PEASANT [*While* MOTHER COURAGE *covers the body.*]: Find him then. Leave *her* to us. We'll give her a proper burial. You needn't worry.

MOTHER COURAGE: Here's money for the expenses.

[*She pays the* PEASANT. *The* PEASANT *and his son shake her hand and carry* KATTRIN *away.*]

THE PEASANT WOMAN [*Also taking her hand, and bowing, as she goes away.*] Hurry!

MOTHER COURAGE [*Harnessing herself to the wagon.*]: I hope I can pull the wagon by myself. Yes, I'll manage, there's not much in it now. I must get back into business.

[*Another regiment passes at the rear with pipe and drum.*]

[MOTHER COURAGE *starts pulling the wagon.*]

MOTHER COURAGE: Hey! Take me with you!

[*Soldiers are heard singing.*]

> Dangers, surprises, devastations,
> The war moves on, but will not quit.
> And though it last three generations,
> We shall get nothing out of it.
> Starvation, filth, and cold enslave us.
> The army robs us of our pay.
> But God may yet come down and save us:
> The campaign will not end today.
>> Christians, awake! Winter is gone!
>> The snows depart! Dead men sleep on!
>> Let all of you who still survive
>> Get out of bed and look alive!

Mother Courage and her Children was copyrighted in the U.S. in 1940, and first published here, not in German, but in English, in 1941: the translation was by H. R. Hays, and the play appeared in an anthology of new writing entitled *New Directions, 1941* published by New Directions. An Eric Bentley version of the play, with the cuts made by Brecht for the German production, appeared in *The Modern Theatre*, volume two (Doubleday, Anchor, 1955). A second Bentley version, even more heavily cut for a projected American production, appeared in *Seven Plays by Bertolt Brecht* (Grove Press, 1961).

The world première of the play (and this *was* in German) took place in 1941 at the Zürich Schauspielhaus; the director was Leopold Lindtberg.

The now famous production of the Berlin Ensemble dates back to 1949 (though the Ensemble did not yet exist) when Erich Engel and Bertolt Brecht put the play on at the Deutsches Theater in Berlin with Helene Weigel (Mrs. Bertolt Brecht) in the title role.

The first Broadway production of *Mother Courage and her Children*, in a version by Eric Bentley, opened at the Martin Beck Theatre, New York City, on March 28, 1963. Produced by Cheryl Crawford and Jerome Robbins, directed by Jerome Robbins, and with the music of Paul Dessau, it featured Anne Bancroft, Zohra Lampert, and Barbara Harris. Other professional productions of the play, adapted by Eric Bentley, have been staged in London, Bristol, Dublin, Cleveland, and San Francisco. It has also been presented by BBC-TV.

The music to the world première in Zürich was by Paul Burkhard, and there is an as yet unused score by Darius Milhaud, composed expressly for English lyrics of Eric Bentley, but the music generally associated with the play is that of Paul Dessau, for which the lyrics in the present text were written. Part of Dessau's score can be heard, with the words in French, on a Vanguard Record (VRS-9022); part with the words sung in German by the Berlin cast, on East German records usually available from Deutsche Schallplatten, Deutscher Buch Export, Lenin-strasse 16, Leipzig

C.I. Two lyrics from the play, one set by Dessau, the other by Hanns Eisler, are to be found on *Bently on Brecht* (Riverside Records, RM 7017).

AUTHOR'S NOTES TO
Mother Courage and her Children

The world première of *Mother Courage and her Children* in Zürich during the Hitler War, with the outstanding Therese Giehse in the title role, made it possible, despite the antifascist and pacifist stand of the Zürich Schauspielhaus (mainly staffed with German emigrants), for the bourgeois press to speak of a Niobe tragedy and of the overwhelming vital strength of the mother animal. Duly warned, the playwright made some changes for the Berlin production. The original text follows.

From Scene One, pages 38-39

MOTHER COURAGE: . . . all of you: be careful, you'll need to be. Now let's climb on the wagon and move on.

SERGEANT: I don't feel very well.

RECRUITING OFFICER: Maybe you caught a chill when you handed over your helmet in all this wind.

[*The* SERGEANT *grabs his helmet.*]

MOTHER COURAGE: And you give me my papers. Someone else might ask for them and I'll be without. [*She collects them in her tin.*]

RECRUITING OFFICER [*To* EILIF.]: You can at least take a look at the boots. And we can have a drink, just us men. I can advance you money: come behind the wagon, and I'll prove it.

[*They go behind the wagon.*]

SERGEANT: I don't understand. I always stay in the rear. There's no safer spot for a sergeant to be. You can send the others on ahead in quest of fame. My appetite is ruined. I can tell you right now, I won't be able to get anything done.

MOTHER COURAGE [*Going over to him.*]: You shouldn't take on so,

just because you can't eat. Just stay in the rear. Here, take a
slug of brandy, man, and no offence. [*She gives him something
to drink from the wagon.*]

RECRUITING OFFICER [*Who has taken* EILIF's *arm and is making
off toward the back.*]: You die anyway. You drew a cross, so
what? Ten guilders in advance and you're a soldier of the king
and a stout fellow and the women will be mad about you. And
you can give me a smack in the kisser for insulting you.

[*Both leave. Dumb* KATTRIN *lets out harsh cries, for she has
seen the abduction.*]

MOTHER COURAGE: Coming, Kattrin, coming. The Sergeant isn't
well, he's superstitious, I didn't know that. And now we'll be
going. Where's Eilif?

SWISS CHEESE: He must have gone with the recruiting officer.
He was talking with him him the whole time.

From Scene Five, pages 70-72

MOTHER COURAGE: What, you can't pay? No money, no brandy!
They can play victory marches, they should pay their men!

SOLDIER [*Threateningly.*]: I want my brandy! I arrived too late for
plunder. The Chief allowed one hour for plunder. He's not inhuman, he says. So I suppose they bought him off.

[*The* CHAPLAIN *staggers in.*]

CHAPLAIN: There are more in the farmhouse. A family of peasants.
Help me, someone, I need linen!

[*The* SECOND SOLDIER *goes off with him.*]

MOTHER COURAGE: I have none. I sold all my bandages to the
regiment. I'm not tearing up my officers' shirts for these people.

CHAPLAIN [*Calling back.*]: I said I need linen!

MOTHER COURAGE [*Rummaging around in her wagon.*]: Not a
thing! They have nothing, and they pay nothing!

[*The* CHAPLAIN *stoops over a* WOMAN *whom he has brought on.*]

CHAPLAIN: Why did you stay out there in the line of fire?

WOMAN [*Weakly.*]: Our farm . . .

MOTHER COURAGE: Expect *them* to leave? My beautiful shirts. My officers will be coming tomorrow, and I won't have a thing for them. [*She throws some stuff down.* KATTRIN *takes it to the* PEASANT WOMAN.] What am I doing, giving stuff away? I didn't start the war.

FIRST SOLDIER: They're Protestants. Why should they be Protestants?

MOTHER COURAGE: Protestant, Catholic, what do *they* care? Their farm's gone, that's what.

SECOND SOLDIER: They're not Protestants anyway: they're Catholics.

FIRST SOLDIER: In a bombardment we can't pick and choose.

[*A* PEASANT *is brought in by the* CHAPLAIN.]

PEASANT: My arm's gone.

[*From the house comes the cry of a child in pain.*]

CHAPLAIN [*To the* PEASANT WOMAN.]: Don't get up.
MOTHER COURAGE: Get the child out of there.

[KATTRIN *runs off.*]

MOTHER COURAGE [*Tearing up shirts.*]: Half a guilder a shirt. I'm ruined. Don't move her when you're bandaging, it may be her back. [*To* KATTRIN *who has brought a young baby out of the ruins and is rocking it as she walks around.*] Another baby to drag around—you must be pleased with yourself! Give it to its mother this minute. Or do I have to fight you again for hours till I get it from you? Are you deaf? [KATTRIN *ignores all this.*] I have nothing but losses from your victories. Now, make do with this, Chaplain, don't waste any of my linen, do you hear?
CHAPLAIN: I need more. The blood's coming through.
MOTHER COURAGE [*Referring to* KATTRIN.]: There she sits, happy as a lark in all this misery. Give the baby back, the mother is coming to! [*As* KATTRIN *finally and reluctantly gives the child back to the* PEASANT WOMAN, MOTHER COURAGE *rips up a new shirt.*] I'm giving nothing, I *can* give nothing, I have myself to think of. [*To the* SECOND SOLDIER.] Don't stand around gawking, go back there and tell them to stop that music, I can see their victory without it. Have yourself a glass of brandy, Chap-

lain, don't say no, I have enough to cope with. [*She has to get down from the wagon to snatch her daughter from the* FIRST SOLDIER, *who is drunk.*] You beast! You want another victory, do you? Well, you don't get away from me without paying up! [*To the* PEASANT.] Your child is all right. [*Pointing to the* WOMAN.] Get something down her. [*To the* FIRST SOLDIER.] Then leave this coat. It's stolen goods anyhow.

[FIRST SOLDIER *staggers away.* MOTHER COURAGE *goes on ripping shirts.*]

CHAPLAIN: There's still someone in there.
MOTHER COURAGE: Don't worry, I'll tear up all I have.

From Scene Seven, pages 80-81

[*A highway. The* CHAPLAIN, MOTHER COURAGE, *and* KATTRIN *pull the wagon. It is dirty and neglected, but new wares are hanging from it.*]

MOTHER COURAGE [*Sings.*]:

> So many seek a bed to sleep in:
> Each ditch is taken, and each cave,
> And he who seeks a hole to creep in
> Finds he has dug an early grave.
> And many a man spends many a minute
> In hurrying toward some resting place.
> You wonder, when at last he's in it,
> Just why the fellow forced the pace.

[*She plays the refrain,* "Christians, awake!" *on the harmonica.*]

From Scene Twelve, page 104

PEASANTS: You must leave, woman. There's only one regiment to go. You can never get away by yourself.
MOTHER COURAGE: She's still breathing. Maybe she's fallen asleep.

Of the Peasants' War, which was the greatest misfortune of German history, one may say that, socially considered, it pulled the teeth of the Reformation. Its legacy was cynicism and business as usual. Mother Courage (let it be said to help performances in the theatre) recognizes, as do her friends and guests and nearly everyone, the purely commercial character of the war: this is precisely what attracts her. She believes in the war to the end. It never occurs to her that one must have a big pair of scissors to take one's cut out of a war. Those who look on at catastrophes wrongly expect those involved to learn something. So long as the masses are the *object* of politics they cannot regard what happens to them as an experiment but only as a fate. They learn as little from catastrophe as a scientist's rabbit learns of biology. It is not incumbent on the playwright to give Mother Courage insight at the end—she sees something, around the middle of the play, at the close of the sixth scene, then loses again what she has seen—his concern is that the spectator should see.

B.B.

THE WICKED COOKS

A Drama in Five Acts

Günter Grass
translated by James L. Rosenberg

Characters

Herbert Schymanski, called "The Count"
Petri, a Cook
Green, a Cook
Vasco, a Cook
Stock, a Cook
Benny, a Cook
Kletterer, a Cook
Martha, a Nurse
Theresa, Vasco's aunt
Mrs. Coldwater, a laundress
Some Cooks in **Kletterer's** employ

Act One

Night. Down left, a small room is indicated. HERBERT SCHY-
MANSKI, *called "*THE COUNT,*" is sitting at a desk before the
window and writing. In the center of the main stage area,*
PETRI, *the cook, is crouching on a footstool and blowing on
a huge trumpet, which is pointed toward the floor. At each
trumpet blast, the cook,* BENNY, *comes up a step through the
trapdoor from the cellar. In the shadowy background, the
arching silhouette of a bridge.*

BENNY: Not so loud, Chief. Piano, piano. [*A last trumpet blast.
Benny, completely out of the cellar, leaps to his feet and digs
into his ear with his forefinger.*] There! [*Laughs.*] Give it a rest
before you start again.

PETRI: Don't laugh, my boy; your laughter could turn back on you.
[BENNY *laughs again;* PETRI *approaches him.*] Stop laughing!

BENNY: What's the matter? I can't hear, Chief. What is this? A
holiday?

PETRI: Go on, get out! [*Points to the trumpet.*] Take that, and
bring me a hammer! A hammer and my everyday trumpet!

BENNY: Hammer?

PETRI: You heard—and hurry up! [*He indicates a small trumpet.*]

BENNY [*Whistles significantly.*]: Big holiday, little trumpet! [*He
whistles again, picks up the footstool, rolls the big trumpet offstage, returns with a hammer and a small version of the big
trumpet.* PETRI *awaits him with folded arms.*]

PETRI: How's your hearing now?

BENNY: Better, Chief. I'm all ears!

PETRI: Then we can proceed. [*He blows a series of strange notes.
In the background, a huge egg appears and, without rolling,
slides forward.*]

BENNY: Fresh as the morning dew! [*Hands* PETRI *the hammer.*]

PETRI: It's still warm. I'm very curious, even though I already know . . . [*He hangs up the trumpet and strikes the egg cautiously. The egg breaks in two, and the cook,* GREEN, *a small pan in each hand, leaps lightly out of the shell.*] Who else could it be but Green?

GREEN: Aren't hens thoughtful nowadays? They provide not only yolks with their eggs, but frying pans as well! Who's for tennis? [*He tosses a pan to* BENNY, *and they pantomime a tennis match.* PETRI *blows an angry blast on his trumpet.*]

PETRI: Stop this nonsense! Put that stuff away—we've got work to do!

GREEN: Go on, Benny, fetch him the shovel; he's in a big hurry today! [BENNY *puts the half-shells together and holds them playfully over his head.*]

BENNY: Whose window shall I put the shells under? [*He laughs idiotically.* PETRI *glares at him threateningly;* BENNY *falls silent, goes out quickly, and returns with a shovel.*]

PETRI: Some day you're going to laugh your teeth right out of your head. [*He blows on the trumpet. Out of the floor there rises a cone-shaped hill of salt as tall as a man.*]

GREEN: I'll bet there's a little mouse in there. [*He nibbles at the cone.*] Hmmm. Salt—innocent, simple table salt. And so much? Who needs so much salt for his soup? [*He curtsies.*]

> "What is sweeter than salt?"
> Sang the dear little goat
> With a tinking bell round her throat
> As she licked the sole of my shoe
> And cunningly tried to undo
> My secret passion for salt.

[PETRI *takes the shovel from* BENNY.]

PETRI: A remarkable goat, obviously; she could make a stone speak. [*He sticks the shovel into the salt; the cook,* VASCO, *jumps out as if he'd been stuck. The salt hill collapses.*]

VASCO: No, no! I've told you everything already. I've told you more than I know.

GREEN: Ah, how frightened he is, good old Vasco.

PETRI: Always suffering from a guilty conscience.

BENNY: Maybe he's in love!

GREEN: Oh? With whom?

BENNY: With Martha.

GREEN: So he goes and buries himself in salt up to his ears.

VASCO: Petri, you know me, you know how I've always stood by you. It's just a matter of pity, of human feeling! [*He bites his fingernails.*]

PETRI: But, Vasco, must such things be? Eh? Must you constantly chew on your fingernails? The Count doesn't like that, you know.

GREEN: He could get a touch of appendicitis and—poof!—we're out in the street. And then that would make us so sad that we would weep great tears—sweet, salty tears!

PETRI [*Counting his men.*]: There's one still missing!

GREEN: So? Still not enough? You mean you're going to toot on that damned thing again? Please. We already know that you're musical. Our ears are ringing from it.

PETRI: But I tell you there's one missing!

GREEN: Okay. But without music, eh?

PETRI: Sensitive, that Green, very sensitive—a mass of little feelings. So I must take his delicate feelings into account—I, the Chief! I daren't blow on my horn when I want to. But there are other ways of doing it! [*He claps his hands. In the background, it starts to snow heavily on one spot.* PETRI *claps again. The snowfall lessens, then stops, and the cook,* STOCK, *steps forward out of the flakes.*]

STOCK: Well, well, well! In the middle of August! The things old Petri can do! [*He makes a snowball, throws it, hits* BENNY, BENNY *throws one back; they play like children for a moment until* PETRI's *trumpet signal restores order.*]

PETRI: Let's try not to forget the object of our business! We find ourselves in great danger; our vocation is under attack; people are turning away from us; they no longer approve of our taste.

VASCO: They want to tear us down.

PETRI: To tear us down, to tear down our tackle and rigging, to move us out and fumigate the kitchen! They want to mock at us!

STOCK: We'll become sacrifices! They'll slaughter us! Soon they'll be sticking cooks instead of pigs!

PETRI: We must consult; we must delve into ourselves. [*Shouts.*] All for one and one for all! No one must stand back! Death to the man who fails! [*He inspects the cooks carefully.*] Benny, bring in the heavens!

[BENNY *runs out and brings in a black cloth canopy mounted on four legs.* PETRI *and* BENNY *stand under it, while the others form a loose circle around them.*]

PETRI [*Sings.*]: One cook . . .
BENNY: Two cooks . . .
PETRI AND BENNY: Two cooks left the kitchen.
PETRI:

> A little cook left the house,
> Still as a little mouse,
> Into the dark, dark night,
> When his cap flew out of sight,
> Out of sight in the night.

PETRI AND BENNY:

> The night is full of cooks!
> The night is full of cooks!

[GREEN *and* VASCO *step under the canopy.*]

PETRI: One cook . . .
BENNY: Two cooks . . .
GREEN: Three cooks . . .
VASCO: And four!
ALL FOUR: With room for one more!
GREEN:

> Four cooks left the house,
> Like a little bouquet of white
> That bloomed in the black, black night
> And they laughed and laughed and laughed!

ALL FOUR:

> The night is full of cooks!
> The night is full of cooks!

[STOCK *steps in under the canopy.*]

STOCK:

> Five capital cooks,
> Like figures out of books!

PETRI AND BENNY:

> And each one had a spoon
> To dip into the moon

GREEN AND VASCO:

> The moon is a potato,
> The stars are small tomatoes!

STOCK:

> A night of dancing moons;
> A night of wicked spoons
> That stir the deep, dark soup—
> The night is like a soup!

ALL FIVE:

> The night is like a soup.
> The night is like a soup.

[*They start out slowly.*]

PETRI:

> And everywhere are cooks,
> In all the holes and nooks . . .

ALL FIVE:

> The night is full of cooks,
> The night is full of cooks.

[*Lights come up on the* COUNT'S *room. He rises, reading from*

*the letter he has been writing; meanwhile, the Cooks and their
canopy disappear into the shadowy background, and we hear*
PETRI's *trumpet signal fading away.*]

THE COUNT [*At the window*]: How wild they are tonight, singing
and blowing on that horn! [*He reads.*] "My dear friend, if you
only knew what terror you had left me in, you would come and
stand by me." [*He lets the letter fall.*] What a liar I am! Even
if he knew, he wouldn't come; he wouldn't dare. He was here
at the beginning and what did he do? Bought a railway ticket
and ran. And now he sends me these postcards which politely
say nothing. And I go through the motions of answering him.
What am I answering? These scattered pencil-scrawled greetings? [*He reads again.*] "To be sure, it was stupid of me. I should
never have gone into the kitchen. I should have remained a
customer and left the kitchen to them. But was it conceited
of me to put on an apron now and then? Did I beg them?
They invited me. Schuster, the host, gave me no peace. Really!
And now they want the recipe!" [*He puts the letter down.*]
But I won't tell them. Yet, how simple it would be just to
go and say: "Boys, here it is! Good luck!" [*He reads.*] "And
so now I'm afraid. They take my breath away sometimes
when they creep up behind me. They never leave me alone.
Every time it snows and the laundry hangs on the line, white
against white, the cooks are hiding there. You don't know. If I
see a white swan, I am suspicious; I almost suspected this white
paper on which I'm writing. I wrote as fast as I could!" [*He folds
up the letter, puts it in an envelope, and addresses it.*] How long
will it go on? They'll give me no rest; they'll hunt me down.
One action will follow another, nothing is too unimportant for
them. First they take the spectacles away from the nearsighted
man, then they dispossess the possessive pronouns. They'll force
me to wear a glass necktie so they can look into my heart and
read what is there—for I will never speak! They know that.
[*He looks out the window.*] Now it's quieter out there. Even
cooks grow weary! [*He wraps a scarf around his neck.*] Finally
a man must rely on the mailbox. I almost believe that nothing
holds the world together any more except the postal service.

[*He leaves the room. The cook* VASCO *appears in the background.
They both start for the bridge, from opposite sides.*]

THE COUNT [*Hesitates, then collects himself*]: Aha, a riddle! What can that be? It stands upon the bridge, dressed all in white like a bride, only not so innocent, and nibbles at its fingernails.

VASCO [*Coming forward.*]: Count . . .

THE COUNT: And now it calls me "Count." But no, my friend, I'm not even a wax mannikin of a count. Simple, stealthy, a common—and very worried—citizen, that's all.

VASCO: But they all call you that. The customers; Mr. Schuster. Doesn't he bow and scrape and speak in a hushed voice whenever you come in? [*He bows.*] "Ah, my dear Count, what an honor!"

THE COUNT [*Laughing*]: But you, my friend, you know my rightful name.

VASCO: Don't you call me "Vasco," as though that were really my name?

THE COUNT: But it is. Aren't you the great explorer, the man who will not believe that the continents have all been discovered and the seas have all been named?

VASCO: I am a cook, that's all—a cook!

THE COUNT: Who can deny it? Well? What do you want?

VASCO: Please! [*He clutches at the* COUNT, *who moves back.*]

THE COUNT: Yes?

VASCO: I want the recipe! Why do you ask? How many times have I come to you and begged you to give it to me?

THE COUNT: And your friends? You shouldn't bite your fingernails like that, you know. Do you think your great namesake was so nervous when he discovered the route to the Indies?

VASCO: I'm not here to talk about colonies: The recipe! If you would be so kind, that is.

THE COUNT: Now, I wonder what good old Petri would say about this? I mean, does he know that you are here, in secret and in full costume, bothering harmless passersby?

VASCO: No.

THE COUNT: Aha!

VASCO: Are you going to tell him?

THE COUNT: I take it you are joking.

VASCO: He'll never know. He'll think I'm at my aunt's because she's sick, and Martha . . .

THE COUNT: How *is* Martha?

VASCO: Look—please—you've already said it's dangerous for us to stand here too long, so make it snappy, and then we can both get out of here!

THE COUNT: Who is with your aunt then? Who's her nurse?

VASCO: What difference does that make now? Are we going to waste time talking about sickness? The soup! The recipe!

THE COUNT: No, Vasco, this isn't the night for it. The clouds are too uncertain. Go on, run home with your chef's hat, before the black night plucks it off your head! Go! [*He claps his hands, then starts away, but* VASCO *stops him.*]

VASCO: What are you clapping for? Do you think I'm a chicken that will fly away when you clap your hands? Give it to me!

THE COUNT: My scarf? Gladly! [*He drapes it around* VASCO's *neck.*] Now, as for my necktie or my suspenders, I'd rather not. What about my shoelaces? [VASCO *hands the scarf back silently.*] You don't care for it? What else do I have that might please you? [*He starts to check through his pockets.*]

VASCO [*Turning away.*]: I won't use it, you know—maybe just a little, for myself. I'll learn it by heart. I'll repeat it over and over, like a poem, in front of my mirror. You too, you do it with me, so later you can't say: He's learned it wrong, that Vasco! [*He makes a leap.*] It will be our little joke. We'll say it to each other, when we meet, like fellow lodge-members. [*He looks at the* COUNT.] We could stand back to back, if you felt embarrassed or afraid.

THE COUNT: I am neither embarrassed nor afraid. I simply say "No." What more do you want?

VASCO [*Shouts.*]: Give me the paper! My God, what must I do to make you give it up? Do you want me to climb up this streetlight [*He does so.*] and gnash my teeth? [*He slides back down.*] Or fall to my knees [*He kneels.*] and beat my breast and pray to you to tell it to me?

THE COUNT: Are you still talking about the soup?

VASCO [*Jumps up.*]: What else? It has a certain color; I don't know how or why. They all call it "the gray soup," and they come back in the kitchen in their black tuxedos with their blonde women smelling of rouge and perfume, and they say, "Cook some for us, Vasco." What should I do? Should I admit that I don't know how? That I'm a bad cook? No, I must go to the Count, who has cooked it for them two or three times and in so doing has driven them crazy to taste it again.

THE COUNT: Mr. Schuster asked me to.

VASCO: And now the customers are asking *me!* [*He drops down and claws at the ground.*] Here, shall I take some dirt and throw it in the soup to make it what they call it—"the gray soup"?

THE COUNT: I never called it that.

VASCO: But other people do!

THE COUNT: Don't listen to them. It has no name. [*He paces up and down,* VASCO *following him.*] I'll grant you, there are lots of possible names. November Soup, Phoenix Soup, the Gray Eminence. You know, at one time I wanted to name it after old Holstein. He was a great cook.

VASCO [*Shouts.*]: It doesn't matter what it's called! Do I cook with a sound? Do I taste with my ear?

[MARTHA, *dressed as a nurse, enters from left.*]

MARTHA: Stephen!

[*Both men start at her voice.*]

VASCO [*Angrily.*]: What do you want? Why are you running around in the night instead of staying in the hospital where they need you?

MARTHA: The Head Nurse let me go so that I could stay with your aunt.

VASCO: Well, why aren't you there, giving her her medicine?

MARTHA: I've *been* there. She asked for you.

VASCO: "Auntie, auntie!" How often do I have to hear this? Suppose you repeat "Aunt" a hundred times, then ask yourself what it means. Something to put aside, to shut up, to throw away! And that's all!

MARTHA: Stephen!

VASCO [*Holds his ears.*]: I can't hear you, you see? Haven't I forbidden you to come to me like this? Is my name a hook for everyone to hang his complaints on? Don't you see who's here with me?

MARTHA: Oh, I'm sorry.

THE COUNT: Not at all, my child. The words we were speaking here fall into the water so lightly they wouldn't disturb a dreaming fish.

MARTHA: Should I go now?

THE COUNT: Vasco will go with you. He is such a conscientious cook that he has forgotten all about his old aunt.

VASCO: I have forgotten nothing! Let her go now and leave us alone!

MARTHA: But . . .

VASCO: Do you want to say that word again, as though I had ears to hear it with? Do you know what we're talking about here? Do you want to make me furious with you? [*He starts to hit her; the* COUNT *catches his arm.*]

THE COUNT [*To* MARTHA]: Please, go now. [*She backs out hesitantly.*]

VASCO: She and her "Stephen." Some day she'll come with my aunt's flesh, I suppose, and try to pry open my mouth.

THE COUNT: You want to appear harder than you are. [*He lets him go.*] Calm yourself.

VASCO: What does she want from me?

THE COUNT: She mentioned your aunt.

VASCO [*Whistles.*]: Really? And does she think that means anything to me? Does she think I'm going to drop everything and run after her at the mention of that magic word?

THE COUNT: You're very unfair. She *is* your aunt, after all.

VASCO: My aunt, my aunt! Must I *possess* her? Must I run around shouting "I possess an aunt"? Isn't that nurse enough to worry about? Did you see her face? When I look at her, I become all confused. I forget—important things. She's like a—like a narcotic to me.

THE COUNT: I can see that. You look half dead.

VASCO: Yes. [*He stares in a sort of bewilderment.*]

THE COUNT: I'll be on my way, then. You should too, Vasco. We've talked enough.

VASCO: About what?

THE COUNT: Nothing important. I'll just run along and mail this letter.

[*The* COUNT *starts away;* VASCO *looks up sharply.*]

VASCO: Letter? [*He stops him forcibly.*] What have you written there? Is it . . . is it . . . ? [*He presses him against the railing of the bridge.*]

THE COUNT: No, no—I swear it.

VASCO: Ah, now I have you! [*He laughs.*] Now it's all over; now

you'll tell! There's no other ear but mine! [*He shakes him.*] Give
it to me! Give it to me!

THE COUNT [*Laughing.*]: Do I have to talk some more? What is
it you want to hear? That you're a great cook, that there's nothing you can't cook, that I am stirred by your tale? But any spoon
can stir me, Vasco. Enough. Let me go. [*He tries to free himself,
but* VASCO *forces him back half over the railing.*] What's this?
A wrestling match without an audience? I'm no Jacob, after all,
and you're certainly no angel! [*As* VASCO *shakes him again, his
chef's cap falls from the bridge.*] Vasco! [VASCO *stops.*] I want to
inform you of something.

VASCO: What?

THE COUNT: You've lost your hat. Now where do you suppose
it will swim to?

VASCO [*Lets him go and leans over the railing.*]: It doesn't look
right, floating there in the water.

THE COUNT [*Straightening his clothes.*]: Poor devil, you've strug-
gled so hard. And why? Did you want to drown me and the
recipe? Did you want to cook it like a fish? [*He leans over the
railing.*] No, it doesn't look right down there. But did you think
I'd look better? Of course, it may be very nice down there under
the water. Down there, it doesn't rain or blow, and it's bullet-
proof. There are no newsboys shouting their headlines. Life is
simple there—and sweet. [*He claps* VASCO *on the shoulder.*]

VASCO: You're a great joker, aren't you?

THE COUNT: Not at all. There are things in this world which I
find quite uncomical. For example, that you want to buy me.
You want to do business with my own little spark of life. But
just stop and consider the value of this brief bit of breathing
in and out. [*He leaps up onto the railing and balances a moment
like an acrobat.*]

VASCO: Here, stop that! Get down!

THE COUNT: Why? Don't you like it? Would you care for something else? Oh, yes! The letter! [*He takes it from his pocket.*]
I'll tell you what—I'll send it after your hat so that they can
chat together. [*He throws the letter off the bridge.*]

VASCO: Come, now.

THE COUNT: I must announce this discovery and patent it. I could
make a fortune! Postal service via running water!

VASCO: Please!

THE COUNT: Indulge me just a moment, eh? Up here I feel so independent, so inventive, so free in spirit! You see, we could consolidate the postal service and the waterworks into one department, thereby bringing about a considerable economy in public administration . . .

VASCO [*Pulling him down from the railing.*]: I can't see it.

THE COUNT: How sensitive you can be at times.

VASCO: Count . . .

THE COUNT: No, not "Count." No more. Or ask me again to describe the soup. Listen. It's a cabbage soup, a perfectly ordinary cabbage soup. The only thing I do is this: I sprinkle a certain amount of very special ashes into it. Although—take note!—you don't really need special materials to make special ashes. Now go, Vasco, with or without your hat. You don't look right standing here like this. [*He crosses the bridge to the right, turns back.*] A cook in the night on a bridge—no, that doesn't look so well. Believe me, even two, three, four, five cooks—they wouldn't look well! No, not even five cooks, with that inflamed moon as an assistant . . . [*He shakes his head.*] And Vasco, you really must stop biting your nails!

[*He goes quickly out. The cook, STOCK, runs in from the left.*]

STOCK: Well, well, well—if you could only see yourself now! Nothing on your head and chewing on your fingernails! Didn't you hear what he said? [VASCO *turns away.*] What are you looking at? Is there something there? He's gone!

VASCO: There he goes, as though there weren't a single person here.

STOCK: Two!

VASCO: His back is expressionless.

STOCK: Vasco, listen—there are two of us here! And I tell you, you can be thankful that this is me and not Petri. [*He gives him a push.*] Hey, look at *me*—not over there!

VASCO: It makes no difference to him whether one person is standing here or two. He comes on his silent feet, sly as a cat. He calls me "Vasco" and you "Stock." "Petri," he says, and "Green," and claps us on the shoulder with this hand or that, it makes no difference. He's going to finish us off, all of us!

STOCK: Well, let's finish *him* first!

VASCO: No. If there were ten of us and we worked slowly and carefully, it would be no use. He will finish us. [*He leans over the railing.*]

STOCK: Don't do that, it's bad for your eyes.

VASCO: Maybe it caught on part of the bridge.

STOCK [*Laughs.*]: Sure—or maybe somebody fished it out with a fishing pole? [VASCO *straightens up;* STOCK *steps back.*] Did I say I had?

VASCO: If you've got anything of mine, give it to me!

STOCK: I've got nothing! [*He turns out his pockets.*] There!—There!—Look!—What do I have? Why are we talking about hats? Why don't we talk about the Count or—better yet—Martha? She is a nurse, you are a cook. A boring pair, both dressed in white! What do you talk about when you're together? Eh? Do you say, "Martha, what is that? Flu or a nosebleed?" And does she say, "Vasco—" No—that's right—she calls you "Stephen," doesn't she?

VASCO: Shut up!

STOCK: If you hit me, I'll tell Petri!

VASCO: Get out!

STOCK: But I can't leave you here all alone—bareheaded.

VASCO [*Seizes him angrily.*]: I'll take care of you! [*He picks up a stone and starts to throw it;* STOCK *runs off, then stops short.*]

STOCK: Just think it over. That's my advice. Think it over.

[*He goes out.* VASCO *throws the stone into the water.*]

VASCO: Splash! as though it were a word. [*He starts out, but* MARTHA *comes in with a small package under her arm. They stand for a moment facing each other.*] Did you talk to him? Answer me—you must have seen him! Did he tell you that he was wicked? Don't stand there like that!

MARTHA: I was at Mrs. Coldwater's.

VASCO: But you must have passed him! What were you doing at old Coldwater's place?

MARTHA: Fetching the laundry. [*She shows the package.*]

VASCO: Was it ready?

MARTHA: Not all of it, only . . .

VASCO [*He grabs the package and tears it open.*]: Why didn't you say what you had? [*He takes out a chef's cap and puts it on.*] How does it fit?

MARTHA: Where is your other one? Stephen, what were you
saying to . . . ?

VASCO: Nothing. He lives, and still he doesn't speak a word. How
is my aunt?

MARTHA: She asks for you.

VASCO: I don't know what good it will do me to watch her die.
But maybe I will have to take my hat off again for another five
minutes—and maybe for another five minutes I can stop being
a cook!

[*They go slowly out toward the left,* MARTHA *first.*]

Curtain

Act Two

*The aunt's apartment. Two rooms. In the left room, half-
sitting in her bed, is* THE AUNT. *A cuckoo clock on the wall
above the bed. A crucifix in the upper left corner of the room.
Right of the bed, a small mirror. In the right room, which is
empty, bed sheets are hanging on lines. Front, far right, a
large tiled oven, with a chimney seat. In the middle of the
room, a chair. The left room is illuminated, the right room in
shadow.* MARTHA *and* VASCO *enter from the left. The cuckoo
clock strikes irregularly.*

VASCO: Is that thing still striking? Why doesn't someone tear it
off the wall and throw it away?

MARTHA: She says she likes to hear it.

THE AUNT: Is that you, my child?

MARTHA: Yes, Auntie. And I've brought Stephen with me.

THE AUNT: Oh? Was he at church with you?

MARTHA [*To* VASCO.]: Please.

THE AUNT: Look at him, my child, and tell me if he was there.

VASCO: I feel chilly.

THE AUNT: Ah—then you were there! Tell me—how was it?

VASCO: The same as always—drafty and cold.

THE AUNT: Martha, why won't he tell me what it was like?

VASCO: I'm telling you! Not many people, and all of them cough-
ing as though that were the only reason they came in off the
street.

THE AUNT: And you? Did you pray?

VASCO: Since I was there—and there was nothing else to do.

THE AUNT: To whom?

VASCO: First to St. Anthony—because I had just lost something—
and then, as always, to the Blessed Virgin.

THE AUNT: And, what did you lose, Stephen?

VASCO: Oh, these stupid questions! Pettiness! Trifles!

THE AUNT: But you said . . .

VASCO: First to St. Anthony. Why not? But then I left and came
here.

THE AUNT: And then?

VASCO: And then nothing! What do you think—she chatted with
me?

THE AUNT: Stephen, Stephen, what are you coming to? Always
before you would come to me and tell me everything.

VASCO [Laughing]: Oh, yes—before. I had different ears then. I
used to hear the angels whistling. And the Virgin would explain
to me just what a virgin was.

THE AUNT: You were such a lovely child. So pious! So religious!
[The cuckoo strikes.] You hear that, Martha? Fifteen times!

VASCO: Seventeen, Auntie, you miscounted.

[THE AUNT sits up straight.]

THE AUNT: Ehhhh! There he is again—that Stephen. Always
knowing better than we do. Here he comes and says: "The
cuckoo clock is wrong." Go away! Go away! He keeps lying, and
he won't tell me what he has lost. He was never with the Blessed
Virgin, never! Perhaps with St. Anthony, but not the Blessed
Virgin!

VASCO: Look—I don't know what you want. You counted wrong,
that's all. Why not—when you're sick and do nothing but lie
here all day?

MARTHA: Next time we'll count all together, all right? Or perhaps
I should take the clock away tomorrow and have it repaired.

Maybe there's only a little mechanical flaw, and you can get it right back.

VASCO: There—you hear, Auntie? I'll pay for the repairs. Or I'll buy you a new one, if you prefer! [To MARTHA.] She doesn't hear me—or maybe she doesn't want to. What nonsense! As if I couldn't count. I think she's getting foolish in her old age. There's no cuckoo in there, there's a dog. And it doesn't go "cuckoo," it barks!

THE AUNT [In a loud voice.]: Take off your hat, Stephen! You must remove your hat! [VASCO takes off his hat.] Sit down on the bed! Not there—at the foot. Ah, you look so evil without your hat! [VASCO jumps up.]

VASCO: I can put it back on if I want to.

THE AUNT: Sit down, I said! [He sits again.] No, no, no, it's no use. You still look evil with your hat on. I had hoped you would look less so if you took it off.

MARTHA: You're getting too excited. Perhaps we should wait in the next room.

THE AUNT: Ah, alas! Why do you look like that? Stephen! Come closer; are you still working with that Petri? Are you still a cook, and do you still run to them when they call?

VASCO: Why not?

THE AUNT: My brother, your father—you must never forget that my brother Charles was your father.

VASCO: Yes, yes! Are you going to start on all that ancient history again?

THE AUNT: Your father was a cook, too. Ah, Lord Jesus, and what a cook he was! He would order me about, you know, and yes, sometimes—only think, Martha!—sometimes he would strike me! Actually! Oh, why are all cooks so wicked? Always. And do they make their spoons wicked? And when they stir with their wicked spoons, do they make the soup wicked?

MARTHA: Auntie, Stephen has come to visit you and was happy to do so.

THE AUNT [Giggles.]: Happy? He comes here and is happy and yet he will not tell me what he prayed and why cooks are wicked and what he lost because he prayed to St. Anthony and not to the Blessed Virgin.

VASCO: But I explained to you already . . .

THE AUNT: Silence. What is wrong with you? When you have

your hat off, you look evil. When you put it back on, you still look evil. Holy Mary and Joseph, what will become of us? And I always thought, when a cook takes his hat off, he looks like a veritable Christ. You hear, Stephen? A Christ! [*She cries; vasco jumps up.*]

VASCO: Are you finished? Why do I come here? Always the same catechism—catechism and agony, over and over!

MARTHA: Stephen—Please—

VASCO: Stephen, please! Please, Stephen! And she? She has no name—just Auntie, that's all! Did her father name her "Auntie"? No, her name is Theresa! And when he called her that, she knew what he meant. And you, why do you call her "Auntie"? Is she your aunt? No! So you're used to the hospital—all right— and everyone there is called "Brother," "Sister," "Aunt," or what have you. All right. But is this a hospital here? No! Why are the two of you here anyway? Why don't you go to the hospital?

MARTHA: She wants to stay here, you know that.

VASCO: But what about you? Are you off-duty—and for how long?

MARTHA: The sisters said it was only right that I should stay here and care for her. The Head Nurse was so understanding.

VASCO: Oh, was she, indeed? And you were too, I suppose? And what am I, then?

MARTHA: I didn't mean it that way.

VASCO: I am wicked! Didn't she say so herself?

MARTHA: Be still now. She's getting restless; her fever is coming back.

VASCO [*He picks up his hat and stands before the little mirror.*]: Just look! Hat on—wicked cook! Hat off—wicked cook! Behind, in front, to the side, left, right—evil—always evil! What kind of a word is that? Is that a word like "hat" or "stove"? "Evil"—is that a kind of soup? Is that a whitefish longing for lemon? Is that a pig's kidneys shrinking from the heat of the frying pan? Is that salt? Is salt evil? And has the salt lost its savor? Or the hen, stuffed with herbs and sage? [*He stares in the mirror.*]

THE AUNT: Stephen. You have put your hat on again.

VASCO: You said it made no difference.

THE AUNT: My child, has he put his hat back on?

MARTHA: No, Auntie, he has taken it off.

VASCO: I have it *on—on*, do you hear?

THE AUNT: Come here! [VASCO *goes to the bed.*]

VASCO: Well?

THE AUNT: Your hat!

VASCO [*He hurls his hat away;* MARTHA *picks it up.*]: I laugh when you give your commands.

THE AUNT: Kneel!

VASCO: Jesus Maria, what now?

THE AUNT: Strike him down, Martha! Force him to his knees.

MARTHA [*Quietly.*]: Do it.

VASCO [*Kneels carelessly.*]: All right. How's this?

THE AUNT: Begin!

VASCO: Oh, no!—I'm not going to have to pray again?

THE AUNT: Don't look at me. Look up—toward your God! Go on!

VASCO: I don't feel like it.

THE AUNT: Come, come, the prayer. "In the name of the Father . . ." Come! [*The cuckoo clock strikes slowly and irregularly.* VASCO *jumps up.*]

VASCO: Let the cuckoo pray! He's learned it by now; he knows it by heart! He prays more than you want him to. Sorrows and joys and wreaths of roses and wreaths of—of coffee—and I don't know what else! To hell with it! [*He runs bareheaded into the right-hand room and sits in the chair.*]

MARTHA: Stephen!

THE AUNT [*Laughs.*]: There he goes, running again!

MARTHA: What is wrong with him?

THE AUNT: Why do you ask? Do you want to become like him— always asking questions? He is full of melancholy—and melancholy comes from Satan.

MARTHA: If you say so, Auntie. I'm not sure.

THE AUNT: Yes—cooks are like that, you know. Always a little melancholy. [*She laughs.*]

MARTHA: Are you feeling better? I see you are able to laugh again.

THE AUNT: I wonder, though, why he always bites his fingernails?

[*In the first room, it grows darker—In the second, lighter.* VASCO *sits up. As he speaks, the objects around him—the bed, sheets and the tiled oven—grow hazy.*]

VASCO: Why does she go to all this trouble just to die? And now

she wants to give me her advice—me, and everyone else.
"Stephen," they call me, and "Vasco." He was the first one to
come to me and say: "They call you 'Stephen'? What nonsense!
Vasco, Vasco—Discoverer, Voyager to the Indies, Fetishist of
Spices!" I've been learning for a long time, haven't I? And my
father—one Sunday while my mother was sleeping, he said to
me: "Go to Mr. Petri." And on Monday I went, and he gave
me money for my cook's uniform, and I was so happy when I
said to him: "This is for my uniform; I will learn with you; and
I bring you greetings from Father." How Petri laughed! And
then the years passed—"Do this. Do this." And it was done.
And now she lies there, my old aunt, and screams: "Take off
your hat!" [*He reaches for his hat and jumps up.*] Where is it?
Oh, if he should see me now—Petri—if he should see how
empty my head is now!

[*The cook* PETRI, *a small trumpet under his arm, steps forward
from behind the bed sheets.* VASCO *sinks back into the chair,
raising his hands in terror.* PETRI *blows softly on the trumpet.*]

PETRI: What do I see here? A man sitting in the cold sweat of
    terror. Why? Wherefore? Could it be because he has lost his
    white cap? Could it be that the gentle tones I blow on the
    trumpet have frightened him out of his wits? Vasco, where is
    your cap?
VASCO: My aunt, Petri—
PETRI: The aunt, the aunt. Always the aunt.
VASCO: I was standing by her bed; it was hot, because of the
    windows being closed . . .
PETRI: And so you threw it away.
VASCO: No!
PETRI: Tell the truth! You took it off and threw it away—away—
    out there somewhere in a field of turnips or under a bridge—
    away—out there in the night, as though the night were a filing
    cabinet for chefs' hats [*He blows softly.*] What will the man
    think who finds such an abandoned hat?
VASCO: No one will find it.

[PETRI *polishes his trumpet.*]

PETRI: He will pick it up, and he will say: "How laughable! Look, here a cook has come running through the night, like a twin who has murdered his brother, armed with a spoon and planning to cook up some sort of a dark, dark soup."

VASCO: No, no—why should I think of such a thing?

PETRI [A *trumpet call*.]: A—what is the word?—an ash-gray soup.

VASCO: No! There must be some mistake!

PETRI: Ah! But that's just what *he* will say—the lucky man who finds your lost cap. "A most unhappy mistake. For how is a poor lonely devil of a cook going to prepare his soup in this dark and cloudy night? Now if there were more of them—say, five—*then* they might bring it off. But one man alone?"

VASCO: Petri, please . . .

PETRI: Does he think he is going to stir the night with his spoon? Doesn't he see that, if he's not careful, it might boil over?

VASCO: May I be struck dead if I ever thought such a thing!

PETRI: It would be most dangerous for you to do so.

VASCO: Please, you must believe me. I've been here with my old aunt . . .

PETRI: Why, what's this? What's this? A little prayer? What do you think—that I'm the Blessed Virgin or St. Anthony, to whom one prays, I believe, when one has lost one's hat?

VASCO: Please, Petri!

PETRI: Stand up! [VASCO *straightens up*.] "Oh, please; oh, oh, oh!" A lovely, round "O." Now don't tell me you're going to turn into a poet who says "Oh!" and "Ah!" and similar lovely things? "Oh!"—always "Oh!" if he can't think of anything else to say. Silence! [*Trumpet blast*.] I know all about you. The great discoverer, the poet. Well, we can play that game, too, you know. Green! Green!

[*The cook* GREEN *jumps down from the tiled stove as though he had always been there.*]

GREEN: That wasn't so easy!

PETRI: Why? Didn't you get it all?

GREEN: Sure, sure, sure. But it wasn't so easy.

PETRI: But you've got enough?

GREEN: Weighed out—nine bags full.

PETRI [*Laughing*.]: Children! Children! [*Trumpet blast*.] Come out, come out! Stock, come out! [*The cook* STOCK *comes rolling out from under the stove.*]

STOCK: The spoon! [*He holds one up.*]

GREEN: Just the thing! Now let's have good old Benny! Without music, if possible.

PETRI [*Puts down his trumpet.*]: Ta, ta, ta! [*Blows in his hands.*] Come forth, my child, laden with fire! [*The oven door springs open and* BENNY *leaps out with a pot in one hand and a torch in the other.*]

BENNY: Right, Chief! What do you want with me?

PETRI: A little cooking job, Benny. The way it must be. [*Trumpet blast.*] My dear Green, what have you dreamed up?

[GREEN *begins to ladle the contents of his paper bag into* BENNY's *pot.*]

GREEN: "Dream up"—that's good! Am I a poet, to dream things up? Eh? No, I am no dreamer. I have counted and figured and weighed out and calculated until my head is swimming.

[*All but* VASCO *laugh.*]

VASCO: Please—what's this all about?

GREEN: Why, look who's here! Good old Vasco—and without his hat.

STOCK: Maybe that's why he nibbles at his fingernails as though they were hors d'oeuvres.

PETRI: Do the rest of you agree with me that he looks terrible like that—with a bare head?

GREEN: I might almost go so far as to say that he looks naked.

BENNY: Maybe he'll catch a chill.

STOCK: But where can he have left his hat?

BENNY: Maybe he sold it. Or maybe he made it into a little apron for his sweet little bride?

STOCK: What does a nurse need an apron for?

[*All except* VASCO *laugh.*]

PETRI: All joking aside, though—

GREEN: We really ought to reveal to him what it is we are making here in this pot—aromatic, delicious, and slowly taking on a strange color.

STOCK: Let's tell him. He looks curious as hell.

PETRI: Where shall we start? Perhaps there, eh? In the blue sack.

GREEN: Mmm. Something bitter. Only it makes things bland, not bitter.

PETRI: And that?

GREEN: Something to make men sad.

BENNY: And that?

GREEN: Something sweet for the bees and good for diabetics.

STOCK: Ah, ah, ah! No, I don't care for that at all. That one there! What's that?

GREEN: I don't understand! That is the most precious of essences! Do you know what is here? Pin seeds! Ah, boys, and when these sprout—what a spring is there! Then come all the tailors and the seamstresses, the housewives, and the old maids, all those whose traffic is with pins and needles—then they come to admire the blossoms and pick themselves a spray of sharpness! [*They laugh.*]

VASCO: Who is that pot for?

PETRI: Ah, dear God, the sweet innocent angel. [*Trumpet blast.*]

BENNY [*Imitating* VASCO's *tone of voice.*]: "Who is that pot for?"

STOCK: Ah, if he only knew, if he only knew! But he's a dreamer—that's all—a dreamer!

VASCO [*Jumps up, falls back in his chair.*]: I'm wide-awake—a wide-awake cook—not a dreamer!

GREEN: What's the opposite of a cook? A chimney sweep, right? Shall we make him into one?

PETRI: We could find a chimney without much trouble.

GREEN: And a broom.

STOCK: We will send him up like the smoke off a sausage.

BENNY: But what would little Martha say to that?

VASCO: All of you, get out of here. This is my aunt's house.

GREEN [*Whistles.*]: He wants to throw us out!

PETRI: And did you hear how he said: "My aunt's house"?

STOCK: Are you your aunt's keeper? You pretend to be a clever man and yet you talk such nonsense! You'd be smarter to tell us where your hat is.

VASCO [*Points to the other room.*]: In there. I told you. In there.

STOCK: Where in there?

VASCO: By the bed. By my aunt's bed.

PETRI: You notice? Always we come back to the old lady.

[STOCK *and* BENNY *dance and sing.*]

STOCK AND BENNY:

> Who's got my hat, my hat, my hat?
> My sick old aunt has found it.
> She used it for her handkerchief
> And blew her nose upon it.
> My old aunt's nose, my sick aunt's nose,
> That's the way the saying goes!
> If the cook could find his hat,
> That would be the end of that,
> But a cook with no hat to his name
> Is a cook whose life is full of shame—
> Shame . . . shame . . . shame . . .

[*Trumpet blast.*]

PETRI: Cut it! Do you want to upset the pot?
STOCK: Jesus, that would be the last straw!
PETRI: Ready, Green? Our little friend is hungry.

[VASCO *shrinks from him.*]

GREEN: All ready!
PETRI: Stand by!
STOCK: Me?
PETRI: That's right!
STOCK: Why not Benny?
PETRI: The text is clear. Let's go! [*Ritualistically.*] Spoon?
STOCK: Moon!
PETRI: Spoon empty?
STOCK: Humpty dumpty?
PETRI: Spoon bright?
STOCK: Star light!
PETRI: What do you think?
STOCK: God be praised for food and drink!

[*All laugh*—except VASCO.]

PETRI: Excellent. So—my little friend. You still haven't learned—
    Silence!—You still haven't learned that one cook alone . . .
VASCO: I was never alone in the night!
PETRI: Then where is your hat? Fifteen seconds. [*He takes out
    his watch.*]

VASCO: I, I . . .

GREEN: Speak up, dear boy!

PETRI: It might help if you stopped biting your nails.

STOCK: Just tell us where it is!

BENNY: It's just a formality, Vasco. You needn't be so afraid.

PETRI: Or would you rather have your dose? Five seconds.

VASCO: My aunt, my aunt . . .

STOCK: Well, well, well—I guess he's going to have to swallow it.

VASCO [*Screams.*]: No! Martha! Martha!

[*The cooks shrink back swiftly and silently and disappear behind the bed sheets. The oven door closes.* VASCO *jumps up as* MARTHA *enters.*]

MARTHA: Did you call, Stephen?

VASCO: I was dreaming. The sheets seemed to move, and the stove was alive and came toward me.

MARTHA: You see—it was nothing.

VASCO: Yes. [*He touches the bed sheets.*] Where is my hat?

MARTHA: You left it behind in there. [*She hands it to him.*]

VASCO [*Puts it on.*]: How is she?

MARTHA: Quiet.

VASCO: Is she still counting every time the clock strikes?

MARTHA: Come now—it's late.

VASCO: To your place? Will it be quiet there? You won't question me? And listen to me and think that I'm lying to you? And you won't talk when I fall silent? And, if need be, you will even hold your breath? Will you promise me this? [*The cuckoo clock strikes slowly.*] What's that?

MARTHA: You mustn't count. Please.

VASCO: Oh, but it's so hard not to count along with it, yet merely to *believe* that it is late!

Curtain

Act Three

The kitchen; the cooks' heads, obscured by clouds of steam, are visible behind a dirty-white half-wall. On the audience side of the wall hang a number of soiled hand-towels. The cook, PETRI, is sitting on a footstool down center wrapping up his trumpet in paper.

PETRI: It's a mystery to me—simply a mystery. How could this happen? Benny! Benny! I don't know, I must have dropped it or knocked it against something.

BENNY [*Comes out in front of the wall, hastily drying his hands.*]: The little trumpet has a sore throat, eh? You want me to take him to the doctor?

PETRI: More or less. Take it to Moser. And make it snappy. Tell him to fix it and get it back to me. And don't forget to tell him who sent you. Give him my best and—remember—tell him I need it by tomorrow night. Tell him we're having a party.

BENNY: And you're going to play a solo. [*He takes the trumpet.*]

PETRI: Beat it! [BENNY *starts out, turns back.*]

BENNY: No kidding—what's wrong today? Too much humidity?

PETRI: Get out! [BENNY *exits.* GREEN *comes out from behind the wall, dries his hands, and takes a small notebook out of his pocket.*]

GREEN: Don't tell me you've let your blowpipe out of your hands?

PETRI: If by "blowpipe" you mean my trumpet, you're right. What's up?

GREEN: We've got to arrange the menu. I'll take care of the fricassee.

PETRI: What else does he want?

GREEN: He says there's not enough soup.

PETRI [*Excitedly.*]: What does he think we're running here—an army mess hall? Now, let's see. We'll have beets. Borscht. Fifty cents. What about bouillabaisse?

GREEN: Not on Tuesday.

PETRI: Put down "borscht." Fifty cents. With cream—seventy-five cents. Yes—our aristocratic friend is always in such a hurry. I was thinking so yesterday. I was talking to him, and he just suddenly turned on his heel and rushed away.

GREEN: Did you send Stock after him?

PETRI: Naturally! We can't let this slip past us. If Schuster were to find out—well—Let's say, for the fricassee, oh, about a dollar and a quarter.

GREEN: Chicken curry or calves' liver?

PETRI: Put down the curry. Stock felt that he didn't get anywhere with him, you know. They got into a quarrel.

GREEN: The whole thing is absolute nonsense. Schuster overestimates the situation. In another five weeks everyone will have forgotten all about this soup.

PETRI: It's a mistake to assume that the people have anything to do with it. Be sensible, Green. What are we doing this for, after all?

GREEN: We still need another kind of soup! [Going.]

PETRI: Onion soup! with Parmesan cheese. Seventy-five cents. [Exit behind the wall.]

[A trapdoor opens and the cook STOCK comes up, carrying a basin on his shoulder. In the basin there lies a whole boar's head.]

STOCK: Ah, it's nice down in the cellar! Now to make some jelly. What do I care about the rest of them? To hell with them. [Sets the basin down, looks at the boar's head.] You're lucky, old boy—You're not being hunted any more. But I've got to chase people around and then run back here and tell what they said. And now all hell will break loose when I tell him I don't know anything at all! Here I'll lie like a boar's head in my own jelly, while they poke at me with their spoons. [He laughs, starts to pick up the basin again. VASCO comes out from behind the wall, drying his hands. He stops. For a moment, he and STOCK stare at each other.]

STOCK: Well?

VASCO: What did you find out? [Seizes him.] Tell me!

STOCK: Nothing!

VASCO: Listen . . .

STOCK: How can I listen while you're pulling and tugging at me?

VASCO: You followed him. You talked with him. [*Lets him go.*]

STOCK: Nothing! I told you.

VASCO [*Shoves him angrily.*]: Oh, you're a little angel! You know nothing, you did nothing! And what about Petri? What's the matter with him, then?

STOCK: Maybe he's worried.

VASCO: I'm telling you to keep your mouth shut, or—or—

STOCK: Well, well, well! What's this? Are you threatening me? What am I going to tell him? Aren't we in this together? Didn't we stand there on the bridge like brothers, thinking what an indifferent back he had as he walked away?

VASCO: Schuster talked to Petri and Green.

STOCK: They're worried—those three.

VASCO: And *we* should be worried! Don't you see, it won't work for all of us! Five are too many! He'll only laugh if he sees five of us.

STOCK: But he won't laugh at two?

VASCO: He always laughs a little—at everything. But two are less laughable than five. He doesn't like crowds, you know.

STOCK: And suppose he sees a real crowd? Not just five, but . . . ?

VASCO [*Grabs him.*]: You've been to see Kletterer! Listen, if you think you're going to . . . !

STOCK: Look out! Petri! [*Both start drying their hands.* PETRI *joins them and starts to dry his hands also.*]

PETRI: So busy? Now what could that be, to make the two of you so very, very busy?

STOCK: Preparing jelly for the boar's head.

PETRI [*Laughs.*]: Ah, so the two of you are standing here discussing the mysteries of making jelly!

VASCO: Not at all! We were—we were discussing Martha.

PETRI: Better and better! Green, come here—quickly!

[GREEN *comes out.*]

GREEN: Aren't there enough cooks here already? [*Dries his hands.*]

PETRI: Oh, no—too few! Listen to this. It will be worth it, I promise you. These two cooks—ordinarily very hardworking, I assure you—have been standing here talking about jelly and Martha, and then about Martha and jelly—or maybe the menu, for the discussion went in this order: boar's head, Martha, jelly, baked potatoes—and then Martha again, because she's so pretty, and then for dessert, a little boiled water soup.

[STOCK *slips out.*]

GREEN: Now I call that remarkable! Very!

VASCO: Now look, you're making a joke out of it because we were standing here and chatting a little instead of working, but . . . where's Stock?

PETRI: He beat it—to chat some more with his boar's head! But—enough nonsense! To business! How is Martha these days? Is she sleeping well? Good appetite? Her shoes don't pinch? And at the hospital? Busy taking pulses, emptying bedpans, keeping the books? Eh? Tell us, how does she spend her days there—running around with a cheerful face? Or doesn't she ever confide in you?

GREEN: What's her real name, by the way?

VASCO: Petri, I give you my word. All we ever discuss is . . .

PETRI: Yes?

VASCO: My aunt's illness.

PETRI: How it all fits together. You notice, Green? Jelly, Martha, the Aunt.

GREEN: And what was your uncle's real name?

PETRI: Not so fast! Now, Vasco, about the old aunt . . .

VASCO: You've got to understand, she's ill. I sat up with her last night. She didn't even speak.

GREEN: What a shame! But Martha perhaps? I take it she hasn't been struck dumb? What's wrong?

VASCO: What about Martha?

GREEN: Now what are we to make of that? I merely mention the name of the sweet little bride and what happens? The even sweeter little bridegroom becomes terrified!

PETRI: Maybe, since the old aunt was as still as the grave, little Martha managed to put in a word now and then, eh? [VASCO *moves uneasily.*] Do you think that, if we put it to her very delicately, she might come here and . . . [VASCO *starts out.*] Stay here!

GREEN: What's the matter with you? We're having such a pleasant little chat, too!

VASCO: The laundry is ready, I think!

GREEN: We're talking about coffee and cookies—he wants to talk about laundry! Isn't it always the way? No, no—stay here with us! We'll fix you a cup of coffee—although that's not really our specialty. And maybe a little piece of apple pie—

PETRI: With whipped cream—you see how generous we are?

GREEN: She'll look very nice, in that modest little nurse's cap of hers. We want everything to be friendly, you understand—and yet proper. We'll have a nice, easy little chat.

VASCO: She knows nothing.

GREEN: Nothing about what?

VASCO: I told you, she doesn't want to go to the hospital—my aunt—she doesn't . . .

PETRI: To hell with the aunt! What is it that Martha doesn't know about?

VASCO: Nothing! Everything!

PETRI: Ah, but who would be so rude and so tactless as to suggest that his little bride was a dumbbell? That's hardly courtly, you must admit, Vasco. It seems to me that it's up to us to protect the honor of your betrothed and—what is the phrase?

GREEN: Restore her good name. It's the least we can do for a lady.

PETRI: And the sooner, the better! Is Benny back yet? Benny! Benny! [*Benny comes out from behind the wall, a frying pan in each hand.*] Is my trumpet all fixed up?

BENNY: No trouble, Moser said. He said he'd have it ready in an hour.

PETRI: All right. Then go fetch Martha, and on your way back pick up the trumpet. But be nice to her, you hear? [*He takes the frying pans from him, gives one to* GREEN.]

BENNY: I'll be very careful. What are you two going to do?

GREEN: We're going to have a tennis match—a very elegant tennis match—until the lady arrives.

BENNY: What? Without a ball?

GREEN: Naturally. Ready, Martha?

PETRI: Whenever *you* are, Stephen. [*They pantomime a tennis match with the frying pans and imitate* MARTHA's *and* VASCO's *voices.* BENNY *laughs.*]

GREEN: Hurry up and fetch her!

BENNY: I'm there already. [*Runs out.*]

GREEN: And be sure to bring me Mr. Petri's trumpet. You know how helpless he is without music and noise. Ah, ah! You must play gently, Martha.

PETRI: Yes, Stephen! [*Quietly.*] What's that about the trumpet?

GREEN: Use your backhand, Martha, your backhand! [*Quietly.*] Just a little joke between musicians. Please, Martha, not *into* the net—*over* the net.

VASCO: She won't be at home.

GREEN: Will you be at the hospital, then, Martha?

PETRI: No, Stephen!

GREEN: Why not?

PETRI: Yes, Stephen!

GREEN: No, yes. What kind of an answer is that? Don't you know how to talk like a human being?

PETRI: Please, Stephen!

GREEN: "Please, Stephen!" Just say where you're going to be, that's all.

VASCO: Not in the hospital—that's certain.

GREEN: Where will you be, then?

PETRI: With your old aunt, Stephen.

GREEN: And then where should Benny go?

PETRI: To the aunt's house, Stephen.

GREEN: And whom will he find by her bed?

PETRI: Martha, Stephen.

VASCO: No—what is all this? You're supposed to be the chief here— what's this all about?

GREEN: What is all this, Martha?

PETRI: I don't know, Stephen.

VASCO: Well, *I* know! I'm a cook, not an orator!

GREEN: Ah. You hear? Cook, not orator.

PETRI: No, Stephen.

VASCO: Yes—a cook! A cook! And I'll go to Schuster and tell him so! [*He starts out, but* PETRI *stops him. They toss the frying pans aside.*]

PETRI: Let's leave poor old Schuster out of this. After all, we were only joking. You know us—we didn't mean any harm. Let's not talk any more about the old aunt or about Martha—to whom Benny is now running on his quick little feet. Let's talk about something else. Let's talk—for instance—about your uncle.

GREEN: Yes. What is his name?

VASCO: I have no uncle!

PETRI: Oh, this wicked world! He denies his uncle!

GREEN: He wants to put him in a dark barrel and roll him into the deep cellar. He is a monster!

VASCO: Do you want me to stand here and lie? I'm only a cook, I tell you! My job is to warm over the red cabbage and baste the kidneys! And what about the laundry? Mrs. Coldwater has brought it, and here we are, standing here in dirty clothes!

[PETRI *holds him back.*]

PETRI: Do you see a fleck of dirt on him?

GREEN: His cap is pure as the driven snow.

PETRI: But where do you suppose his old cap is?

[VASCO *tries to get away.*]

VASCO: Please! That's enough! What do you want from me?

PETRI: I'm speechless! We've told you what we want. The name of your right reverend uncle.

VASCO: I was talking about my aunt, that's all. That's all I've ever talked about!

PETRI: Oh, please—don't cry, dear boy. Now, what was *her* name again?

VASCO: Theresa.

PETRI: Aha. That is, to be sure, a rather common yet undeniably pretty name. Hmm. Now where have I heard that name before? No matter. Aunt Theresa, then. And now for the uncle! Speak! [*Seizes him.*]

VASCO: No! Not another word!

GREEN: We're not asking you to swear a vow, you understand!

PETRI: Maybe he wants to be a saint in a cell?

GREEN: Or maybe he wants to be a deaf-mute. Or he wants . . . Ah, I have it!

PETRI: Yes?

GREEN: He wants a little spoonful.

VASCO: No, no—not that!

PETRI: But didn't you just say that not a single word more would cross your lips? And now you want us to believe that you're ready to tell all? What are we to think?

VASCO: We were at my aunt's . . .

PETRI: But now it's a holiday! [*They twist* VASCO's *arm behind his back.*] Stock! Come here, my boy.

Stock [*Looking out from behind the wall.*]: What is it?

Petri: Bring us a spoonful.

Stock: Jesus, I didn't mean it this way, Vasco. I only told them what I'd seen, that's all.

Vasco: You! A fine friend you are!

Petri: Or maybe we'll need *two* spoons?

Stock: No, no, no—right away, Petri! Just give me a minute to dry my hands! [*He dries his hands and disappears again.*]

Petri: Still silent? Well, I don't blame you for biting your fingernails like that, my boy. But I *do* think it would be better if you were to talk.

Vasco: If only the Count hadn't said anything . . . [stock *returns with the spoon and places himself in front of* vasco.]

Green: So the Count is your uncle, is that it? An aristocratic transformation! Tell me—what do gentlemen in high society talk about?

Stock: Come on! Talk! [*As they all watch* vasco, *the* count *enters from the right.*]

The Count [*Laughing.*]: Well, what's this? [*They release* vasco *hurriedly and with smiling embarrassment.*] What are you going to do—give Vasco his medicine? Such a strong, healthy fellow as that?

Petri: It was just a joke, Your Excellency. You know how cooks are. [*To* stock] Beat it! [stock *exits.*]

The Count: Yes, I learned a little bit yesterday about cooks.

Green: Oh. Something pleasant, I trust? [vasco *withdraws silently.*]

The Count: That's a matter of interpretation. I got a good laugh out of it. Where is Vasco, by the way?

Petri: Shall I call him?

The Count: No—never mind, Petri. Probably he's feeling a little ashamed of himself. Flight doesn't seem to agree with him. Yes, gentlemen, last night under the darkness of Heaven he made a sort of trial flight. He stood there before me, as you are now—with a chef's cap on his head—white in the moonlight.

Green: He's always been a little bit strange.

The Count: He seized me, there on the bridge, and demanded something of me.

Petri: Not money, surely?

THE COUNT: No, no, no. I'm not sure just what it was. You see, the girl came along just then.

GREEN: Martha?

THE COUNT [*Thoughtfully.*]: Sometimes, in my mind, I see her as Ruth, gleaning in the fields. The stubble hurts her feet, but she does not shrink. Even if she were blind, she would work. She is patient.

GREEN [*Laughs.*]: I could almost believe it!

THE COUNT: Don't laugh, you fools! What do you know about patience? Your patience is like that of a tough piece of beef, but Ruth's . . .

GREEN: Look, we were talking about Martha. What happened next?

THE COUNT: She came along; we talked. What about? Hmm. I don't remember. Whatever one talks about on bridges. Oh, yes—Vasco! He wanted something from me—in fact, he had even tried to shake it out of me!

PETRI: By force?

THE COUNT: Oh, he shook me the way you shake a nut tree. Only no nuts fall from my branches. Then he wanted to throw me into the water. Me and my recipe.

GREEN: Aha!

THE COUNT: And now it seems to me that you too also want . . .

PETRI: Oh, certainly not, Your Excellency. We certainly do not approve of these methods.

THE COUNT: Good! Then let me propose something: You all close your eyes—eh?—and I will put it in the pocket of one of you.

PETRI: Which one?

THE COUNT: You or Green.

PETRI: No, no, no—Out of the question! [*The* COUNT *shrugs, starts to go.*]

GREEN: But why not?

PETRI: Because I said "No"! [*Turns, sees the* COUNT, *runs over and blocks his exit.*] Wait! You can't leave like this. Why not simply tell it to all of us? We're all cooks together, aren't we? Now, obviously it's some sort of borscht or a cabbage soup. Only they say you sprinkle ashes in it . . .

THE COUNT: Ah, you have described the process exactly. But

enough of this. My mind is firm. I will never give it to you, you headhunters.

GREEN: Why the devil not?

THE COUNT: Because you want it. Period.

GREEN: But I . . .

THE COUNT: No, not even you, Green. I'm really very sorry, because I know you have ulcers and yet are still a fine cook—a cook who must cook with his brain, not his taste . . .

GREEN: A good cook . . .

THE COUNT: Never tastes the broth, I know. I know the proverb. The wisdom of an invalid.

GREEN: And Vasco? Did you tell him? Did you give him the recipe? [*The* COUNT *draws back.*]

PETRI: You shouldn't have done that. Even though he *is* your favorite.

GREEN: Aren't we your friends? Why him—him alone?

THE COUNT: Let me go! You talk of friendship and look at me like a newly purchased, enterprising piece of India rubber! Let me live and—[*He searches through his pockets.*]

PETRI: Are you looking for something?

THE COUNT: Nothing unusual, some notes . . . What was I saying? Yes—let me live! Where are they? Gone! Lost!

GREEN: What—here? In the kitchen? [GREEN *and* PETRI *drop to all fours and start searching.*]

THE COUNT: Really—it was nothing important. Please—stop.

GREEN: Was it a small tablet—or a notebook?

THE COUNT: A little notebook—yes. But you must let Vasco live—not just me. It's true, he's my favorite—but he knows nothing—just as you do!

PETRI: Find anything, Green?

GREEN: Not a trace. Was it white?

THE COUNT: White as innocence—but written on a little. And please, don't fight when you find it, boys, and beat each other over the head. Like this. [*He strikes* GREEN *lightly on the cap and runs out, right, laughing.* VASCO *comes out from behind the wall and observes the scene.*]

GREEN: Why is he laughing?

PETRI: Because we're crawling around here like fools looking for a notebook in which we *assume* something is written. That's why.

VASCO: Something written? What? He taps you on the cap, yet

you believe him. He flatters you, calls you by name—he says
"My dear Green" or "Dear old Petri"—then you fall to your
knees and he laughs a bit and runs off. He doesn't even turn
around. And you? You decide you want to give me a spoonful—
or maybe two—in the hopes of making me talk. What now, eh?
What now? Do you still want to give me my dose?

PETRI: Nonsense! We just thought . . .

VASCO: Yes?

PETRI: . . . that you wanted to keep the whole business to yourself.

VASCO: So I did—at first. Because I thought the Count didn't like
dealing in groups of people. [STOCK *comes in with a package.*]
And I know him. Don't I know him—eh?

STOCK: I can testify to that. Petri will believe me.

VASCO: All he believes in is his spoonful. That's his one and only
truth. [STOCK *throws the package down.*]

STOCK: Here's the laundry! Old Coldwater complained about it . . .

GREEN: Why? [*The cooks put on clean aprons and caps.*]

STOCK: Who knows? When *doesn't* she complain?

GREEN: We ought to be friendlier with her. She may come in
handy some day. Send her some jelly and a few little tidbits.

PETRI: Listen. I still decide what's to be worn in this kitchen.

STOCK: Sure, sure, sure—and, after all she's part of the business,
too—old Coldwater.

PETRI: Look—enough of this chatter! Everybody listen! The situation is simple: if we don't get together and do something—and
quickly—we're finished! Schuster has told me that if the business isn't back on its feet again within three weeks . . . well, you
know what I mean! As for you, Vasco, no more sneaking off on
your own. That was very, very stupid of you. [*Helps him tie his
apron.*] I never doubted you, but Green is always a little hasty.
However, I never really believed you would go that far.

GREEN: We just wanted to scare you a little, that's all.

STOCK: I thought all along they were just trying to teach you a
lesson. Would I have brought them the spoon if I didn't? [BENNY
shoves MARTHA *into the room. He is carrying the trumpet.*]

VASCO: So this is what it means! Very polite apologies with nothing behind them. She goes—*now!*

BENNY: Don't get excited. Chief's orders. Ah, she didn't want to
come and leave her poor old auntie. But I persuaded her. Here's
the old blowpipe, Chief—good as new. [*He hands over the trum-*

pet; PETRI *unwraps it.*] Ha—old Coldwater's been here! [*He changes clothes.*]

MARTHA: Stephen?

BENNY: Isn't that sweet, the way she says "Stephen"?

PETRI: Shut up! She can go—we don't need her now.

MARTHA: Stephen—your aunt . . . [*He turns his back.*]

PETRI: What about the aunt? Did you go in?

BENNY: No, Chief. She wouldn't let me in the room.

MARTHA: She is dead! [BENNY *laughs.*]

PETRI: What's there to laugh about? Shut up! You can go, little girl—go on, go! Stephen will be along soon to help you. [MARTHA *goes out hesitantly.*] Well—so it goes. We were just speaking of her and now—kaput! [*He blows on the trumpet and sets it aside.*] The aunt is dead! [*Everyone, except* VASCO, *laughs.*]

STOCK: You should laugh, too—she's dead!

VASCO: Yes, yes, it's really very funny. [*The cooks go behind the wall, laughing.* PETRI *detains* STOCK, *center.*]

PETRI: You—finish up the chicken, then pack up some jelly and five slices of bread for Mrs. Coldwater. I'll take it to her myself! [*He exits.*]

[STOCK *draws near the trumpet, picks it up, turns it around and around, then holds it to his eye like a telescope, sets it down again.*]

STOCK: Music! Music! [*He bows deeply to the trumpet.*] The chicken! I'll finish it up. We'll see, we'll see. [*He goes to the wings, brings back a chopping block, puts the trumpet on the block.*] Music? Music? [KLETTERER *enters from the left and stands observing* STOCK *for a moment.*]

KLETTERER: So—is this what you've come to? Killing a trumpet and making trumpet soup?

STOCK [*Without turning around.*]: Jesus—Kletterer!

KLETTERER: Hmm—an elegant shop you've got here! Lots of light, good drains—no cooking odors. Like a health resort!

STOCK: How did you get in here? [*Turns around.*] Did he see you?

KLETTERER: Evidently not. [*He seizes* STOCK *by the apron.*] Well, how goes it? Has he talked?

STOCK: No, no—it's all nonsense! He led them around by the nose and then stood there laughing while Green and Petri went root-

ing around on the floor like pigs looking for truffles! Now go
on, get out! If he finds you here, there'll be hell to pay!

KLETTERER: And now? [*Picks up the trumpet.*] What are your
plans now? What's next on the program?

STOCK: Don't ask me! [*He brings a basket in from the wings; there
is a live chicken in the basket.*] Here, watch. I'm going to kill
this chicken and pack up some jelly and bread to send to old
lady Coldwater. Petri is going to deliver it in person.

KLETTERER: What the hell do I care about your jelly?

STOCK: Oh? Not interested, eh? Not even if Petri is delivering the
goods in person? Eh? Aha—yes—now I see the light going on in
your head!

KLETTERER: You mean . . . ?

STOCK: Big deal— I'm telling you. They're going to rent the laundry
room and throw a big party—with the Count invited!

KLETTERER [*Whistles thoughtfully.*]: When?

STOCK: Leave it to me!

KLETTERER [*He seizes* STOCK.]: But you'll give me the straight story,
won't you, Stock? You would never be so stupid as to destroy
your friendship with Kletterer, would you? You understand that
I intend to be among the guests when you throw your big
party. Because—you see—I love parties.

STOCK: What's the matter? What are you shaking *me* for? You're
always grabbing people and messing up their clothes—you and
Vasco! Relax. Don't worry. I'll send you a message—by carrier
pigeon.

KLETTERER: You know where I live. [*He goes out quickly, left,
the trumpet under his arm.*]

STOCK [*Noticing the trumpet is gone.*]: Music! Music! Music!? [*He
puts the basket on the chopping block, then back on the floor.*]
Music! Music! [*He imitates the flapping of the hen, then does a
handstand before the basket, staring the hen in the eye. He
crows. He jumps up, opens the basket, takes out the squawking
chicken, and raises his hatchet.*] Music! [PETRI *rushes out from
behind the wall.*]

PETRI: How often have I told you not to kill chickens onstage?!
Do you want to convert all the paying customers into vegetarians?

Curtain

Act Four

The laundry room: MRS. COLDWATER *is taking down the laundered aprons, stockings and caps of the cooks.* GREEN *sits at a table writing and keeping an eye on her work.*

GREEN: You can leave the last line full if you like.

COLDWATER: What is it you want the room for? I don't care, mind you, if you want to have a little party here. Boys will be boys. I don't even care that you don't let me know about it till the last minute! But to come like this and wake me up out of a sound sleep—! "Let's go, let's go!" Eh? What's it all about?

GREEN: We're going to throw a birthday party.

COLDWATER: Ha! As though you cooks care anything about birthdays! What kind of craziness are you fellows up to, eh?

GREEN: How long have you been working for us now? Several years—right? Every week two uniforms per man, along with the napkins and towels, the tablecloths—everything. Right?

COLDWATER: There's enough to do—I can't complain.

GREEN: Precisely. And my advice is: those who have no complaints should ask no questions.

COLDWATER: All right, but a person can speak a word or two now and then, can't she? Oh, ta, ta, ta—Mr. Green! Big man! He sits there and writes. Very important. What, I wonder? Maybe place cards—or birthday verses?

GREEN: Are you finished?

COLDWATER: It looks like it.

GREEN: Then tell Martha to come in here! [*Points to the door.*]

COLDWATER: Ah, yes, Martha! Now you listen to me, young man! Is that any way to behave, leaving her to stand out there in the weather like that? Hah? Doesn't she have enough to put up with, with that—that—what's his name?

GREEN: Vasco!

COLDWATER: Yes—that's the one! And not only that—the poor little thing has just lost her aunt.

GREEN: It wasn't *her* aunt.

COLDWATER: Well—anyway—it was the only person in the world she had any real connection with.

GREEN: Mrs. Coldwater—if you don't mind! [*Points to the door imperiously.*]

COLDWATER: All right, all right, I'm going! [*Opens the door.*] Poor little thing! These are modern manners, eh? [*Brings* MARTHA *in.*] And to make her stand here under the wash!

MARTHA: Hello, Mrs. Coldwater. [*Takes off her raincoat.*] Good evening, Mr. Green.

GREEN: You can warm you hands there at the pipes, if you like. I won't need you any more, Mrs. Coldwater. And I beg your pardon for this—er—little irregularity. It won't happen again.

COLDWATER: I thought you said it was a birthday?

GREEN: All right—that doesn't happen very often, does it? Once a year. And if someone asks you about this . . . ?

COLDWATER: I say, it was a birthday party. Okay. Is Mr. Schuster coming?

GREEN: Probably.

COLDWATER: Did he say so?

GREEN: I said, "probably"! [*He stands up.*] In consideration of the late notification, etcetera, your usual rental fee will be doubled. [*He hands her an envelope.*] All right?

COLDWATER: Naturally, if I thought it was *really* a birthday party, I wouldn't have said a word.

GREEN: Good night, Mrs. Coldwater! [*Hands her a second envelope and steers her to the door.*] Sleep well!

COLDWATER: Easy, now, easy! Is this my room or am I a visitor here? Eh? I'm warning you, now, you leave Martha alone! You hear? Now listen, child! Don't let these fellows get fresh with you! Keep an eye on them—you know what I mean? After all, they're only little cooks trying to act big!

MARTHA: Mrs. Coldwater . . . [*She moves toward her.*]

GREEN [*Shoving* MRS. COLDWATER *out of the room.*]: You stay right here! There's nothing to be afraid of, my angel. So . . . you were able to get off work, eh?

MARTHA: The Head Nurse wasn't willing, at first. But then Sister Dora—she's the night nurse—put in a good word for me.

GREEN: That was very sweet of her.

Martha: We—understand each other, Sister Dora and I.

Green [*He fiddles with her blouse; she wards him off weakly.*]:
But what, but what? You understand yourself, too—eh? Does
she have a friend? [*He clasps her in his arms.*]

Martha: Please!

Green: Does she have a friend?

Martha: I think so. Please don't, Mr. Green! [*She breaks loose.*]

Green: All right—if you insist! [*Wipes his hands on his apron.*]
What were you saying, now? Oh, yes! Sister Dora's friend. What
is he—a postman, a taxi driver—perhaps a cook?

Martha: Is that what you think? Do you suppose that all nurses
have cooks as sweethearts?

Green: Oh, no—that would be too much! Too much. [*Paces up
and down.*] Such an idiot! Talented, he has a real feeling for
cooking, he doesn't even need the money, everything falls into
his lap—so what does he do? Starts running around with a nurse!
Do you see that you are simply standing in his way? Why, with
his talent, that boy could make a fortune! But, as I say, what
about this little friendship? A cook and a nurse—what a combination! What do you intend to do—set up a hospital kitchen
for invalids? Oh, yes! How nice! But not for the rest of us! You
stand in his way, my child! You're a stumbling block! Stop
crying!

Martha: But he said . . .

Green: He is an idiot! Young, dazzled with love—he can do nothing. It's up to you. You must decide, you must say "no," you
must sacrifice yourself. As a nurse, you shouldn't find it too
difficult. You should be used to that sort of thing.

Martha: But he's not sick.

Green: Oh, but he is! Deathly sick—as sure as my name is Green.
That hospital odor is destroying him. Chlorine, carbolic acid,
acetic acid. Have you ever known a cook who could stand that
sort of thing? And always that little cap on your head. Sooner
or later, that will make your hair grow thin and then fall out.

Martha: What is it you want me to say?

Green: I just want you to think this over very calmly, and then—
at the proper moment—sacrifice yourself a little. After all, it's
Stephen's happiness we must think of—right?

Martha: Yes.

Green: And then you will . . . [*Hears something.*] Shh! Stop your crying! [PETRI, *in a black raincoat, comes in, takes off the rain-coat and tosses it to* MARTHA *to hang up.*]

PETRI: Well? Everything all right? What did Coldwater say?

GREEN: She's gone off to bed.

PETRI: So—?

GREEN: Just waiting for the others. Everything's all ready. She's been crying.

PETRI [*Pats her soothingly.*]: All right, all right. What's she doing here, anyway? Was that necessary?

GREEN: I suppose so.

PETRI: I hate all this confusion and fuss. I ordered you to go easy on the expense. No expense, and a nice, neat motivation. Period. Now, would you mind explaining to me . . .

GREEN: She's here, and that's that! What about the boss? Is he coming?

PETRI: I couldn't care less.

GREEN: I asked you a question. Is he coming?

PETRI: No.

GREEN: But he promised.

PETRI: I don't like this. I don't like the girl being here.

GREEN: We should be a little more polite, I think.

PETRI: Oh, no, listen, will you? Green has tender feelings! Schuster has asked me to tell you that he feels his appearance here would be unnecessary. He is fully confident and, indeed, convinced that matters here will be successfully carried out according to his—er—conception, quite calmly and without undue rashness.

GREEN [*Whistles meaningfully.*]: What a philanthropist!

PETRI: I see that you understand me.

GREEN: If only *you* understood the rest of us. You have forgotten your trumpet, haven't you? Now, how are you going to make yourself understood without it?

[*The door bursts open.* BENNY, STOCK *and* VASCO, *carrying packages, push the* COUNT *into the room. The cooks are in raincoats; the* COUNT *wears a shawl over his morning coat.*]

THE COUNT: Petri! Green! What a surprise! After being rudely awakened and rather impolitely transported here—lo and behold! I find myself among friends. Ah—are you here, too, Martha—and at this late hour?

Vasco: Who brought her here? That wasn't part of our bargain.

Petri: I quite agree. But calm yourself, my boy, we'll settle all this later. [*To the* count.] I hope you haven't suffered any impoliteness at the hands of these louts, Benny?

Benny: He didn't want to come.

Stock: He wanted to stay sleepybye.

Petri: All right—skip it! Out!

The Count: But why? Now that I am here safely on shore, as it were, all these little unpleasantnesses are as good as forgotten. Well, well—isn't this cozy here? It doesn't exactly smell good, though, I must say . . .

Vasco: That's cabbage you smell. It's the perfume of poor people.

The Count: To be sure. You have a very delicate sense of smell. It's too bad that you can't live by your nose. Cabbage, of course! And why not? Considered purely optically, this little room is a feast for the eyes. These hangings! These are prospects! Landscapes! My dear Green, is there any significance in this little tableau?

Green: None. Pure coincidence. A laundry room is sure to be warm—that's all.

The Count: Ah. I am reassured. For a while there I almost had the feeling that I was being confronted with a symbol, or—worse yet—that I was going to have to spend the rest of this night under the burden of symbolism.

Petri: You may set your mind at rest, Count.

The Count: I have no choice but to believe you, do I? And now—?

Stock [*Quietly.*]: Let's get started, let's get started.

Petri [*Quietly.*]: What the matter?

Stock: They've gotten wind of it. They were hot on our trail.

Petri: Damn! How could that have happened? Vasco? Benny?

Benny: Beats me, Chief. Somebody must have blabbed.

Vasco: What are you looking at me for? Green was there—so was Stock—They both had a chance to talk a little!

Stock: And this noon—where were you?

Petri [*Loud.*]: Silence!

The Count: But Petri! Let them go. I get the feeling you scold your men too much. Certainly you shouldn't squabble before a young lady. [*To* martha.]: I will anticipate these gentlemen by offering you this chair. [*She sits down timidly.*] And, with the permission of Green, our chief of protocol, I will seat myself from time to time to time, here on the edge of the table! So. Now—to business! I gather we are going to discuss—for the hundredth time—this problem concerning the recipe for the soup.

VASCO: Speak up! Tell it to us—quickly! I beg you! Or, if you want to give it just to me, why not? Haven't I sworn to you that it would be buried forever—here, in my heart? [PETRI *pulls him back*.]

STOCK: Why does he always jump in ahead of everybody else?

PETRI [*Quietly.*]: I'm warning you, Vasco! [*Aloud.*] How nice, that you have brought the thing up so clearly and directly! Now we can all talk together like friends. You see, the future of our calling, not to mention the future of gastronomy itself and, indeed, of . . .

THE COUNT: Humanity.

PETRI: Precisely. How well you put it. You have always been a patron of our difficult yet important art. Always you have stood at our side in word and deed when it was necessary to cater to the—er—special tastes of our regular customers. But not enough! Not enough! Now, you are going to magnanimously grant us a look at your writings. Let your collected works—which the boys have rather overenthusiastically brought along—serve here as evidence of your proverbial passion. In these packages . . .

THE COUNT: Which will get damp if you leave them here.

PETRI: Put them over there by the steam pipes! You too, Vasco, you too!

[*They move the packages near the steam pipes.* MARTHA *starts to help. The* COUNT *restrains her.*]

THE COUNT: No. Don't bother. What do these papers have to do with *you?* But go on, Petri—I'm afraid I interrupted you. [*Loud knocking at the door.*] Hmm. It looks like our visitors are going to have the next word.

PETRI [*To* GREEN.]: You speak to them. [GREEN *rises and goes to the door.*]

GREEN: What about? About you? They're not interested in discussing our great virtuoso of the trumpet. [*He goes out.*]

PETRI: Yes, yes, yes. Now—what were we talking about?

THE COUNT: About God and the world and a piece of paper. You look to me like a man who is distracted. Have you been getting enough sleep lately?

PETRI: Right! The packages! Now, suppose we assume that perhaps some notes about this soup are in one of these packages—no one knows which one . . .

THE COUNT: Not a soul. But you are proceeding from totally false assumptions. This isn't a question of some mysterious recipe, but simply of my wretched, completely private secret.

[VASCO *rushes forward.*]

VASCO: Right, your secret. No, let me speak, Petri! Let me talk to him! What do you mean, a secret? Can anything remain a secret? *Should* it? Do you want to die and take it with you? Do you want to lie there with your mouth sealed and your secret locked inside [*He strikes his breast.*] forever?

THE COUNT [*Laughing.*]: What a stream of questions! My, my! But you are searching in the wrong place, my friend. Not here in my breast! Out there, in the street, perhaps in a trash container—there's where to look for this vexing secret. Like a lame dog, limping along from tree to tree and leaving a paltry sign of his inglorious existence. [GREEN *returns, bolts the door behind him.*]

BENNY: I'm going crazy! He's going to best us yet!

STOCK: He's making fools of us. Let Green talk to him instead of Petri. Does he think he can get away with telling us jokes and selling us rotten eggs?

PETRI: Silence!

GREEN: They're out there, Petri—all of them!

PETRI: Kletterer?

GREEN: He knows everything.

PETRI: Ridiculous! What is there for him to know?

GREEN: Ask him. You're exactly the one to talk to him. They say they want to be in on this with us and give us their advice.

PETRI: Benny! Stock! To the door!

STOCK: This is stupid. If he wants to come in here, let him.

PETRI: Make it snappy!

STOCK: But let Green talk. He can do it better.

PETRI: I give up. Why not?

GREEN: He treats me as though I were his son. He would even give me his shining trumpet—if he only had it here. [*The cooks laugh.*] [*To the* COUNT.] All right! Pay attention! I've already talked things over with our friends out there. They're ready for any-thing! They don't have our—er—patience. They simply grab a man first and ask questions later. So—use your head. Here is paper, ink, everything you need. Write, for God's sake, write— and we promise to protect you from that gang out there!

THE COUNT: Hmm. You're not very good businessmen, I must say. You bring your client into danger and then demand some-thing from him. You ought to make *me* an offer! Go ahead! Make me an offer!

PETRI: How much? [*Loud knocking at the door.*]

GREEN: You hear that? They're strong fellows! He means money. How much?

THE COUNT: I'm afraid your money doesn't interest me much. [*Louder knocking.*] Let them in. They must be freezing out there.

PETRI: You're very playful, aren't you?

STOCK: To hell with this bull! He doesn't want money. What, then?

THE COUNT: Can't you see? I want to go home; I want to go back to bed. Why don't you quietly discuss what you want to offer me and then come back again? Poor Martha. She must be very tired. [*Pounding on the door.*]

STOCK: They're going crazy out there!

BENNY: What crap! Let's take care of them right now!

STOCK: Now even Green knows the score here. Let's turn him over to them! [*Meaning the* COUNT.]

BENNY: Let's give him a spoonful if he wants us to offer him something!

GREEN [*To the* COUNT.]: You see? Your own people are getting restless. Write—now!

BENNY: He can have *two* spoonsful if he'd like! [*He comes away from the door and takes a bottle and spoon out of his pocket.*] How would *that* be? It tastes best when it's cold.

THE COUNT: Petri, will you ask your unwashed Benjamin to stand downwind of me? I don't like the smell of his toothpaste.

BENNY [*Stamps angrily.*]: That for your "toothpaste" and for your "unwashed" and all the rest! What do you say? [*To the others.*] Shall I?

STOCK: The dike is breaking! Who am I supposed to be—Hercules—to hold this damned door by the hour? [*Splintering, the door breaks open. In the opening, a crowd of cooks, led by* KLETTERER. *He has* PETRI's *trumpet and blows a blast on it.* STOCK *jumps aside.*]

KLETTERER: Well, well, well, what's all this? What do you call this little game? Can we sit in on it? Looks like things are moving right along. The good old spoonful—we know that one—it makes people talkative. [*To the cooks behind him.*] Take it easy, boys, we're going to join in. What's this? [*Points to the packages.*]

THE COUNT: The gentleman is referring to my modest collection of recipes.

KLETTERER: Quiet out there! So—you are the Count? My name is Kletterer. You've never heard of me? Well, prick up your ears—we're going to become good friends, you and I.

THE COUNT: Why not? Many of my warmest friendships were formed at this late hour of the night.

KLETTERER: Aha! A joker! Well, what about the negotiations here? Green?

PETRI: Look here, Kletterer, where did you get my trumpet?

KLETTERER: I was talking to Green. I was inquiring about the negotiations.

GREEN: We are unfortunately going to have to adjourn.

KLETTERER: Nonsense! Let me have a try! [*Pushes* GREEN *away from the table; to the* COUNT.] So. You're being difficult?

THE COUNT: My dear man, I merely want to go to sleep. And I'm sure this young lady does, too.

KLETTERER: Lady? Ah, yes, the nurse. She wants to go to bed, too. And so do I. [*The cooks stir restlessly in the background.*]

GREEN: You've got to haggle with him, Kletterer. He's not interested in money.

BENNY: Look—what did I say? A spoonful, right? [KLETTERER *smacks* BENNY *in the face; the cooks in the doorway laugh.*]

KLETTERER: Shut up, damn it! [*To* PETRI.] The kid doesn't have very good manners, does he? Is that what you teach them?

PETRI: He's stupid—what do you expect?

KLETTERER: Haggle, eh? All right. Listen, Count! What's in this first package?

THE COUNT: Some fish dishes, I believe. Venison. Fowl. Several sauces.

KLETTERER: Any *personal* recipe of yours?

THE COUNT: God—who knows?—they're so jumbled and mixed up . . .

KLETTERER [*Giving* BENNY *a shove.*]: Take it over to the door! [BENNY *shoves a package to the doorway, where* KLETTERER's *people start tearing it open.*] Nothing there? Fine—fair enough! Next? Here—these two! [*Two more packages are torn open.*]

THE COUNT: I must say, your offerings are rather wearying, although I must admit that you're saving me some work. On the other hand—it's one of my little weaknesses—I did a certain amount of selection in advance—you know, I kept some out, collected; in short, what you have here is an edition. You and your people are very thorough, though!

KLETTERER: You hear that, boys? We're getting warmer! Thoroughness!

THE COUNT: Avanti! Let's have the rest, Benny. You're doing your job well.

KLETTERER: Hold on—I give the orders here!

PETRI: But not much longer. Poor Kletterer. He wants so badly to be the chief. But people like him are quickly played out. Well—what else do you have to suggest? Your friends there aren't at all satisfied with you. Listen. They're muttering. You'd better do something—quick—before they bite your head off.

KLETTERER: I'm not going to try to be clever with him. Give me a second to think.

PETRI: Of course. A second—ten seconds! Think carefully. What now? Maybe a game of blind man's buff or pin the tail on the donkey? Maybe a little bit of fortune-telling with cards, eh? [*To the* COUNT.] Or maybe we should tear off his shirt and tickle him a little—our modest little Count!

THE COUNT [*Jumps up.*]: Green!

GREEN: What's this? What's this? So sensitive?

STOCK: How terrified he is when someone mentions his shirt? Do you suppose he is like a young god underneath—hairless and smooth?

BENNY: Or maybe he has a pair of pimples hidden somewhere?

STOCK: I wonder if he has hair on his chest—or elsewhere?

BENNY [*Giggles.*]: I wonder if he has *anything!*

STOCK: You mean . . . ? Oh, that would be *horrible!*

BENNY: Take a peek.

STOCK: Do you mean to imply that the mighty Count can't—do anything?

BENNY: What with?

STOCK: You mean he makes pee-pee through some sort of little pipe?

THE COUNT: Petri!

STOCK: Ah—you hear?—he calls for help! He's getting nervous! What would happen if he no longer had a shirt? Without a shirt, does he stop being the Count?

KLETTERER: Silence! All of you! What's the matter with you, Green—do you think I can't keep up with you?

GREEN: Let's make a deal. You talk with your boys—tell them to go on home like good fellows. Naturally, *you* will stay here. After all, what could we do without you and your little trumpet?

KLETTERER: And then . . . ?

GREEN: No sooner will your gang have disappeared then Vasco will stop nibbling so hungrily at his nails and settle down to talk a little business with us. And with the Count. You understand, Vasco, what it is that you're going to have to do?

VASCO: Wait a minute! Why now? Why did I have to go along there with Stock and Benny? What does good old Petri think I am? A little cook who hops when he says "Jump!"—is that it?

GREEN: Ah—you've insulted him, Petri! You'd better say something.

PETRI: Go ahead. Do whatever you want to!

THE COUNT [*Excitedly.*]: Don't let them do this, Petri! What will Schuster say when he hears about it?

PETRI: As you see, at the moment I am powerless.

VASCO: Aha—now we have it! He can't do anything without his music! Take your people away, Kletterer!

KLETTERER [*Shoves his grumbling followers out the door and locks it.*]: Go on—clear out! I'll take care of this. Don't worry. I won't give in. You wait out there.

VASCO: How much fresher the air is, now that they're gone! Now things will move fast!

THE COUNT: What do you have in mind?

VASCO: Just to talk a little about this and that.

THE COUNT: You won't be able to prove anything. Rumors—gossip—nonsense—that's all! Who cares what people say?

VASCO: But I don't say *what* they say. I just say that they *talk* about things. Maybe it doesn't mean much, what they say, but it means *something!* You know what they say? [*Whispers.*] That the Count doesn't like women!

GREEN: I don't believe it!

VASCO: That's what they say. And all the wicked gossips whisper that he prefers handsome young boys. I've even heard that he—er—made approaches to poor little Benny here.

BENNY: That's right! I can swear to that!

GREEN: You beat it! Nothing but a stupid rumor!

VASCO: Green is right! We, who know the Count so well, naturally we say: That could never be. Of course, he's a little shy. When Martha comes into the room, he gets red in the face and says: "Young lady . . . dear lady . . ." Now I ask you, what is that? Is that love? Green—Kletterer—what do you think? And why not? Hasn't he grounds enough? Hasn't she come to me and wept and said: "Oh, the poor Count . . . ?"

MARTHA: Stephen—please!

VASCO: What shall I do? Betray everything that you have said to me about him? Isn't it *my* shame if I betray it all? Haven't I always said to myself: "Why do I keep running after her when all she thinks about is the Count?" And when she calls me "Stephen," why does it always sound like "Herbert"? His name. [*To* MARTHA.] No, no—not a word—and don't speak my name again!

PETRI: Go on, Vasco, go on.

VASCO: Right away. You are silent, Count. But you are not silent because I am wrong, but because I am right and I have touched you on a sore spot! So—let people talk, I said. Let them say that the Count has no heart. But now I know that you have and that I have touched it! Right? Have I?

THE COUNT: Yes, Vasco, you have. You are a great discoverer, after all.

VASCO [*Exhausted.*]: Good. I've done all I can. You take over, Green.

MARTHA: Why are you talking like this? Stephen, what have I done to you to deserve this?

VASCO: All that was between us is over now. Now you must go to him and call him by name. Go! Go on!

GREEN: I believe that Martha is in full accord with us now. I have already had a word or two with her. You remember what I said, Martha?

MARTHA: No.

GREEN: What—you've forgotten already? Didn't I say: "That's no match—a cook and a nurse!" Didn't I?

MARTHA: Something like that. [*To the* COUNT.] But . . . you . . . ?

THE COUNT: I have nothing more to say, my child. Vasco has said it all.

GREEN: Enough! The deal is as good as served up. Read this over at your convenience and here, on this line, sign your aristocratic name, my friend. Do you want a chair?

THE COUNT: No. You have almost won.

GREEN: Almost? We *have* won!

PETRI: But *you* have won, too! Such an attractive girl. Healthy, clever, patient, never disobedient. I can see your future now— a lovely little home, some children . . .

THE COUNT: If that's what Martha wants. We could go off on a little holiday in the country at first. I have a manor house with a garden—you could live there like a visitor if you wanted to. No, no, let me finish. And then—after a while—if you decided you wanted to live there with me, not as a visitor, I would be—very happy. Give us this time.

GREEN: But why should she? She's already said "Yes." It couldn't be sweeter even in church.

STOCK: Just what I was thinking. Why do they bother with a wedding? Don't they already have blessings enough?

BENNY: He wants to pull the wool over your eyes.

GREEN: Vasco, what do you think?

VASCO: Let them go. Give them their holiday. Then we'll follow.

GREEN: Kletterer? Petri?

PETRI: Make him write it down. Then we'll have him.

KLETTERER: Only if I sign it, too!

GREEN: You can blow on it with your horn! [*The cooks laugh and put a paper on the table before the* COUNT. MARTHA *comes forward.*]

MARTHA: Why don't you ask my opinion? I was to have been on night duty tonight, but you came and dragged me away, and now . . .

THE COUNT: Would you rather stay with him?

MARTHA: With Stephen? [*She gets down and starts collecting the torn pieces of paper.*]

THE COUNT: No, child, never mind the papers. They need it more than you do. [*To the table.*] My name? [*He signs.*] You have a rapid kind of handwriting, Vasco—so rapid, you may never be able to catch up with it! [*Goes back to* MARTHA. *Before* PETRI *can pick up the paper,* KLETTERER *seizes it and studies it.*]

KLETTERER: I'll just take the precaution of holding on to this document—as well as your delightful trumpet! So—there it is. I always thought he wasn't really a Count. See? His name is Schymanski. Herbert Schymanski. [*Sits down and polishes the trumpet.*]

THE COUNT: It's almost morning. Shall we go and have some breakfast, Martha? [*He puts her coat around her shoulders.* GREEN *hands him his shawl.*]

MARTHA: Stephen, I'm going now! [*She and the* COUNT *exit.*]

STOCK: A charming pair. [*To* VASCO.] Why are you looking like that?

VASCO: It's getting light.

STOCK: But you are gazing after her as though you are saying goodbye forever. Why?

VASCO: So that she will think of me. So that I will be like beef between her teeth.

[MRS. COLDWATER *comes in with bucket and mop.*]

MRS. COLDWATER: Well, how was the birthday party? Everyone looks happy, I must say! [*She sweeps away the recipes around the door, then notices the broken lock.*] All right, now! Who did this, eh?

GREEN: Never mind, Mrs. Coldwater. Here—have a new lock put in—but don't talk about this. Good? There's been enough talk here for one night. Enough hot air to dry your clothes.

BENNY: Why did you just let them go? [*They all cross to the door.*]

STOCK: I don't get it, either.

VASCO: So that he can have his time with her—and sit at the table with her and be in bed beside her—now that she is a woman and not a nurse.

COLDWATER [*Taking down the laundry and throwing it over the cooks.*]: What's the matter with him? Always biting his fingernails and planning for the future!

CURTAIN

Act Five

The garden: A wall of medium height encircles a garden and a small country house. To the left, the garden gate; to the right, the front of the house—gable, window, door. In the garden, some flower beds, a small fountain. A flagstone terrace immediately in front of the house. A table and two chairs on the terrace. Two-thirds of the wall is whitewashed; the rest remains dirty-gray. A bucket and paintbrush stand on a low stool.

The count *and* martha *enter through the garden gate. Both are dressed in summer clothing. They are barefoot, carrying their shoes in their hands.*

The Count [*Seizes the paintbrush.*]: And now the last stroke! It will be like a holiday—innocent and a little boring.

Martha [*On the terrace.*]: Please, Herbert—let's eat first! Ooh, this feels good—standing here on these cool stones!

The Count [*Leaving the paintbrush and coming up on the terrace.*]: Ah, yes—it's cooling to the feet, clear up to the top of your head!

Martha: Look at your dirty feet!

The Count: And yours. Let me see, child. [*He puts his shoes and hers on the table. They sit. He takes her feet in his hands.*]

Martha: Don't look at them, Herbert. They're too big.

The Count: They're so dusty. And reddened and scratched underneath the dust.

Martha: Please!

The Count: No, let me. I don't know whether your feet are beautiful, but they are good. You ought to go barefoot all the time.

Martha [*Laughs.*]: Like your Biblical Ruth, gleaning in the fields. As though I had nothing else in the world to do but to go hopping through the stubble. Well, at any rate, my feet are now going to get washed. Yours should, too.

The Count [*Stops her.*]: Stay—just for a moment! Foot-washing and wall-painting—those things can wait!

MARTHA: And you've put our shoes on the table! Now, how do you think that looks?

THE COUNT: I think they look very peaceful—and a little tired. [*He mixes up the shoes.*] You see? No matter how you arrange them, they remain our shoes. Even if I look at their soles—like this—and compare how we have worn down our heels. Look— you've stepped on a beetle. As though you could ever harm a beetle!

MARTHA: Take them off the table, Herbert.

THE COUNT: No! Leave them, I say! They have earned it. Let others wander for miles and return home with a whole bouquet of wild flowers and put them in a vase on the table. Others come home as though from plundering the fields and forest. We come back bearing only our good old faithful shoes—with maybe a new knot in the shoelaces!

MARTHA: How you go on!

THE COUNT: What's that? Do you mean to say that our somewhat shriveled leather flowers can't compare with the tulips or the poppies? Well—in that case—there is only one thing to do; transform them into vases. [*He picks a few flowers and sticks them in the shoes.*] So!

MARTHA: All right. Let them stay there—for now. But then . . .

THE COUNT: Then you will come with plates and silverware and a checkered tablecloth, and suddenly they will turn back to shoes again—with us in them, as though we had been born there. But right now you are still the barefoot girl running through the stubble—whose feet are so big she's always a step ahead of me even though we run side by side! [*She picks up a bucket.*]

MARTHA: May I say something now?

THE COUNT: But . . . [*He tries to hold her, but she draws away from him.*]

MARTHA: No "buts." I'm going to the fountain with this bucket [*Does so.*] and I'm going to bring it back to you, half-full.

THE COUNT: And the poor goldfish?

MARTHA: There's enough left for him. Now—no more talking, no more brilliant new ideas or creations of new flowers—wash your feet!

THE COUNT: And what will you do in the meantime?

MARTHA: I'll watch you.

THE COUNT: And then? [*He washes his feet.*]

MARTHA: Then I'll take a towel and rub your feet till they're dry.

THE COUNT: Then, when it's my turn to bring you a bucket full and watch you wash your feet, I'll take *two* towels—and they will barely be large enough for your two little toes.

MARTHA: Talk, talk, talk! Everything about me is too big, to hear you talk.

THE COUNT: You're a giantess! When I pass my hand over your back, I make a long voyage—say, from Rome to Copenhagen.

MARTHA: But before you travel to such distant cities, I suggest that you let me dry your feet—so that you don't catch cold and arrive at your destination as a sick man! [*She bends down and dries his feet.*]

THE COUNT [*Leans back; the heads of the cooks appear, peeping over the wall.*]: It's hot today. I'll wait until after dinner to finish painting the wall. Don't you think that would be better, Martha? [*They both look at the wall, see the cooks, and start in terror.*]

STOCK: Ah—look there! She is washing his feet and drying them. Such sweet humility!

BENNY: And then he does it for her. One little foot washes the other.

STOCK: I call that "true love."

BENNY: I wonder if they are so helpful to each other in other ways? [*They laugh;* KLETTERER, *with the trumpet, leaps up onto the wall, walks to and fro, and then peers through the trumpet as though it were a telescope.*]

KLETTERER: A charming garden—charming. Too many flowers, perhaps. And no vegetables.

BENNY: I don't understand it. They must eat the roses.

STOCK: Here. This is their menu: [*Seats himself on the wall.*] First, pansy soup, with primrose croutons.

BENNY: Then stuffed bluebells, with violet sauce, and filets of forget-me-nots.

STOCK: And for dessert—a piece of carnation cheese!

BENNY: And after dinner [*Squats atop the wall.*] if they have some indigestion, the young vegetarians can drink a little bit of dew from the Mayflowers!

STOCK: And tenderly wash each other's feet until it's time for love-making again and "Ooh—ooh," "ah—ah," "isn't life sweet?"

[STOCK *and* BENNY *embrace each other elaborately.* KLETTERER *blows a loud blast on the trumpet.*]

KLETTERER [*To the* COUNT.]: You, there! It's really very charming here! I've often imagined people living like this.

THE COUNT: You like it?

KLETTERER: Well—not completely. I don't often have much to do with flowers, for example. How does that go, Benny? What is it that the poet says?

BENNY: "Let the flowers speak!"

KLETTERER: Right! And that's why we're here. We want to make our two little flowers speak. [*The other three cooks laugh loudly.*]

THE COUNT: Well, now, don't squat up there on the wall like a flock of white ravens. Come in, boys—it's been a long time. Vasco, Petri, Green! Why don't you say anything?

KLETTERER [*Swinging his trumpet.*]: Here is the music. They have nothing more to say. Now listen, Count. I'm the chief now, and when Mr. Schuster wants something, he comes to me and says: "Kletterer, straighten this out for me. Things were awfully sloppy when Petri was in charge. But I can rely on you, right?" And he can, believe me—he can.

THE COUNT: You're a poor public speaker, Kletterer, but you have a good figure—I'll say that for you.

GREEN: You needn't take him too seriously, Count, you know Schuster. Today, one boss; tomorrow, another. But not everyone knows how to blow the trumpet.

STOCK: Petri has come down in the world a bit.

GREEN: And Kletterer has come up a little—perhaps a little too far.

STOCK: Nevertheless we're all of us still good friends—Vasco, Green—all of us . . .

GREEN: And of course we're not simply going to let good old Petri sink out of sight.

STOCK: It's just that he's come down in the world. So what? Who can predict who will be the top dog tomorrow?

KLETTERER: Certainly not you!

STOCK: Who knows? Who knows? [VASCO *seats himself on the wall.*]

VASCO: How different she looks! No more the nurse. She's done her hair up differently, too. What made me think that she was blonde?

PETRI: Did you hear them billing and cooing? The next thing you know, he'll be hauling out a guitar and singing about his lost happiness.

VASCO: I always used to think that she had no neck—and now suddenly she has one—lovely. And her hands, the way she moves them, as though they could perform miracles, as though each finger had a special sense of touch.

PETRI: How is this going to end? Do something, Kletterer! Show us what you can do.

GREEN: You're too severe, Petri. He's only been in charge of things a short while.

STOCK: He needs to learn the ropes.

GREEN: We ought to help him.

KLETTERER: To hell with your help! Things are going to move fast now! Hop! [*Trumpet blast;* BENNY *and* STOCK *jump down into the garden; the* COUNT *rises.*]

THE COUNT: Look out! You're trampling the flowers! Can't you come in through the gate, you blockheads?

BENNY: Did he say "blockheads"?

STOCK: He thinks we're the Benny and Stock he used to know.

THE COUNT: Now you're stepping on the borders! Petri, get your people out of the garden! [PETRI *indicates* KLETTERER.] All right, then—you, Kletterer!

KLETTERER: But you see the situation. We've been more or less invited here.

BENNY: Three times before we had you on the spot.

STOCK: And each time the bird slipped out of our hands.

THE COUNT: I repeat my request. Call off your dogs.

KLETTERER [*Trumpet blast*.]: Everybody stop! Back! March! March! Now then, what's this? They're not obeying me any more. Something wrong here? [*Peers into the trumpet.*]

BENNY: Let's go! [*Pulls a notebook from his pocket.*] Here—please write clearly, preferably in block capitals! [*Starts to put the notebook on the table.*] Well! What have we here? Shoes on the table! Very jolly! Whose gunboats are these?

MARTHA: Mine, Benny.

BENNY: And this junk?

MARTHA: The flowers? Just a game.

BENNY: It had better not be some kind of trick.

STOCK: Let them play their little games. Do we have time to talk about stupid trifles? Three times we had him cornered, three times he slipped away—and you want to talk about games!

BENNY: I only wanted to make room on the table. [*Pushes the shoes off the table and lays the notebook down.*] We've got to have order!

THE COUNT: This is nonsense, Kletterer! I have no intention of doing business with these louts.

KLETTERER: But why the hell not? What difference does it make, who brings you the paper? [GREEN *and* PETRI *laugh.*]

PETRI: This is just the way I thought it would be.

GREEN: Kletterer had a great idea—to send Benny to speak to the Count. You know—the real proletarian.

KLETTERER: But . . .

PETRI: That was a misfire, I would say! Green, you take over. [*He climbs up onto the wall.* GREEN *disappears behind the wall and comes in through the garden gate.*]

KLETTERER: All right, if you think he can do better. I'd love to be surprised.

BENNY: They're just trying to bluff you, man. We'll get it.

KLETTERER: I said, let Green try! Shut up! Go on—guard the gate! Stock, you too!

STOCK: All right, all right—whatever you say—you're the boss. [*They station themselves at each side of the gate.*]

GREEN: You must excuse the behavior of the—er—louts, my dear Count. As always, we will try to make things short and sweet. You will remember our last meeting, I'm sure; if not, I have the record of it down in writing. Here is your signature. Needless to say, such a signature speaks volumes; it is the signature of an honorable and respected man.

THE COUNT: You want the recipe. I am sorry.

KLETTERER [*Jumps down from the wall.*]: Sorry? What do you mean?

THE COUNT: I have told you over and over again, it's not a recipe —it's an experience, a living knowledge, a way of life. You must know that no cook has ever succeeded in making this soup twice.

KLETTERER: All right—all well and good. But what are you so sorry about?

THE COUNT: I see I must make myself clearer. These last few months with Martha, my wife—isn't it true, child?—may I say it at last?

KLETTERER: Yes, yes—what about these months?

THE COUNT: They have simply rendered this recipe superfluous. I have forgotten it.

KLETTERER: The recipe? The re——? What—what are you trying to say?

THE COUNT: I really would have liked to help you. But, to explain precisely: After the first few days here—indeed, after the first few hours . . . how soon was it, my child?

MARTHA: We came here; you made breakfast for us . . .

THE COUNT: . . . and you asked me if you could have two cubes of sugar for your coffee.

KLETTERER: You have an astonishing memory!

THE COUNT: Everything is very clear in my mind.

KLETTERER: Except for the recipe, is that it?

THE COUNT: I have never even thought about it—until this moment.

MARTHA: I have thought about it. I have lived in fear of this day.

KLETTERER: You have very good reason, my girl, you and your comic opera Count! I will, I will . . . [*He seizes the* COUNT.]

PETRI: What will you do, Kletterer? [*He climbs down from the wall ceremoniously.*] What overly clever idea do you have now in your childlike little mind? You world-famous discoverer of baked potatoes, you barley-soup mixer, you genius of the cooking pot!

KLETTERER: I'll—I'll show him—and you, too! I'll force him to talk!

PETRI: No, no, my dear fellow—that will never do. In all friendship, I must say you're somewhat lacking in gentility.

GREEN: Let him go! No one has said that you weren't chief any longer.

PETRI: I even let him have the trumpet. You see the result. Tarnished, battered, no proper care. What do you say, Count? Is that any way to treat a costly instrument?

THE COUNT: You should have hidden it somewhere.

PETRI [*Laughing.*]: I should have hidden it! Did you all hear that? Such advice—from him—the secretive, the forgetful! [*Seriously.*] Now listen to me. We've known each other for quite a while, you and I. You know that so far it has been I who have ordered that our transactions be carried out quietly and politely. [*Shouts.*] But I can behave quite differently—I warn you.

THE COUNT: I have no doubt of it.

PETRI: Toward both of you! You needn't think that I am going to be softened by this mild air, this nearly white wall, the flowers, this little fountain—Benny, what's the little fish's name?

BENNY: I'll ask him. [*Fishes in the fountain with his hand and hands* PETRI *the goldfish.*]

PETRI [*To the* COUNT.]: Here! Take a look! A moment ago, he was happy and safe—now he's gasping at the air! That doesn't please him at all—that you still don't want to tell us your story. And what I am about to do will please him even less. I am going to stick him in my pocket—very carefully—and then pat it a little, so, then maybe *he'll* tell me the recipe, eh?

THE COUNT: What has this little fish done to earn your anger? Punish me if you must, Petri. You may even enjoy it. But put this little life back into the water. You may be famous for your skill with trout and pike and tench, but I really don't think you're quite ready to tackle a goldfish.

PETRI: My dear fellow, shut up! You're merely provoking my true nature; you see, I'm slowly coming to understand your methods. Now. Take your former nurse by the arm, go into the house there and talk it over. Then we will come in and ask you one more time, very briefly—you understand! And then you will cry "No!" Both of you will cry: "Oh, Petri! Petri! Oh, this Petri!"

THE COUNT: And you, Vasco? What do you say? You sit there on the wall.

VASCO: I'm looking at her, but she doesn't look at me and call me "Stephen" any more. Why?

MARTHA: Let's go. It's getting chilly in the garden.

THE COUNT: Right away, my child. What a shame! I would have liked to have finished the wall. Maybe you can do it for me, Vasco. It doesn't look right—unfinished, like that. [*The* COUNT *and* MARTHA *go into the house.*]

VASCO: He wants me to paint the wall? Why not? He has Martha, and I paint his wall for him.

KLETTERER: And the recipe?

PETRI: The whole thing. I'll pull it out of him piece by piece.

GREEN: Are you so sure? He would give it to us if he knew it. He has no reason now to go on keeping it a secret. He has what he wants.

STOCK: The Count would never lie. But we can't just give in and say that there's nothing to be done. We've got to act as though he still knew it and finish what we've started!

PETRI: You're talking utter nonsense! He doesn't want to—he keeps wanting to put it off. Maybe . . .

VASCO: Maybe nothing! The Count tells the truth. You want to go up there and get what he hasn't got? You want to go up those steps into the house, full of authority, and say: "Where is the soup? How do you make it gray? How many ashes and what kind of ashes make it gray?"—and then to start all over again— "How many and what kind of ashes, and why?" Is that what you want to do? Hand me a shoe, Benny! Or do you want to be like a Pandora who doesn't know what's in the box she's opening? You want to stand there like Rasputin and look threatening, pretending to be sinister? Give me the shoe—the big one!

PETRI: Go on, give it to him! All right, you know him, Vasco. Let's hear what you have to say.

VASCO: What shoes she has! And look how she's worn down the heels.

PETRI: Suppose he *does* know something?

VASCO: Well, then—you're the clever one. You know how to do things to make someone tell what he knows. But what if he *doesn't* know it any more—if love has acted like an eraser and obliterated it all from his brain and from his heart so that he no longer remembers how many ashes and what kind of ashes. What then? Personally, I think I'll go back to Schuster and sell shoelaces. [*He loosens a knot in the laces with his teeth.*]

KLETTERER: Maybe he's reconsidering.

GREEN: Right. That takes time. Maybe . . .

PETRI: He'll just go on saying he doesn't know forever.

VASCO: What do you mean "forever"? Is that eternity—"forever"? Is that something you can buy in the church, with song and sweet incense? Oh, how clever we are! [*He gets up on the wall.*] When did he know it, do you suppose? When did he know it and where did he forget it? What a hard knot this is! When did he know—eh? [GREEN *and* STOCK *laugh.*]

STOCK: Good old Vasco—what a character!

GREEN: Squatting there on the wall, eating his heart out for Martha.

STOCK: Untying knots in a shoelace with chewed-up fingernails and teeth—and meditating while he works.

KLETTERER: You mean—you mean, he wants to have the nurse back again?

GREEN: Our recent boss is a little slow-witted. Explain it to him, Stock.

STOCK: All right, all right. But when a brain is that innocent, it's sort of like a virgin—and I would hate to disturb *that*. What's to explain? Vasco will get Martha back, and the Count will suddenly remember what love had made him forget. [STOCK *and* BENNY *join hands and dance.*]

STOCK AND BENNY:

> Dollar, dollar, you must wander
> Like a silly goosey-gander,
> Silly as a foolish scholar,
> From one odd place to another.

[VASCO *stirs restlessly.*]

PETRI: Quiet! What's the matter, Vasco?

VASCO: But suppose she doesn't want to leave him?

PETRI: Did she want to go with him originally?

GREEN: Maybe he'll be very happy to be alone again. Basically, he doesn't care much for women.

BENNY: Then he can finish painting his wall in peace.

VASCO: That's right. He said he wanted to finish the wall.

[*Two pistol shots offstage in rapid succession. The window shutters over the door burst open.* VASCO *lets* MARTHA's *shoe fall.*]

STOCK: What's he shooting for?

GREEN: Now Vasco will *have* to finish the wall.

[VASCO *crosses and stares in the open window.*]

STOCK: What is it? What are you doing? Has he shot you, too?

PETRI: Vasco!

VASCO [*Turns slowly to them.*]: The recipe!

KLETTERER: What about it?

STOCK: He knows it! I can see it!

VASCO: No, no.

BENNY: I think you're right, Stock.

[KLETTERER, STOCK, *and* BENNY *close in on him.* VASCO *leaps up on the wall.*]

VASCO: I won't tell you anything! Nothing! [*He jumps down behind the wall; they climb the wall and go after him.*]

KLETTERER AND STOCK AND BENNY [*Off.*]: Vasco, Vasco! Here—he ran off this way! By the slope! He's trying to get to the railroad embankment!

VASCO [*Off.*]: No, no, no!

[PETRI *and* GREEN *stand on stage, listening.*]

PETRI [*Picks up the trumpet and tries to blow it.*]: No more sound. Well, well. There they go. Do you understand why?

GREEN: They think with their legs.

PETRI: And the recipe?

GREEN: An excuse for running. No one asks about it any more. It's not even a question of the soup.

PETRI: Why aren't we running?

GREEN: We'll just wait a little while. When they're worn out— and when their shoes are worn out—then we will make a few efforts.

PETRI: Good old Vasco! Now he will never have time to go to Schuster. Restless and barefoot, he must wander through the world.

GREEN: He won't even have a few seconds' rest to stop and bite his fingernails.

PETRI [*He takes the goldfish out of his pocket.*]: I wonder if he will be as silent and sparing of his words as this beautiful and luxurious and quite useless—fish? [*He throws it into the basin.*]

GREEN: Now, the occupant of this fountain has several things in common with all the swimming beasts of the great world. Not in vain do men praise the delicacy of fish dishes!

PETRI [*At the edge of the fountain.*]: He has turned up his belly. He has no further desires.

GREEN: And you and I—anyone who wields a spoon and acts as a cook—no one can ever again force him to be a goldfish and go swimming away before our eyes. [PETRI *polishes the trumpet.*] Nothing more can happen here. [*He goes out.*]

PETRI: There he goes. And somehow I seem to feel in my legs the stirring of a desire to move on toward some unknown goal.

[*He quickens his steps and hurries on out.*]

The End

VASCO

A Drama in a Prologue, Four Scenes, and an Epilogue

Georges Schehadé

adaptation by Lucia Victor

CHARACTERS

SEPTEMBRE, a lieutenant in the cavalry
CESAR, cart owner and merchant
MARGUERITE, his daughter
TWO PEASANTS
MOTHER HILBOOM
VASCO, hairdresser
EMERITA, his sister
MAYOR CORFAN
FIVE WIDOWS
MIRADOR, General Maravigna
HIS SERGEANT-OF-THE-GUARD
MAJOR BROUNST ⎫
LIEUTENANT HANS ⎬ Three soldiers
LIEUTENANT LATOUR ⎭
ENEMY SOLDIER
SERGEANT PARAZ ⎫
SERGEANT ALEXANDER ⎬ Three trees
SERGEANT CAQUOT ⎭
LIEUTENANT BARBERIS
TWO SOLDIERS
DRUM MAJOR KRANZ
GREGORY, a drummer

*The action takes place during the course
of a war . . . somewhere around 1850.*

Prologue

*A clearing in a forest. At the rear is a cart, covered with a
dilapidated tarpaulin, its two empty arms pointing up. Inside
the cart, a lantern burns. In the trees are ranks of motionless
crows, their eyes shining. The wind is moaning. There is the
sound of someone crashing through underbrush, and* LIEU-
TENANT SEPTEMBRE *appears over the rise. He is young, strong
and handsome, grave. He wears a uniform of black, gold but-
tons and braid, and a hat in the shape of a tricorne. He stops
to catch his breath after his battle with the underbrush.*

SEPTEMBRE [*Staring at the crowd.*]: Those black birds . . . wherever
I go! [*A pause, then he shouts.*] Ravens, come out of those
trees! [*They do not move.*] All asleep . . . in this wind of iron.
[*The wind moans, and through the trees comes the distant hoot-
ing of an owl. He listens.*] Another goddess of the night . . . a
princess of the blood! [*He laughs, then bitterly.*] If only I could
be frightened, instead of filled with sadness and disgust. [*He
looks again at the crows, then draws a pistol from his belt.*] Fly
away, ravens! [*He fires; one bird falls, the others do not move.*]
CESAR [*From inside the cart.*]: What's that . . . what's that . . .
what's that . . . what's that . . . [*He pokes his head out.*]
SEPTEMBRE [*Whirling.*]: Who are you?
CESAR: Cesar! And that name better inspire some respect in you,
highway cutpurse that you are! . . . or I'll stretch you flat with
a swipe of my shovel . . . [*He holds the lantern out, and sees
the pistol.*] . . . or, since I'm an agreeable man, I will bestow
upon you a gift to be quits, O Evil One! [*Calling into the cart.*]
Marguerite, hand me my spectacles! [*To* SEPTEMBRE.] What do
you want?

Septembre: I want . . . [*Then, as* cesar *ignores him to reach in for his spectacles, he continues in wry whimsy to himself.*] . . . what you cannot give, old Troll . . . I want . . . not to do what I must do!

[cesar *has his spectacles and has perched them on his nose.*]

Cesar [*Examining* septembre.]: A cavalryman! Then where is your horse?

Septembre [*Pointing to the empty shafts of the cart.*]: And where is yours?

Cesar: In his old age he gave us one last gift before departing. We ate him. [*A snatch of song is heard from inside the cart.*] Silence, strumpet! [*To* septembre.] Declare yourself, soldier! Are you lost? We offer shelter. Hungry? I will lavish on you filling thoughts. A single man? I will give you my daughter. A deserter from the army? We will lead you back to duty by the ear . . .

Septembre [*Cutting in.*]: I am looking for the house of Vasco.

Cesar: Ohoooo! So it's information you're after. That calls for a great deal of caution. [*With enormous dignity.*] I will take off my nightshirt. [*He disappears within the cart, as a pretty young girl appears in the opening of the canvas.*]

Marguerite [*Seductively.*]: Hello . . .

Septembre: Do you know the house of Vasco?

Marguerite [*Tossing her head.*]: My father will tell you. I know other things. [septembre *turns away.*] You seem indifferent to pleasure. Even this strong wind blowing on us stirs nothing in you. It burns my whole body. [septembre *moves away.*] Look at me. [*He turns. She looks at him a long time. Then, almost shyly.*] What is your name, soldier?

Septembre: Septembre.

Marguerite [*With a shiver.*]: How sad it sounds.

Cesar [*Bustling down from the cart.*]: You're in luck . . . for, fundamentally, I know everything. I am a philosopher! Yes, it is a philosopher who stands before you. A rare find on a deserted path. Did you ever think to find a philosopher in the middle of a forest, a forest . . . ? [*He puts a finger on his mouth, mysteriously.*] . . . inhabited by monks! [*Lowering his voice still more, he indicates the crows in the trees.*] All those crows are monks. [*Pointing at the crow killed by* septembre.] You struck down a monk! In this countryside . . . [SEPTEMBRE *opens his mouth to speak;* CESAR *goes on quickly.*] I beg your pardon? Ah, you didn't say anything. I didn't think so. A well bred man doesn't interrupt when you talk to him. [*Going back to his discourse, as* SEPTEMBRE *smiles in amusement.*] In this countryside, the transmigration of souls is the infallible rule. Yesterday while I was going through the village I strangled a rooster who insulted me. I recognized him instantly: it was the soul of a bootmaker I used to owe a little money to. My daughter can bear witness to this. [*To her.*] Marguerite, what was it that rooster said to us . . . the one we ate last night? [MARGUERITE *bursts into laughter.*] I'll beat that girl . . . [*He takes off his shoe.*] I'll dust her off with this. It isn't enough that she mocks me, her father . . . but with a guest, a stranger, as an observer!

SEPTEMBRE: Listen to me, philosopher . . .

CESAR [*Like one who has lost his train of thought.*]: Yes. . . yes . . . where was I?

SEPTEMBRE [*Wryly.*]: Nowhere.

CESAR: Then where are you?

SEPTEMBRE: *With* you.

MARGUERITE [*Laughing.*]: Give it up. You'll never get finished with my father.

SEPTEMBRE: On the contrary, I have finished. Good night. [*He starts off.*]

CESAR [*Disappointed.*]: And the information I specially got dressed to give . . . don't you want it any more?

MARGUERITE [*Calling after him.*]: Lieutenant Septembre! [*He stops and turns. She speaks to her father.*] Go on, help him if you can. Talk like an ordinary man.

CESAR: But I am not an ordinary man. And we must begin at the beginning. The question is complex . . . [*He suddenly notices the shoe in his hand.*] Whose shoe is this I'm carrying? [MARGUERITE *laughs;* SEPTEMBRE *can't help laughing, too.* CESAR *murmurs like a man who is afraid he is losing his faculties.*] Give me a little water, Marguerite.

SEPTEMBRE [*Holding out a flask.*]: Here.

CESAR [*After drinking.*]: That's army water. I can smell it. [*To his daughter.*] Haven't we something to give the lieutenant in return?

MARGUERITE: Nothing, father.

CESAR: What do you mean, nothing? Not even a bee? a dried fruit?

SEPTEMBRE: You could give me what I asked for . . .

CESAR [*Intent upon his own problems; uneasily.*]: Then what are we going to eat tomorrow, Marguerite? [*His glance falls on the dead crow.*] God will provide . . . and of course, your father. [*To* SEPTEMBRE.] Now that we're at ease on the happy outcome of our fast, I put myself wholeheartedly at your service.

SEPTEMBRE: I thank you.

CESAR [*As a crow on a branch croaks.*]: They're at it again. Listen!

SEPTEMBRE [*Giving up, he starts to go.*]: Good night.

CESAR [*Quickly, calling after him.*]: And do you know what they're saying? The way to the house of Vasco! You see what helpful crows?

SEPTEMBRE [*Stopping; skeptically.*]: Not yet . . . philosopher. But I am open to evidence.

CESAR [*As the crows croak again.*]: Wait! This part is for me.

SEPTEMBRE: Then keep it. Where is the house of Vasco?

CESAR: Ssh! They're talking about my daughter . . . and in what terms! [*Shaking his fist at the crows.*] Devils of the dustbin! Changeling soldiers that lay black eggs! [*To the lieutenant, as the crows croak again.*] They claim they were only joking, but I shall stand my ground. Lend me your pistol . . .

SEPTEMBRE [*Raising the pistol by the barrel, in a gesture of half whimsical despair, half real irritation.*]: I think perhaps I will . . . butt end foremost.

CESAR [*Retreating.*]: Marguerite! Quick, hand me the shovel!

MARGUERITE [*Running down from the cart to stand between* CESAR *and the lieutenant.*]: Hit my father, would you! What did you come here for, anyway?

CESAR: That's right.

MARGUERITE: We put ourselves out to entertain you . . .

CESAR: To instruct him, my dear.

MARGUERITE: . . . and you threaten my father. For a little joke about his crows!

CESAR: Which are useful, too.

SEPTEMBRE: Forgive me, I was only going to crack hazelnuts.

MARGUERITE: I'll tell you where your house of Vasco is, without even knowing the place! It's probably the village beyond the river . . . if you're so desperate to go. [*They are face to face.*]

SEPTEMBRE [*After a pause.*]: I *must* go, Marguerite. [*Another croak from the crows.*]

CESAR: They say it's the second village beyond the river. Where the Portuguese live.

SEPTEMBRE [*His gaze still on* MARGUERITE.]: That sounds logical.

CESAR: I wouldn't know anything about it, myself.

SEPTEMBRE [*Moving to her.*]: Forgive me . . . [*He holds out the pistol.*] . . . I was only going to crack hazelnuts.

[*They are close together. For a moment it looks as though they might almost meet in a kiss.*]

MARGUERITE [*Suddenly.*]: I have changed my mind. I only want to be with you, and talk to you under the trees, like two friends of a hundred years who have nothing left but the soul.

SEPTEMBRE [*Shaking his head.*]: The soul is a dream, and the world is real, Marguerite . . . and very strong.

[*She looks at him for a moment, then turns and runs to the cart, and goes in.*]

CESAR: Complete silence now. [SEPTEMBRE *looks at him. He points to the crows.*] They are waiting for the rise of the moon to resume our discussion. You'll see what will happen then. And if it doesn't stand your hair on end like a little gazelle's tail, a corkscrew . . .

SEPTEMBRE: This gazelle, Cesar, cannot wait for the moon. [*He starts to go.*]

CESAR [*Trotting after him.*]: But where is your horse, lieutenant?

SEPTEMBRE: I left him. He had lost a shoe.

CESAR: That leaves him three. It's not so bad . . . how many have you?

SEPTEMBRE: Two—which I must put to use. Goodbye, Cesar.

CESAR: It would take a bloodhound to find the way in this dark . . . and the wind . . . [*No answer.*] Don't go that way. The path is full of jagged rocks and brambles!

SEPTEMBRE: Then it is surely the path that I must take. [*He disappears from view.*]

CESAR [*Calling to her in the cart.*]: Marguerite, get your needle and thread ready. That path is pitiless . . . it has already devoured several of my breeches. [*He looks at the trees a moment.*] When is that moon coming up? This wind must be holding it back on the other side of the earth. [*He stretches.*] I must walk my dogs a bit. I've neglected their health too much. The other day I noticed a deep-seated anemia lying behind their agate eyes. [*He paces, a prey to his reflections, then calls.*] Marguerite! Did you let the dogs out? Marguerite! Daughter!

MARGUERITE [*In a strange voice.*]: I am dreaming . . . let me be.

CESAR: With what dream, Marguerite? That's important. A dream is a window. Who knows how a lie can slip into a soul . . . and grow? Dream aloud so that I may tell. [*She does not answer.*] I tell you, dream out loud! Or I'll wake you up!

MARGUERITE [*In the voice of a sleeper.*]: I am with someone . . .

CESAR: Already? You certainly make time, my girl! [*Worried.*] You aren't with a crow, are you?

MARGUERITE [*Slowly.*]: I am in church, father.

CESAR [*Reassured.*]: That's good. [*On second thought, astonished.*] But what are you doing there?

MARGUERITE: I am dreaming . . . leave me alone. I walk on flag-stones . . . [*As she speaks, light glows softly behind the transparency of the canvas, and we see her, dreaming . . .*] . . . in a church adorned with shepherd children, each with two flutes at his lips . . .

CESAR: This could lead to trouble. [*To* MARGUERITE.] Hurry . . . get out of that holy place!

MARGUERITE: . . . and I am so richly dressed, father . . . so poor and so beautiful . . . [CESAR *begins to be absorbed in the dream.*] . . . that they throw me flowers . . . which I do not see . . .

CESAR [*With respectful curiosity.*]: Me neither.

[SEPTEMBRE's *voice is heard calling softly from offstage:* "Cesar!"]

MARGUERITE: I move on, miraculous and forsaken . . . guarding my steps . . . as if I were a hazelnut . . . or thistledown . . .

VOICE OF SEPTEMBRE: Cesar! [*He enters.* CESAR *moves toward him, one arm stretched out for silence, the other pointing toward the dreaming* MARGUERITE. SEPTEMBRE *stops, and stares fascinated toward the cart.*]

MARGUERITE: Here, shadows are a second light, which repeats everything I see. Thus, the shadow of a rose, is a rose more delicate . . .

[*An airy little strain of music is heard.*]

CESAR [*Kneeling; softly.*]: The wind has stopped.

MARGUERITE: . . . and I wonder why I am so happy? I am not the most beautiful . . . and my loved one is not the greatest. [SEPTEMBRE *turns slowly away from the cart.*] Now, the day withdraws, and leaves me with its hands and its violet steps in a garden. And I meet, near a fountain . . . a young hairdresser. The water makes no sound . . .

CESAR [*On his knees.*]: My angel, Marguerite!

MARGUERITE: He touches my hair, gently mourning . . . and opening his scissors, makes of them two flames! my heart, and his . . . united forever!

[*There is a bitter smile on* SEPTEMBRE's *lips. He stands absolutely still.*]

CESAR: Amen.

MARGUERITE: And so I have become, Father, Madonna . . . and the betrothed of a young hairdresser. And I should be dead of hunger in this place of light, were it not for a manger filled with cornflowers and with bread.

CESAR [*His face aglow, to* SEPTEMBRE.]: This dream is the most beautiful dream of our lives. My white hairs this evening are a garland of love for my child. [*Suddenly* MARGUERITE *starts to snore; he listens in surprise, hardly able to believe his ears.*] She is snoring? [*He stands up.*] You were snoring, Marguerite? After the things you said? You weren't seeing visions, then . . . you were sleeping! [*Furiously.*] She has tricked me! [*He picks up a stick.*]

SEPTEMBRE: No. Cesar! [*Harshly; as much in self-accusation as to Cesar.*] It is vile to break the dreams of innocence.

CESAR: But she snored! Hussy! Hussy! Hussy! [*Despairingly.*] Marguerite, my angel.

SEPTEMBRE: She has run away from us . . . where we would try in vain to follow.

[*Crows croak.*]

CESAR [*Brandishing his stick.*]: Go somewhere else and get your-selves whitewashed . . . gargoyles! [*A short silence.*] You came back.

SEPTEMBRE [*Bitterly.*]: I told myself I'd wait for the moon to rise.

Cesar: You see? It's one thing to get in here. To get out is quite another.

Septembre: True.

Cesar: Turn around, let me see. What about the breeches?

Septembre: It's all right.

Cesar: It seems that I was angry, since I'm holding a stick in my hand. But at whom? I need a massage with fresh grass. [*Rubbing his forehead.*] With your permission, I'll extinguish the lantern. What's the use of illumination for a lieutenant from the wars, who is dressed in black.

Septembre: Extinguish it, Cesar.

Cesar: And besides, I am too poor to assume this expense personally.

Septembre [*Pulling some money out of his pocket.*]: Here is compensation . . . and enough to let you drink my health some evening. And, Cesar—don't touch the crow. Let him rot.

Cesar: I am touched. Keep your money. I don't want to rob you, I'd rather . . . like you. Buy something from me. I may be a philosopher, lieutenant, but I am also a merchant.

Septembre: Gladly. And I'll double the sum.

Cesar: Then buy from me . . . a dog.

Septembre [*Laughing.*]: Most unusual merchandise . . . in a forest.

Cesar: Oh, they're not ordinary dogs. My animals don't fidget around or dirty things. I sell dogs, it's true, but I sell . . . the ideal dog. A philosopher knows how to do things right.

Septembre: I ask nothing better than to see . . . while waiting for the moon.

Cesar: Follow me with the lantern. [*They disappear behind the cart; then reappear,* cesar *carrying a large case, and the lieutenant still with the lantern.*] It's a unique collection. [*He opens the case, and pulls out first an enormous dog stuffed with straw, with bared fangs frightful to look at; he places the dog on the ground.*] This is Jaguar. I'd advise you not to get too near, nor to risk the lightest pat . . .

Septembre: I'd be afraid to meet him in the dark.

Cesar: Actually, he's a watchdog.

Septembre: And very well stuffed.

Cesar: Don't fool yourself . . . he bites! I'll stir him up and prove it!

Septembre: Never mind, never mind . . . I believe you.

Cesar: Thank you, but I insist that he howl . . . or you may think I'm joking.

Septembre: But *I* do *not* insist. [*Abruptly and dryly.*] Leave the soul of this poor dog in peace!

Cesar [*Moved.*]: You hear, Jaguar? This is the first time that anyone has really respected you, my poor dog. [*To* septembre.] For someone of your profession . . . how shall I say it? . . . you are a good man.

Septembre: Let's take a look at the others.

Cesar [*Taking another from the case.*]: Ulysses! He should have been an actor. He fell in love with a lark, and sighed for her all day long . . . look at him . . . the way he gazes at the sky. [*A pause.*] He died of grief. I stuffed him with feathers.

Septembre: He deserved it, indeed.

Cesar [*He continues to take dogs out of the case.*]: This one is historic! I ask you to examine him closely. He went to prison with his master, an Englishman. Wears a hat in winter, and knows how to count. [*Lowering his voice.*] Ask him the name of his master, the banker. [*A pause.*] What was your master's name, Charlie?

Marguerite [*From the cart, changing her voice.*]: Wood. [cesar *jumps with fright; the lieutenant starts, slightly.*]

Cesar [*With a glance toward the cart, and as easy as can be, gesturing to the dog.*]: You see?

Septembre [*Laughing.*]: A very remarkable animal.

Cesar [*Taking out three little dogs, one by one, and standing them on the ground.*] Anna, Rosa, Pepy. [*With certain condescension.*] Three little ladies of easy virtue . . . play the piano occasionally. Of no importance in my business.

Septembre: And so . . . [*With a laugh.*] . . . which one would you advise me to acquire?

Cesar: Wait! You haven't seen this marvel yet! [*He takes from his case a little dog, seated on his haunches, head atilt.*] Fidele! My deeply lamented friend. Four-footed Christian, if ever there was one, without the grace of baptism but through the compassion of God. My pearl! My favorite! [*He bends over and takes Fidele to his heart, overcome with emotion.*] He is still warm with his devotion to me. A true dog, this one.

SEPTEMBRE [*Softly to himself.*]: Strange encounter . . . here in
the dark of night! [*To* CESAR.] All right, I'll take Pepy . . . little
playtime girl. That's all a soldier needs.

[*At this point a brilliant red light grows on the horizon, bathing
the trees, and glowing tragically on the faces of the dogs.*
SEPTEMBRE *rushes up a nearby slope, followed by* CESAR. *The
two men stand there for a moment without speaking. Then,*
CESAR *looks at the lieutenant.*]

CESAR: Your face is bloody, lieutenant.

SEPTEMBRE [*His eyes fixed on the horizon.*]: One of our battles,
Cesar.

CESAR: A great crimson battle, with its demons! [*To himself.*]
Filthy . . . war. Scum!

SEPTEMBRE: And all the fires of the earth raise their heads . . . all
the fiends of the night fly on their wheels! [*To* CESAR.] A village
is burning, Cesar.

CESAR [*Following his own thoughts.*]: I am thinking of the chickens that must be flying to extraordinary heights, to get away
from the war.

SEPTEMBRE: The wind is doubling . . . so as to spare nothing.

CESAR: Look at the dogs! [*The red glow is lighting their faces.*]
They're terrifying now. [*In horror.*] They will devour us!

SEPTEMBRE: Beasts who rise against man, eh?

CESAR: I'll go find a whip.

SEPTEMBRE: No, Cesar, sugar. These animals haven't done anything to you. They even seem too gentle . . . for this night. [*He
moves farther up the slope, the better to examine the flaming
horizon.*]

CESAR [*Alone, near the dogs.*]: Sugar? Where will I find some
sugar . . . to calm them?

[*The sound of a cannon is heard in the distance.*]

SEPTEMBRE: Cannon now? [*To* CESAR.] Do you like that noise?

CESAR: Excuse me, I didn't hear. I was concentrating on the
problem of sugar. [*Little by little, the brilliant red light disappears from the horizon.*] It seems to be over. The night is darker
now.

SEPTEMBRE [*To himself.*]: Those fires were toward the north . . .
[*To* CESAR.] . . . weren't they?

CESAR: For me, the north is all the things I love. We do not have the same compass, Lieutenant.

SEPTEMBRE [*Dryly.*]: We do not have the same life . . . that's all.

[CESAR *puts the dogs back in the case.*]

CESAR: I won't sell any more. These beasts are too savage . . . I am an honest merchant. [*He has finished.*] So then, good night.

SEPTEMBRE: Good night.

CESAR: The same to you.

SEPTEMBRE: Thank you.

CESAR [*Grumbling.*]: But it's a shame to miss such a good sale . . . because of the fires of an army!

[*He blows out the flame of the lantern and ascends the cart to go to sleep. The sound of the cannon can still be heard. The lieutenant sits on a stump.*]

CESAR [*Calling from the cart.*]: Are you still there, Lieutenant?

SEPTEMBRE: Yes.

CESAR'S VOICE: That hat you're wearing . . . I just thought of it . . . it's a little ship!

SEPTEMBRE: Now what are you thinking of?

CESAR: Well, if I were in your place, I'd give it to some children . . . if they had a pond.

SEPTEMBRE [*After a moment.*]: To play with?

CESAR: To play with.

[*A moment passes. The lieutenant rocks his hat like a little boat; then calls.*]

SEPTEMBRE: Cesar!

CESAR: Yes?

SEPTEMBRE: About my hat . . . I think your idea is charming.

CESAR [*After a moment.*]: Are you sleeping, Lieutenant?

SEPTEMBRE: Hardly.

CESAR: What does a general do when it rains?

SEPTEMBRE: He gets wet. Doesn't he?

CESAR: No! He looks silly.

SEPTEMBRE [*Laughing.*]: That's true.

CESAR: Just the same, I would have liked to be a general, for a change. [*A pause.*] Lieutenant?

Septembre: Yes? [*After a moment, realizing that* cesar *does not speak.*] Cesar!

Cesar: Yes. [*A pause.*] What good friends we have become all of sudden! [*Another pause.*] Why are battles always red? A great green battle, Lieutenant, would be so pretty!

Septembre [*Nostalgically.*]: Then it would be the springtime, Cesar.

Cesar: And a battle . . . blue as the immense sky . . . that's not bad either.

Septembre: Try and tell that to the men! [*A moment passes. He gets up. Harshly.*] I, lieutenant of the war . . . I am drawn by a halter! [*The wind suddenly begins to blow again.*] I go against all the friendly stars. I want to shout how heavily my native land weighs upon my soul tonight . . . and no one hears me. [*He cries out.*] Cesar, listen! [*There is no response.*] Cesar? [*No response; after a moment, in a faint voice.*] Are you sleeping?

[*Darkness envelops him . . . and the wailing of the wind . . . Then a soft light of morning glows, and the wind has turned to a lilting tune . . .*]

Scene One

In the growing light of dawn, several brightly colored little houses move on to form a village square, with a well in the center. On one of the houses, up center, is a balcony with pots of flowers, and a sign in Gothic lettering: vasco, hairdresser. *Inside, can be seen a hairdresser's chair, and some shelves filled with atomizers, bottles of perfume, etc.*

By now the light is golden and the music is gay . . . a sprightly little scherzo, to which two old peasants *enter, carrying pails and hopping on shaky old legs. The scene of the Peasants is, in fact, almost a funny little ballet . . .*

FIRST PEASANT [*Holding up his pail.*]: For my carrots.
SECOND PEASANT [*From the opposite side of the stage.*]: For my onions.

[*They meet at the well.*]

FIRST PEASANT [*With a skip and shuffle.*]: When gardeners meet in Sosso . . . [*He bows ceremoniously.*]
SECOND PEASANT: Good day. [*And he, too, bows.*]

[*They throw their pails into the well in rhythm together.*]

FIRST PEASANT: Our gardens may be rivals, but . . . [*They pull their pails up.*] . . . we pull together at the well.

[*They execute a turn, and start off, each to their own side, calling as they go.*]

SECOND PEASANT: For my parsley.
FIRST PEASANT: For my peas.

[*And the minute they are off, the door of the house up center opens, and* EMERITA *tiptoes downstage with the music. She looks off right, then off left; and just as she opens her mouth to call up to the balcony, a quavering voice is heard offstage.*]

VOICE OF MOTHER HILBOOM: Jero-o-o-ome!

[EMERITA *scampers back into the house just as* MOTHER HILBOOM *enters.*]

HILBOOM [*Wandering toward the well.*]: Jerome! Where are all the boys? I never see them anymore.
FIRST PEASANT [*Entering with his pail.*]: What is it, Mother Hilboom? You've startled my apricots.
HILBOOM: Jero-o-ome!
SECOND PEASANT [*Entering with his pail.*]: Jerome's gone off to the war with the others.
FIRST PEASANT: We've told you and told you. Your poor head doesn't hold onto anything anymore.
HILBOOM [*Looking at the houses as she moves downstage below the well.*]: All shut up. Is it Sunday? Or Good Friday?
SECOND PEASANT [*To the* FIRST PEASANT, *as* HILBOOM *sits on the ground in front of the well.*]: All women are a little bit crazy, but the old ones . . . ! [*He shakes his head; they throw their pails*

into the well, and pull them up again.] Papa Rondo . . . [*He bows ceremoniously.*]

First Peasant: Papa Trapu . . . [*He, too, bows ceremoniously.*]

Second Peasant [*Starting off.*]: For my radishes.

First Peasant [*Starting off.*]: For my beans.

Second Peasant [*As he is nearly off, triumphantly; he has the last word.*] For my ARTICHOKES.

[*Once more the door of the house up center opens, and* EMERITA *tiptoes out. Again she looks right and left, and is about to call up to the balcony.*]

Hilboom [*Suddenly mumbling, out of her old woman's daydream.*]: Jero-o-o-ome! [EMERITA *scrambles back into the house.* HILBOOM *gets to her feet.*] Jerome! I wonder why I never see him anymore. [*She throws her pail into the well. As she pulls it up, she peers anxiously down toward it.*] Ever since yesterday I keep seeing a face in the water . . . always the same one.

First Peasant [*Entering with his pail.*]: What did you draw up today, Mother Hilboom?

Second Peasant [*Entering with his pail; eagerly.*]: Maybe some honey? Like in the days when our boys were at home?

Hilboom [*Frightened.*]: Another face! [*She swirls the pail.*] There . . . it's running down to the bottom now . . . and another floats up to the surface.

First Peasant [*Patting her shoulder, gently.*]: Go on, Mama Hilboom . . . go to my garden and pick up the apricots that fell when you called.

[*She moves off muttering.*]

Second Peasant [*As he tosses his pail into the well.*]: For my lettuce.

[*The window on the balcony opens, and* VASCO *sticks his head out.*]

First Peasant [*Tossing his pail into the well.*]: . . . My tomatoes.

[*They pull their pails up.* VASCO *pops back in and closes his window.*]

Second Peasant [*Freezing in position.*]: Seems like a cloud passed by.

First Peasant [*Also freezing.*]: Something white swam into my eye. [*A pause, then they resume their movements.*]

Second Peasant: When gardeners meet . . . [*He bows ceremoniously.*]

First Peasant [*Shaking his head.*]: No, Papa Trapu. Ever since the battles started, it hurts me to bow.

Second Peasant [*Opening his eyes wide.*]: You got wounded, Papa Rondo?

First Peasant: No, but since my Robert went to war, it's me that does the bending . . . [*He demonstrates.*] Up early, weeding . . .

Second Peasant [*Nodding.*]: Up late . . . hoeing.

First Peasant: Not a young man left to help us . . . except . . . [*He points with his thumb towards* vasco's *house.*] . . . that one! And he's too little and scared for any good use.

Second Peasant [*Musing.*]: My Gaston . . . and my Gregoire . . . how they loved to listen to my fiddle in the evening.

First Peasant: Till they heard the drums one day! [*Illustrating angrily.*] One long ro-o-o-oll . . . three pulls on the bugle . . . and off they go! Over there . . . [*He gestures vaguely toward the horizon.*] . . . loaded with guns.

Second Peasant [*Timidly remonstrating.*] But, Papa Rondo, it's for the "fatherland". Like Mayor Corfan said on the steps of the courthouse . . .

First Peasant: The fatherland! The fatherland is my apple trees! It's your radishes! The fatherland is my cow's behind, to be clear about it!

[*Once again the door up center opens, and* emerita *emerges. She stops short. There is a pause while the three stare at each other.*]

Second Peasant [*Picking up his pail.*]: Yes, my radishes . . . [*He starts off.*]

First Peasant [*Picking up his pail.*]: My apple trees . . . [*He goes off.*]

Second Peasant [*Stopping just before he's off, with a "take" of incredulity.*]: Your cow's behind! [*He shrugs, cackles, and exits.*]

[*The moment they are gone,* emerita *whirls and calls in tears to* vasco's *balcony.*]

EMERITA:

VascO-O-O-O!

Why won't you go to war like everyone else here,

Men and mules?

You mustn't think I'm cruel, but you *have* to go!

They're pointing their fingers at me,

And whispering, "There goes the sister of that Italian barber!

I've become like a military drum, and everyone beats on me.

Lean out of your window and look at your sister . . .

Her cheeks that you used to compare to apples,

Are apples floating in water,

I've cried so much!

A marvelous future was open before you, but now the war has
forgotten you.

Ooooooo! I'm weeping so!

Mayor Corfan said, himself, what an honor for a simple barber,

A country hairdresser . . .

To mingle with important generals who use a handkerchief
when they sneeze in the mornings,

And wear dressing gowns with gold eagles embroidered on them.

What are you afraid of?

A bullet here or there doesn't always mean death . . .

Mayor Corfan said so.

And since you're so small, you've less chance of being hit than
most.

Ooooooooooo! I'm crying so!

Why don't you do like everyone else and go to war!

Press the flag to your lips . . .

Kiss me goodbye . . .

And you could take your combs and scissors with you.

Why, it's almost like vacation.

Wait . . .

I have to blow the tears out of my nose . . . [*She blows her nose.*]

I'm ashamed of you, Vasco, so ashamed.

Your poor sister is going to take the veil.

Nobody here will give me any laundry to do or things to sew or
clothes to iron.

You, yourself, can't get a single hair to cut . . .

Or a moustache!

We're deserted, brother.

There's a convent on the mountain that will give me shelter . . .
Divine organ music will make me forget the laundry . . .
An angel with a flaming sword will take your place and be my
  brother. [*She beats her forehead.*]
How wonderful!
Farewell! Three times farewell! Once for me, once for you, and
  . . . once for the war! [*She goes back in, weeping.*]

[VASCO *peers out, sighs in relief . . . then reaches for his comb
and scissors. With marvelous grace, in loving pantomime he
starts to trim the hair of an imaginary customer. He is happily
at work as the* SECOND PEASANT *enters with his pail.*]

SECOND PEASANT [*Glancing at the window, sees* VASCO.]: He's
  cutting . . . NOBODY's hair! Comb in one hand, and in the
  other . . . [*He imitates the scissors.*] tskk . . . tskk . . . tskk . . . for
  nothing! Vasco's gone crazy! [*He calls.*] Papa Rondo! Papa
  Rondo!

[*The* FIRST PEASANT *comes running on.*]

FIRST PEASANT: Yes? Yes? [*The* SECOND PEASANT *points wordlessly
to the window.* PAPA RONDO *looks.*] Oho!

[VASCO, *circling around the empty chair, continues his hairdressing. Finally he goes through the gestures of curling the
ends of an enormous moustache.*]

SECOND PEASANT: He's twirling a moustache now! Clear up to the
  ceiling it goes!
FIRST PEASANT [*Squinting.*]: Whose?
SECOND PEASANT: Ceiling?
FIRST PEASANT: No . . . moustache.
SECOND PEASANT: You can see for yourself . . . nobody's.

[VASCO *bows ceremoniously before his imaginary client, after
having wiped off his chin with a towel.*]

FIRST PEASANT: And now he's bowing.

[SECOND PEASANT *whistles to mark his astonishment at the depth
of the bow.*]

SECOND PEASANT: Must be somebody very important that he's—in
  a manner of speaking—cutting!

[*At this point,* vasco, *without more ado, jumps up and seats himself in the chair.*]

First Peasant: He's sitting on him!

[mayor corfan *and* lieutenant septembre *enter. The* second peasant *runs toward them.*]

Second Peasant: Mayor Corfan! You'd better take care of this. Look!

First Peasant: He's just mocking us. Judas! [*He calls to* vasco, *waving his fist.*] What are you doing here . . . when all our boys are being blown up?

[vasco *disappears, shutting the window.*]

Corfan [*Shooing the* peasants *off.*]: Leave him to me, old men.

First Peasant [*As he goes.*]: Coward!

Second Peasant: No-good barber! [*They exit.*]

[corfan *turns to* septembre, *shrugs, and indicates* vasco's *house.*]

Corfan: My duty stops here . . . if duty there can be toward a . . . a wig trimmer!

Septembre [*Almost to himself.*]: A pleasant little house.

Corfan [*The oily politician.*]: I regret, Seigneur Officer, that you had to spend the night in the woods . . . and so near to us, too!

Septembre: I have no further need for you.

Corfan [*Bowing, coolly.*]: I will go and have a horse saddled for your return.

Septembre: Two. I will not be returning alone.

Corfan: A horse for you . . . [*Disdainfully.*] . . . a mule for him. Farewell, Lieutenant. [*He pretends to go, but hides at the back of the stage to watch what the* lieutenant *is going to do.*]

Septembre [*Moving toward the house.*]: Vasco! Citizen Vasco! [*There is no response.*] I have an order from Mirador, Commander-in-Chief of all the Armies. Rest easy, I have not come to enroll you by force in the war. You can leave your door locked, and just come to the window. I will be brief. [*The curtain at the window moves slightly, but no one appears;* septembre *grows a trifle impatient.*] For the second time, I ask you to listen to me . . . no more than that! [*Another moment;*

then, without touching his pistol.] In the name of General
Mirador, come to the window or I'll fire!!

[*Inside the house there are little panicky sounds, but no one
appears.*]

CORFAN [*Moving to the* LIEUTENANT.]: Are you really going to
shoot the village barber?

SEPTEMBRE [*Pointedly ignoring* CORFAN.]: Very well, Vasco, I'll wait.
[*He begins to march slowly upstage and down, the clanking of
his spurs distinctly heard.*]

CORFAN [*Edging toward* VASCO'S *house, and dripping honey . . .*]:
Vasco . . . don't be afraid! The lieutenant wants to see you on a
matter of . . . hairdressing!

SEPTEMBRE [*Whirling on him.*]: I forbid . . .

[VASCO *appears. He is young, slim, charming. He stands at his
window, trembling with nervousness. There is a moment's pause.*]

VASCO: Really? For hairdressing?

CORFAN: What else, in heaven's name? You don't think they'd
come to *you* to save the country!

[SEPTEMBRE *makes a convulsive turn away.*]

VASCO: Oh. Then I'll come down and open the door.

SEPTEMBRE [*Sharply.*]: No! [*Duty warring with inclination, and
losing!*]: Stay at your window.

CORFAN [*If that's the way it must be . . . all right. Cooing to*
VASCO.]: Like a lady from her carriage window . . . [*Pointing to
the Lieutenant.*] . . . with him below. The advantage is with you.

SEPTEMBRE [*Turning slowly to look up at* VASCO.]: You are Vasco?
Why are you shivering like wash on a line? [*A pause.*] Does this
pistol frighten you? [*He draws it from his belt, and tosses it up
to* VASCO.] Here . . . catch it! [VASCO *catches it.*]

CORFAN [*Applauding.*]: Bravo! Now you, in turn, throw him a
comb. [VASCO *throws a comb which the* LIEUTENANT *catches.*]
There you are . . . an exchange of pledges! Now, do you feel
better up there on your balcony?

VASCO: Thanks to your frankness, I can breathe again. Only, now
I'm a little embarrassed to have you at my feet.

CORFAN [*Protestingly.*]: But we should be . . . [*With cunning.*]
. . . we are petitioners.

SEPTEMBRE [*Cutting in.*]: Listen, Vasco. [*He takes paper from his pocket, unfolds it and reads, while* CORFAN *assumes a deferential attitude.*] "ORDER TO LIEUTENANT OF CAVALRY SEPTEMBRE . . ."

CORFAN: Septembre . . . that's him.

SEPTEMBRE [*Continuing his reading.*]: ". . . to attain the village of Sosso, and make contact with one Vasco, a barber (or wigmaker, or hairdresser, according to the preference of the gentleman in question) and to arrange with him by any possible means . . ."

CORFAN: Aha . . . !

SEPTEMBRE: ". . . to ally himself with the Army for a Secret Assignment. He will be well paid and fed; and if the opportunity arises, may cover himself with glory. It seems to us that this should be extremely attractive to a barber (or wigmaker or hairdresser) . . . ! Signed, Mirador, General Maravigna. Postscriptum: M. Corfan, the patriotic mayor of Sosso, will lend to the herein named Lieutenant of Cavalry, every assistance." [*There is a pregnant pause, while* SEPTEMBRE *folds the letter and slips it into his jacket.*] There you are. [*Neutral and cool.*] Now it's up to you to decide.

CORFAN [*Touching* SEPTEMBRE's *arm, in a low voice.*]: Truly, Lieutenant, you *need* assistance. You'll never enlist a cat in that fashion!

SEPTEMBRE [*Coldly overriding* CORFAN's *hypocritical counsel.*]: You are free, Vasco, to accept or refuse Mirador's offer. I will wait for your answer just long enough to look at myself in the water of this well . . . and then, I'll be off at a gallop. [*He moves away.*]

COFRAN [*Cooing, to* VASCO.]: Now, war is war . . . but never mind that. Would you like, Master Vasco, to dress the most beautiful head of hair in the country? [VASCO *looks at him, alert.*] To wield your scissors and comb, to make of it a veritable cloud of beauty? Tie it with ribbons, or—if you're in really fine form—create a charm of curls? [*Confidentially.*] That's what the Lieutenant came for. It's written on the back of that paper . . .

SEPTEMBRE [*Striding to him and grabbing his arm.*]: Contemptible . . . !

CORFAN [*Low, to the* LIEUTENANT.]: But to do as you just did, is actually to encourage this rascal to stay here!

SEPTEMBRE [*Through his teeth.*]: That's my affair!

CORFAN [*Wagging a coyly admonitory finger.*]: Ah no, Lieutenant, it is Mirador's! [SEPTEMBRE *lets go.*] And what of your Oath of Duty? [SEPTEMBRE *moves away, and sits on the rim of well.* CORFAN *goes on, ever so sweetly.*] Be careful, Lieutenant, that well is deep . . .

VASCO [*Who has been pondering.*]: . . . The most beautiful head of hair in the country . . . [*To* SEPTEMBRE.] That seems a very honest offer. [*No response.*] Please, is it for a lady?

CORFAN [*With a wink.*]: You are being very curious . . . !

VASCO: Well, could I at least know the color of the hair I'm to dress? [*Apologetically.*] I'm sensitive to yellow.

CORFAN [*Snorts; then.*]: It is . . . russet! The color of autumn leaves.

VASCO: Then that's all right. But one little doubt crosses my mind. You wouldn't be suggesting that I do . . . a beard?

CORFAN [*Scoffing.*]: Noooo! You are going to dress the hair of . . . [*A short hesitation.*] . . . Armando the Third! [SEPTEMBRE *turns to him, incredulously.*]

VASCO [*Worried.*]: Then it's a bishop!

CORFAN [*Losing his patience and, almost, his diplomacy.*]: No, and it isn't the Pope, either! Armando is Armando! Now hurry up and accept, or the Lieutenant will leave!

VASCO [*To himself, almost with terror.*]: And I'll be left here alone . . . without a single client . . . [*To* SEPTEMBRE.] Wait, Seigneur Officer . . . let me pray, and think a moment.

SEPTEMBRE [*Harshly.*]: Yes, Vasco, pray. [*With a sudden sweetness.*] And if you stay here, keep the pistol as a souvenir. It is very good for cracking hazelnuts . . . [*To himself.*] . . . in the spring . . . when battles are green.

VASCO: I will come!

[*There is a pause—*CORFAN *stares at* SEPTEMBRE.]

SEPTEMBRE [*Still seated on the rim, and gazing into the well.*]: How somber the water looks now . . .

CORFAN [*Triumphantly; to* VASCO.]: Take everything you need: powder, scissors, mirror . . .

[VASCO *begins to pack a kit with his barber's blouse and various instruments. Before putting in the atomizer, he sprays it profusely to see if it works; then, closes his window.*]

CORFAN [*Low, to* SEPTEMBRE.]: Don't fail to tell Mirador that Corfan did everything he could. For him, I have emptied the village of its sons, like a sack! And tell him that I'd have been happy to serve under his command, myself, except that . . . [*Confidentially.*] . . . the living is very bad in the Army . . . you understand? [*He laughs nastily.*]

[*The* SECOND PEASANT *appears from left and stands watching, leaning on his hoe.*]

VASCO [*Appearing in the doorway.*]: I am ready.

SEPTEMBRE [*Coldly.*]: Very well, let us go. [*Then suddenly, in a softer tone.*] Turn around, Vasco . . . look at your home!

[*The* FIRST PEASANT *appears a step on from right, leading a rooster on a string. He, too, stands watching.*]

VASCO [*His mind on his project.*]: I have everything in here . . . [*Showing the kit.*] . . . including the curlers. I am burning to work on Armando, Seigneur Officer.

SEPTEMBRE [*Softly.*]: Don't you want to look—one last time—at your little house?

VASCO [*Still concentrated on his mysterious client.*]: Where is this Armando?

[SEPTEMBRE *stares at him a moment, then turns on his heel and goes.* VASCO *turns to* CORFAN.]

CORFAN [*To* VASCO, *mysteriously.*]: Armando lives . . . by a manger! [VASCO *looks at him, startled.* CORFAN *suddenly erupts into laughter and herds him off.*] Ha . . . ha . . . ha . . . ha . . .

[*They are off. The two* PEASANTS *stare for a moment, then the* SECOND PEASANT *moves right toward the* FIRST.]

SECOND PEASANT [*As he crosess.*]: We won't hear his scissors any more . . . tskk . . . tskk . . . peeping away in the morning like a little bird.

FIRST PEASANT: Or the squeek of the crank when he lowers his shutters at noon.

SECOND PEASANT: It's a terrible thing to see . . . [*They start to cross stage together. As the* FIRST PEASANT *moves with his chicken on its string following,* CESAR *emerges from the wings on all fours, nose dead ahead, like a bird dog on point to the chicken on a* *string.*] . . . how they carry off our boys without so much as a doff of the hat or a how-do-you-do!

[*And the* PEASANTS *are off. Just as the chicken's tailfeathers disappear after them into the wings, however, a sound comes from the other side of the stage.*]

VOICE OFF RIGHT [*Imitating a chicken*]: Cocorico! Cocorico!

[CESAR *is torn between a present chicken tied to its owner, and a possibe chicken which is free. He finally plunks for the latter, and heads to the right.*]

CESAR [*Imitating the sound.*]: Cocorico! Cocorico! [*And he vanishes into the wings.*]

MARGUERITE [*Entering upstage right, still imitating her rooster.*]: Cocorico! He can't be far off. Cocorico! [*She exits, searching.*]

CESAR [*Entering.*]: I've found him! [*He, in turn, imitates the rooster crow.*] Cocorico! Cocorico! [*He backs off, peering for the rooster.*]

MARGUERITE [*Entering.*] He *isn't* far off! [*She exits, searching.*]

[*Then both* CESAR *and* MARGUERITE *enter, backing on, and imitating the rooster calls, until they back into each other, and jump in fright.*]

CESAR: It was you, Marguerite! Impertinent! [*To himself.*] This cursed chick plays me some great tricks!

MARGUERITE: But, Father, I saw a real chicken. On top of a dungheap, scratching away.

CESAR: Where, my girl?

MARGUERITE [*Dragging him over and pointing offstage.*]: There, Father.

CESAR [*Looking, disappointed.*]: It's a turkey. And unfortunately I'm on very good terms with turkeys . . . otherwise I'd tackle him.

MARGUERITE: But you might possibly have mistaken him for a chicken. Who could ever know?

CESAR: My conscience. [*A moment's pause.*] Oh, well . . . for once I'll make a deal with it. [*To* MARGUERITE.] You go this side, and I'll go the other. And you shoo him. [*They start their stalking tactics.*]

[*At this point, the two* PEASANTS *enter with their pails. They*

stand amazed, watching the strange behavior of CESAR *and* MAR-
GUERITE.]

FIRST PEASANT [*Observing* CESAR.]: What's this fellow doing?

CESAR [*Hurriedly straightening.*]: I am honoring your village! Take
your hats off! [*Contemptuously.*] . . . Farmers! [*Indicating* MAR-
GUERITE.] This is my daughter. I am a philosopher.

SECOND PEASANT: Good day, Miss. [*Presenting himself.*] Papa
Trapu.

FIRST PEASANT: Good day, ma'am. Papa Rondo.

CESAR [*Pointing to their pails.*]: You are going to look for water
at the bottom of a well, when it falls from the sky? It seems
that you live upside down in this town!

FIRST PEASANT [*Gleefully.*]: All right, then, crawl up a tree and
draw us some water, Philosopher!

CESAR: Why not? Wait till it rains and you'll see.

SECOND PEASANT: He's right, this young man. Everything's upside
down in our town since our sons have gone.

CESAR [*To the* SECOND PEASANT.]: Tell me, gaffer . . . you haven't
by any chance seen anything of a rooster around here with whom
I've been having an argument? Sort of a chestnut color, with red
claws . . . ? who keeps hurling insults at this lady and me?

SECOND PEASANT [*Admiringly.*]: And you understand them? [*To
the* FIRST PEASANT.]: He must be a philosopher!

FIRST PEASANT [*Understanding* CESAR's *game.*]: Around here, roosters cost one and a half coppers.

CESAR: Even if they are scoundrels? What kind of town have we
fallen on, Marguerite, my daughter! [*He looks around the square,
then flatteringly.*] However, the Town Hall Square is magnifi-
cent; the buildings are imposing . . . but the justice is not!

MARGUERITE [*Who has just discovered the sign on* VASCO's *house.*]:
Father! Look, father! "VASCO, HAIRDRESSER".

CESAR: Vasco?

MARGUERITE [*Deeply troubled, in a low voice.*]: Hairdresser . . .

CESAR: Isn't that the house the lieutenant was looking for last
night? Behold, what a memory I have!

MARGUERITE [*To herself.*]: Madonna . . . and betrothed to a hairdresser . . .

CESAR: Yes . . . yes! There was your dream, too, Marguerite. [*After
a moment.*] But barbers swarm like mushrooms in this country

where people wear their hair like scrub brushes. How will you recognize yours?

Marguerite: Father, suppose it's him?

Cesar [*Suddenly angry at the memory.*]: But you snored!

Marguerite [*Pleading.*]: But if it is?

Cesar [*With great authority he takes* marguerite *by the hand and goes to knock at the door.*]: Open up, Monsieur Vasco . . . to your father-in-law!

First Peasant: He's gone away.

Cesar [*Shocked.*]: Left his business? What are you telling me?

First Peasant [*Nodding.*]: With a lieutenant.

Cesar: Oho! What was the lieutenant like?

Marguerite: What was the hairdresser like?

First Peasant: Which one should we answer . . . the lady or the philosopher?

Second Peasant [*To* cesar.]: As for the lieutenant, we saw him just a minute ago, riding off on a livery horse, dressed in black, and wearing a curved sabre.

Cesar: That's the one!

Second Peasant [*To* marguerite.]: And the hairdresser . . . astride the horse in back of the lieutenant, legs dangling, and half fainting.

[marguerite *opens her mouth to question him, but the* first peasant *rambles on.*]

First Peasant: He wasn't a bad chap, even if he did play some funny tricks . . . working away at the chair, with his soap and all, and a customer that was only in his head! Poor little fellow . . .

[*Again* marguerite *tries to speak, but the* second peasant *is muttering now.*]

Second Peasant: Ah, life here is not so beautiful as nature . . . and I keep wondering, why does Spring come back again?

Marguerite [*Breaking in.*]: Monsieur Rondo . . . Monsieur Trapu . . . forgive me for interrupting you, but my heart is beating so fast!

First Peasant: What is it, pretty child?

Second Peasant: Yes, Miss?

Marguerite: Please . . . tell me what he looks like? The one who rode off on a horse a little while ago . . . [*To herself.*] If it's my hairdresser . . . and it can't be anybody else but him! Just as I saw him in my cart, as he appeared to me, raising his scissors like a cross and calling me "my Marguerite" from a window. It was night time . . . windy . . . and the war . . . !

CESAR [*Moved.*]: My angel, Marguerite!

FIRST PEASANT: You must have a good heart, miss, to be tormented like this. [*To the* SECOND PEASANT.] What did he look like? Vasco. You were the last . . . you had your hair cut last Epiphany.

SECOND PEASANT: To tell the truth . . . it's kind of shameful to admit, but I never looked. I was examining myself in the mirror, and discovered I looked quite old. But you, Papa Rondo . . . you used to meet him often picking flowers . . .

FIRST PEASANT: Mmm. Let me think. And on thinking, I must say . . . that he looked like . . . nobody but himself.

CESAR: Very funny!

SECOND PEASANT [*Searching his memory.*]: A little moustache . . . like a mouse. That comes back to me . . . Round like a balloon.

CESAR [*To encourage him.*]: That comes back . . . and lots of other things . . .

SECOND PEASANT: Small, like a sprout.

FIRST PEASANT: Medium.

SECOND PEASANT: As for his character . . . shy. As a falling star.

MARGUERITE: Father, it's him! And I didn't need to listen to what they were saying. The answer has been in my heart for a long time.

CESAR: Since yesterday. And even then, you snored! [*To the* PEASANTS.] Pick up the thread of your toil, farmers, and leave me alone with my child. I'm going to dust her off good! [*He breaks a branch off a tree and tests it for flexibility.*] She brings out more grey hairs on my head every day of the week. This is what she needs . . . the hiss of a switch through the air. I know her. Return to your cucumbers, gentlemen, while I prepare the Farandole! [*He whips the switch right and left, making it whistle.*] Unless you prefer to remain, like knights of old, to witness the slaughter.

SECOND PEASANT [*To the* FIRST.]: This philosopher is youthful and fiery. I'd like to share a bottle with him, and sing the songs of our younger days.

CESAR [*Grabbing the ball on the bounce.*]: Most gladly for my part . . . [*Quickly remembering himself.*] . . . after the slaughter.

MARGUERITE: Don't beat me today, father . . . I'm so unhappy.

CESAR: A bit of correction is just what you need. Right in front of the house of your dream. [*With a gesture toward* VASCO'S *house, then, suddenly breaking out with tenderness.*] Marguerite, my angel!

[*The voice of* MOTHER HILBOOM *is heard, and she enters, muttering.*]

HILBOOM: . . . and the stones will grow in my belly until they are trees. I shouldn't have eaten the fallen apricots . . . should have prayed for them instead. An Ave Maria for each one, like at church on Sundays. [*She imitates the sound of a bell.*] ding . . . dong . . . ding . . . dong . . .

CESAR: This is a most respectable old lady, my girl . . . let us bow.

FIRST PEASANT: Poor woman, she's wandering.

SECOND PEASANT: That's the difference between an old man and an old woman. Otherwise . . .

FIRST PEASANT [*Finishing the sentence with a laugh.*]: . . . otherwise, we'd be pretty crazy, too!

HILBOOM [*As she throws her pail into the well.*]: I'm pulling a load of lead! Everything is heavy down there . . . down in the roots of the water . . .

CESAR: I'll help you, grandmother. [*He pulls the pail with her.*] By God, it's true that it's heavy!

FIRST PEASANT: You're not used to working.

CESAR: My good man, when I stuff a dog, I tell you it is a titanic labor! [*He pulls the pail on the rim of the well.*] Your pail has now reached the light of day, Madame Hilboom.

[MOTHER HILBOOM *looks into the pail and utters a cry. Everyone leans over and looks in.*]

FIRST PEASANT: There's nothing.

HILBOOM [*To herself, as she stares at the water.*]: A sword . . . some scissors . . . and a young girl.

FIRST PEASANT: Papa Rondo, you have better eyes than I have, lean over. I don't see a thing but pure water.

SECOND PEASANT: There's nothing.

CESAR: Well, I see everything she sees, and even more. Speak, sorceress, I beg you . . . for I saw the face of my daughter in the water.

FIRST PEASANT [*Intrigued by* CESAR'S *words.*]: Close up, there *is* something moving.

SECOND PEASANT [*Bending closer.*]: Only some air bubbles still at the bottom, that's all!

HILBOOM [*Her eyes still fixed on the water.*]: I shall go to the bottom . . . there, where lie the life and death of images . . . to seek. [*To the others.*] Touch the water now. It's burning hot. That is an omen. [*Gazing into the pail.*] I can see a brightness in the distance, like a gold coin, thinking . . . thinking . . . and a little light of the Holy Sacrament lost in an immense woods . . . beside some dogs that died a long time ago . . . [*She looks at* CESAR.] . . . on an abandoned wall, some angels, hungry . . . eating roses. All that is a sign of the devil. And . . . there! The first face has come back . . . a second one drives it away! In this burning caldron, a coming and going like the steps of a dance . . . And what could dance so well in the water, if not the soul of a maiden? [*She looks at* MARGUERITE.] Now the water lies quiet . . . there is nothing left . . . but some cold droplets. [*She calls.*] Jerome! Jerome! . . . [*She takes a few steps, as though leaving, but drifts to a stop, upstage.*]

FIRST PEASANT: Any way you cut it, she spins some words, does Mama Hilboom!

CESAR [*Staring at* MARGUERITE.]: I saw you in the water.

SECOND PEASANT [*To* CESAR *and* MARGUERITE.]: Don't think any more about it! Come, eat something, and throw off these sad thoughts.

FIRST PEASANT: Papa Trapu will play on the violin for you, miss . . . at eighty years of age!

CESAR [*Mechanically.*]: A very moving instrument. [*To himself.*] But we have to find Vasco.

[*The door of the house up center opens, and* EMERITA *appears carrying a suitcase, and a large wadded up handkerchief to her eyes.*]

FIRST PEASANT: There goes his sister . . . to enter a convent.

SECOND PEASANT: Too many troubles on earth.

[EMERITA *has turned her back to them in order to fasten a sign on her door. As she turns now, the sign is revealed:* GONE, TO FIND HAPPINESS IN HEAVEN.]

CESAR [*Moving toward her.*]: Mademoiselle! Your brother has gone . . . [EMERITA *looks at him, startled.*]

SECOND PEASANT: On a horse . . .

FIRST PEASANT: With a lieutenant.

EMERITA [*Scarcely daring to believe this good news.*]: My brother has gone—to war?

CESAR: And we must find him! [*To the others.*] His scissors were in the pail . . . along with the lieutenant's spurs. What a lot of hardware.

EMERITA [*With growing excitement.*]: My brother has gone off to war!

HILBOOM [*Suddenly giving out with an unearthly cry.*]: Aieeeeee! [*They turn and stare at her. She moves downstage, pointing to the well; in a voice of tragedy.*] And the water in this well catches fire like a straw . . . And young girls will be widows . . . Even in their dreams . . . [*All look at her in consternation for a frozen moment, except* EMERITA *who is wrapped in her own joy of fulfillment.*]

CESAR [*An outburst.*]: Let us go eat something . . . for the love of God!

[*Rhythmic lamentations in the distance: Ee-oo. Ee-oo. Ee-oo. Those on stage stare at one another.*]

SECOND PEASANT [*Somewhat apprehensively.*]: The Widows!

VOICES [*Approaching in rhythmic chorus.*]: Ee-oo . . . Ee-oo . . . Ee-oo . . .

[*Enter the five* WIDOWS. *Their faces painted like tragic masks, they are dressed in black from head to toe. Carrying black veils, which they wave to and fro, wailing their Ee-oo, Ee-oo, pacing their steps, they form a kind of tragic ballet.*]

SECOND PEASANT: The Widows! The Widows! Make way for their grief.

CESAR: My God, they're terrifying!

FIRST PEASANT [*Confidentially, to* CESAR.]: Don't worry too much about them—they have a way of exaggerating things.

SECOND PEASANT [*Sotto-voce, to* CESAR.]: You should see the way they eat. They go through our larders like locusts.

WIDOWS [*They have finished their round dance, now move single file.*]:

> Ee-oo . . . Ee-oo . . . Ee-oo . . .
> Like Jeremiah, like Zachariah,
> Like so many sewing machines,
> Ee-oo . . . Ee-oo . . .
> We bewail our fate
> As in endless circles we turn.

[*They wave their veils.*]

> Black. Black. Black!
> Black as the darkest night.

> Ee-oo . . . Ee-oo . . . Ee-oo
> Eternal winter is our lot
> The fires that warmed us are forever quenched.
> Ee-oo . . . Ee-oo . . .
> Where are our husbands, our brothers?

> Behold us
> As we behold each other
> Dancing the same monotonous dance.
> Ee-oo . . . Ee-oo!

MARGUERITE [*To* CESAR.]: Oh, I want so much to join them and to weep for my fiancé Vasco.

CESAR: You stay right where you are! I know these women, oh, I know their kind. Before you can take a deep breath, they'll be taking off their clothes for any man who happens by, changing in an instant from black to white, and making a mockery of the holy sacraments.

WIDOWS: Ee-oo . . . Ee-oo . . . Ee-oo . . .

MARGUERITE: We've got to find Vasco, father, or I'll be just the same as they are!

CESAR: You expect me to join the army, at my age!

WIDOWS:

> Ee-oo . . . Ee-oo
> Farewell to sparrows
> To moonlight: milk of goats!
> Native roses!

MARGUERITE: Unless we leave this minute, father, I shall join their dance.

CESAR: What, go off to the wars with my white hairs—just for the sake of blowing things up!

MARGUERITE: For Vasco's sake, father, for the sake of Vasco— whom I don't even know!

[*One of the* WIDOWS *detaches herself from the group, and points to her companion.*]

WIDOW: Alice will wash out her linens tonight, and then all alone in her bed, she will dream of the sweetness of a man's body!

ANOTHER WIDOW: Ee-oo . . . Ee-oo . . .

THE OTHER WIDOWS: Ee-oo . . . Ee-oo . . . Ee-oo . . .

CESAR [*Holding tightly to his daughter, as he cries out.*]: A chain to bind my daughter! A chain for love!

WIDOWS [*Waving their veils.*]: Black. Black. Black.

WIDOW [*Leaving the group, prophetically pointing to the well.*]: The well-water is blazing as if it were straw . . . And the young girls shall be widows, even in dreams . . .

WIDOWS [*Joining together, dancing.*]: Ee-oo . . . Ee-oo . . . Ee-oo . . . Ee-oo . . . Ee-oo . . . [*All* WIDOWS *suddenly rush down, full front, as in unison they utter one piercing, terrible cry.*] Ha!

The Lights Dim Out

Scene Two

The quarters of MIRADOR, GENERAL MARAVIGNA. *Outside, two sentries can be seen, tirelessly marching their beat. As they converge at the onstage limit of their march, they execute together a sharp, staccato stamping turn, then continue their walk in the opposite direction.*

MIRADOR's *epaulettes are agleam with gold. He is old, bald, and obviously a thoroughbred.*

He is standing at his desk, reading his reports with the aid of a lorgnette.

MIRADOR [*As he reads.*]: General of Artillery Philibert . . . devoted

... very devoted ... three stars! What says the devoted Philibert? [*After reading a few seconds.*] That his men are encircled by a river ... and he awaits the summer with patience ... [*He laughs; then looks at the two sentries right and left, still tirelessly pacing.*] Just try and think with those two pendulums! [*There is the sound of a trumpet in the barracks courtyard.*] They're saluting someone. [*Then, the roll of a drum.*] And saying goodbye to another. [*Then the trumpet, and then again the drum.*] The one who left, came back and gets saluted again. Ah! How exquisite is the politeness of the Army! [*He chuckles ironically; then takes up another paper and reads.*] General Inch . . . "Valorous" Inch, if you please . . . Commander of the River Corps . . . announced that he, with all his boats, is circling on a lake. Impossible to set foot on the shores because of enemy fire. [*He stops reading, and raises his brows.*] Thus everything in its proper place. Philibert with his cannon is in the middle of water . . . and Inch with his boats is in the middle of gunfire. Admirable situation! [*He laughs; then takes up another paper.*] This fellow's really in the soup! "With my infantry, we are hidden in a field of beans and cauliflowers . . . no one but the bees can take our measure . . . " [*He puts it down and takes another.*] Well! For variety, here's a comforting report. Adjutant Benz knocked his own sentry senseless, thinking to have found an enemy messenger. He deserves a Medal of Error! [*The stamping turn of the sentries; he bursts out.*] Damnation!

[*The* SERGEANT-OF-THE-GUARD *enters.*]

SERGEANT [*Clicking his heels to attention.*]: Lieutenant Septembre is here.

MIRADOR: I'm expecting him. [*The* SERGEANT *salutes and starts to go.*] Sergeant!

SERGEANT: Excellency?

MIRADOR [*Indicating one of the sentries.*]: Count the steps of that sentry for me. I'll take care of this one. [MIRADOR *and the* SERGEANT *count.*]

SERGEANT: Twelve, Excellency.

MIRADOR: My boy takes eight. And yet they both seem to have about the same height. [*He reflects for a moment, then dismisses the* SERGEANT.] Thank you, Sergeant.

[*The* SERGEANT *leaves.* LIEUTENANT SEPTEMBRE *enters. During the first part of this scene,* SEPTEMBRE *moves like an automaton . . . his responses are icy, as though he had deep-frozen the human being in himself to allow the soldier to carry out his duty.*

MIRADOR *does not take note of the entrance of* SEPTEMBRE, *occupied as he is with observing the two sentinels, his head going from right to left to right. Then:*]

MIRADOR: Is that you, Septembre? [SEPTEMBRE *takes his hat off and clicks his heels to attention.*] Well?

SEPTEMBRE: He is here . . . and ready to leave.

MIRADOR: Unarmed?

SEPTEMBRE: Unarmed. [*A pause.*] Except for his scissors.

MIRADOR: I expressly forbade . . .

SEPTEMBRE: It was necessary, Excellence. He thinks he is going to dress the hair of . . . Armando.

MIRADOR [*Astonished.*]: Armando?

SEPTEMBRE: Armando III.

MIRADOR [*With a great burst of laughter.*]: A beautiful military mission!

SEPTEMBRE: And en route he will deliver a letter to a Mr. Bertrand, who is trout fishing.

MIRADOR [*After reflecting a moment.*]: Are you convinced that this hairdresser has no idea of the importance of his mission, or the risks involved in going to see Mr. Bertrand the trout fisher?

SEPTEMBRE: He seems quite at ease.

MIRADOR [*Abruptly.*]: I trust General Bertrand is not actually fishing for trout.

SEPTEMBRE [*Ironically.*]: I doubt if he has time, under the circumstances. Surrounded, cut off . . . threatened with annihilation . . .

MIRADOR [*Disgustedly.*]: These gentlemen are still quite capable of distracting themselves into forgetfulness. Your message will bring them back to a healthy sense of danger. And they will know from which side we are going to attack for their deliverance . . . [*Pleased.*] Lieutenant, for once I am satisfied. To have put the fate of our armies into the hands of this . . . independent hairdresser . . . has a simplicity which pleases me. Incidentally, was he given some money, and the two-toned whistle to make himself known to our patrols?

Septembre: He refused the money, and took only the whistle, an umbrella and a basket of provisions.

Mirador: Pretty good . . . this little fellow! [*Reaching for the name.*] . . . Coco?

Septembre: No. Vasco.

Mirador: Ah! I was confused. Coco was the name of an army mule. Died a long time ago.

Septembre [*Looking at* **mirador** *for the first time.*]: Vasco, too, will die.

Mirador [*His wise old eyes measuring the hidden disturbance.*]: Aha! So, that's the track, eh? [*In a friendly voice.*] Sit down. Cross your legs. Relax! [**septembre** *sits.* **mirador** *paces up and down, looking at the two sentries.*] Have you ever been a weaver, Lieutenant?

Septembre [*Rising.*]: I don't understand, Excellence.

Mirador: A weaver . . . [*He pantomimes with his hands the movement of the loom.*] . . . the loom.

Septembre: Ah.

Mirador: Command those men not to move another step! [*Pointing to the sentries.*] To freeze on the spot!

[**septembre** *goes to the door.*]

Septembre [*In a calm voice to one sentry.*]: At ease, sentry. [*To the other.*] At ease, sentry.

Mirador [*Admiringly.*]: And behold! Transformed to soldiers of lead! [*To* **septembre**, *who returns.*] Thank you, Lieutenant, I feel much better. You are thinking, Lieutenant, that the equilibrium of an old general is a pretty fragile thing.

Septembre: I don't think much of anything, Excellence, merely because you have stopped the pacing of two sentries.

Mirador: Oh. I wasn't talking about them. I meant that you judge me, at times, rather harshly. [**septembre** *jumps to attention.*] Sit down, Lieutenant, sit down. I have a certain affection for you. You're direct, you're strong, and you think . . . you think . . . privately! That's the word. [*Interrupting himself.*] But perhaps you're sleepy? After galloping around the countryside for three nights in search of this hairdresser . . . [*Stressing the words.*] . . . by my orders.

Septembre: I am not sleepy, Excellence.

MIRADOR: I was saying that it's not pleasant for an old . . . [*With a gesture toward his uniform.*] . . . multicolored general . . . to see a sort of disapproval welling up in the eyes of his aide-de-camp. I am not a villain, Lieutenant, nor a drunkard who plays dice with blood. If I am exposing this poor barber to the worst dangers of body and soul, it is damn well by careful, cold calculation. [SEPTEMBRE *stares at him.*] How many times have you been wounded, Lieutenant?

SEPTEMBRE: None, Excellence.

MIRADOR [*Breaking out strongly.*]: And I, seventeen times! Two ears hacked off by the same sword, and sewed back on by the surgeon major. [*He hunches his shoulders at the memory.*] Scars all over from gunshot wounds. I'm pieced together like an old sack. I have exactly three navels . . . and when the night wind blows . . . [*He points to his right shoulder.*] . . . a musical shoulder bone. I walk straight now, but I know what it is to limp. [*He indicates the paper on the desk.*] This desk is a cemetery, Lieutenant. Thousands of soldiers are stretched out on hills that are as tiny as that . . . [*He holds out thumb and forefinger, an infinitesimal distance apart.*] . . . on paper. Yes!

SEPTEMBRE [*Harshly; his soldier-shell cracking.*]: The crows will eat your soldiers!

MIRADOR [*Mildly.*]: Of which particular meal are you speaking, Lieutenant?

SEPTEMBRE: I'm talking about that army, cut off from everything . . . its regiments dispersed and washed out . . . surrounded . . . which is waiting for your orders to know how to die! Do you think so little of your soldiers as to send them . . . a barber?

MIRADOR: I have picked this boy out of thousands! And not through a wild imagination or a taste for the ridiculous. It is too serious for that. Colonel Piper has made for me a remarkable study of the citizens of this land . . . and all trails led to the barber of Sosso. And do you know why, Lieutenant? Because he is beyond any doubt, the *most timid of men.* Yes! [*He pauses briefly for emphasis, holding* SEPTEMBRE's *eyes.*] He has nothing to do with our affairs? I freely admit it. With our slashing swords, our trumpets, our bullets, our guns, our cartridge belts, this whole batch of military hardware of which I am the pinnacle . . . this fine chap prefers to shave . . . to clip . . .

SEPTEMBRE: And your message will never arrive, because Vasco will be killed!

MIRADOR: Vasco will accomplish his mission . . . because he is afraid!

SEPTEMBRE: No!

MIRADOR [*Frowning; the full arrogant power of the Commander-in-Chief trained on* SEPTEMBRE.]: Did I hear "no"? We are quite alone here, aren't we, Lieutenant? Who could have said "no" to Mirador?

SEPTEMBRE [*Standing his ground.*]: Vasco will not get across the lines, Excellence!

[*A pause.* MIRADOR *decides to soften.*]

MIRADOR: He will pass through the eye of a needle . . . between the glance of one soldier and the regard of another. Because what I have sent, is a shadow! An insect to creep through the grass! The postman who is never noticed! [*Contemptuously.*] As for those brave captains who have volunteered eagerly for the same mission, I have sent them to sweat it out . . . at the canteen! I don't like heroes. They are rarely useful, and always cumbersome. A man who is afraid, is effective . . . and dangerous! Above all, he has an awareness of nuances . . . and I can assure you that's a very important factor in our profession, where most men, including cavalry officers at full gallop, show the flexibility of carved stone!

SEPTEMBRE [*After a moment; almost pleadingly.*]: Order me to go with him! We'll take the road together . . . I, Lieutenant of the war, and he, poor little hairdresser. [*Desperately urgent.*] I am no hero, Excellence.

MIRADOR: But you are an excellent contradictor, Septembre. [*Gently.*] And now if you have any more scruples on the subject of the hairdresser, I pray you to put them in your boots and to trample them. Go . . . and set your friend on his way . . . [SEPTEMBRE *does not move;* MIRADOR'S *voice rings out like the crack of a gun.*] . . . LIEUTENANT! [*Almost visibly,* SEPTEMBRE *freezes into the form of a soldier again. He salutes, and leaves. Alone,* MIRADOR *moves to a large book on the table.*] Let us look again in this ancient Book of War we call the Bible. [*He opens the Bible and reads.*] "In the same day shall the Lord shave with a razor that is hired by them beyond the river, by the King of Assyria, the head and the hair of the feet; and it shall also consume the beard . . . " [*He closes the book, and chuckles.*] So says Isaiah. All things considered, my choice of this barber has good sanction.

[*There is a sudden tumult outside.*]

VOICE OF MARGUERITE: Don't touch my father!

VOICE OF CESAR: Attack a philosopher, will you?

A VOICE: All right, all right . . . clear outa here . . . both of you!

ANOTHER VOICE: You scratch me, kitten, and I'll spank your bottom!

CESAR: My son-in-law is a soldier! Let me go!

A VOICE: Come back here! Be careful of the guard!

ANOTHER VOICE: Don't shoot! His son-in-law is a soldier.

SENTRY: Halt! Who goes there?

MIRADOR [*Goes toward the door and calls out.*]: Sergeant of the guard!

[*The* SERGEANT-OF-THE-GUARD *comes running in one door, and* SEPTEMBRE *enters from the other.* MIRADOR *looks at the* SERGEANT, *inquiringly.*]

SERGEANT: A man and his daughter have made their way into camp.

MIRADOR: And of course everyone was sound asleep?

SERGEANT: No, Excellence! [*After a moment.*] But there's no danger from this fellow.

MIRADOR: And he arrives under my very windows . . . like that! by simply putting one foot in front of the other?

SERGEANT [*Uncomfortably.*]: He was allowed to pass, Excellence . . . his daughter is very beautiful.

MIRADOR: Do you hear that, Septembre! The penalty is light, and officers are so gallant! [*To himself.*] Some day I'll have a dozen of them shot in their underpants as an example. Yes! [*To the* SERGEANT.] What do these people want?

SERGEANT: They demand to see Lieutenant Septembre.

MIRADOR [*A glance at* SEPTEMBRE, *then to the* SERGEANT.]: Bring them in. [*To* SEPTEMBRE.] If you permit it, Lieutenant?

[*The* SERGEANT *goes out, and returns a moment after, followed by* CESAR *and* MARGUERITE.]

CESAR [*Rushing to* SEPTEMBRE.]: Lieutenant! I've been looking for you! [*Aware of the reserved attitude of* SEPTEMBRE.] You remember me?

SEPTEMBRE [*Coldly.*]: Very well.

CESAR: The crows . . . the forest . . . [*Tenderly.*] . . . and your hat, in the pond . . . [*He points to* MARGUERITE.] . . . and my daughter, who nearly slapped you? [MIRADOR *laughs;* CESAR *looks at him, then leans toward the* LIEUTENANT *and whispers.*] Is that a general? I've never seen one close up. What should I say to him?

SEPTEMBRE [*Dryly.*]: Take your hat off.

MIRADOR [*Amused; to* SEPTEMBRE.]: Won't you introduce me to your visitors?

CESAR: One is never better served than by oneself. [*To* SEPTEMBRE.] With your permission . . . [*He moves to* MIRADOR.] Cesar! And my daughter, Marguerite. I am a philosopher. Generally, philosopher's daughters are ugly . . . but mine is beautiful.

MIRADOR: I agree, as to the lady. But what branch of philosophy do you follow?

CESAR: All branches. Ask the lieutenant about my theory of the crows. And ask my daughter of my experiments with roosters. [*Inquiringly.*] But who have I the honor of . . . ?

MIRADOR: That's of no importance.

CESAR: Ah, no! Words must have a destination . . . true, Lieutenant! Either you chat with someone, or you talk to yourself.

SEPTEMBRE [*Trying to urge him outside.*]: Come with me . . .

MARGUERITE [*Menacingly.*]: Let my father talk!

CESAR: In truth, we didn't come here just for a laugh. [*He looks from* SEPTEMBRE *to* MIRADOR.] Although we might well do so. [*To* MIRADOR, *with respectful astonishment.*] A man of your age, sir, dressed up like a windmill! And that one . . . [*In a somewhat irritated tone, indicating* SEPTEMBRE.] . . . all in black like a priest!

MIRADOR [*Laughing.*]: As a matter of fact, Septembre, you do look terribly virtuous.

CESAR: It's in the virtuous ones that you find the worst excesses. There stands a man, who barely two days ago patted me on the shoulder and called me "Cesar," and who today, looks through me like I was a stump!

MIRADOR [*Half to himself.*]: They're all like that, old boy.

LIEUTENANT [*Impassively.*]: What do you want?

CESAR: I want to see my son-in-law, who is a soldier.

MIRADOR: In what regiment?

CESAR: I don't know anything about that.

MIRADOR: Is he cavalry? [CESAR *hesitates*.] Artillery? Infantry?

CESAR: Hairdresser. [*A pause*.] His name is Vasco. [MIRADOR *and* SEPTEMBRE *look at each other in amazement. Seeing the look, and thinking the worst*.] Is he dead? In two days?

MIRADOR: God forbid!

CESAR: So say I! I have come to embrace my kinsman, and to give him a few words of caution.

MIRADOR: Surely . . . surely . . . [*With a meaningful look to* SEPTEMBRE.] The Lieutenant will take care of you.

SEPTEMBRE: It's just that . . . well, he's not here at the moment.

CESAR: What? Why, just a while ago he was measuring out some shaving soap. A corporal told me so.

MIRADOR [*Wishing to finish with this*.]: Very well. Then Captain Nidelbroun will arrange it. Good night. [*He turns to his desk*.]

MARGUERITE [*Moving threateningly toward him*.]: Good night to my father, maybe . . . not to me!

CESAR [*Grabbing her arm, in a low voice*.]: Be careful, Marguerite. This cold old man in the red trousers scares me. The Lieutenant seems like a little boy beside him. Notice his sharpened spurs . . . and the sentries that watch over him outside like frost on a window! [*Admiringly*.] I must report all this to the crows! Between us, he's pretty big stuff . . . this Mirador!

SEPTEMBRE [*Calling*.]: Sergeant!

[MARGUERITE *looks at* MIRADOR *with pleading eyes*.]

MIRADOR [*Raising his hand*.]: Wait, Lieutenant. [*To* MARGUERITE.] What can I do for your fiancé . . . if not for you, my child?

MARGUERITE: I only want . . . to see him!

CESAR [*To himself*.]: Otherwise, their engagement will be . . . incomprehensible! Some day I'll tell all this to the crows. That Mirador . . . he's really big!

MIRADOR [*Profoundly*.]: Go back home and wait for him with confidence. Your fiancé, mademoiselle, is a great military figure. Be proud of him! [*To* CESAR.] Both of you. [*To* SEPTEMBRE.] All three of you! [*To* MARGUERITE.] He will return to you . . . [*To himself*.] . . . as long as he stays afraid! [*A pause; then, to* MARGUERITE *and* CESAR.] And now, you may go. Good night.

[MARGUERITE *and* CESAR *go out slowly. In the distance, a bugle is heard blowing "lights out" . . . and the lights go down on* MIRADOR, *his face careworn, at his desk, and* SEPTEMBRE *standing rigidly in his uniform behind him . . . like a military painting of the period.*]

Curtain

Scene Three

A small hill in the country. There is a hut made of warped planks, on which is painted in whitewash: POST 1. At one side is a hedgerow. A drum is lying nearby.

Three SOLDIERS *are playing cards.*

Suddenly, there is a noise in the brush offstage. The three SOLDIERS *freeze in attitudes of alarm.*

The noise is repeated. The three whip up their guns.

MAJOR BROUNST [*The leader of the three; in an exaggerated whisper.*]: Ready . . . aim . . . [*His mouth is wide open for the "fire" when a thin piping whistle is heard from the direction of the offstage noise. Once more, he freezes. Then abruptly and as one, the three* SOLDIERS *dive behind the hedgerow.* VASCO *enters, holding his umbrella and a basket of provisions. There is a long thin whistle at his lips.*]

VASCO [*Blowing his whistle.*]: Fu . . . fu . . . fu . . . [*He stops, tilts his head, and listens.*] Fu . . . fu . . . fu . . . [*An invisible whistle replies feebly. He then tries a different beat.*] Fufu . . . fufu . . . fufu . . .

THE INVISIBLE WHISTLE: Fufu . . . fufu . . . fufu . . .

VASCO [*With a kind of trill.*]: Fu-fu-fu-fu-fu-fu-fu-fu-fu-fu . . .

THE INVISIBLE WHISTLE: Fu-fu-fu-fu-fu-fu-fu-fu-fu . . .

VASCO [*Circles, giving a short whistle at each step.*]: Fu.

INVISIBLE WHISTLE: Fu!
VASCO: Fu!
INVISIBLE WHISTLE: Fu!

[*The three faces reappear from behind the hedge, and wink coquettishly at* VASCO. *The three* SOLDIERS *are now clumsily disguised as women. They wear wigs done up with clusters of curls and bangs. No false bosoms or makeup. Their dresses barely reach past their knees, so that we see below them, the trousers, and above, the collars of their uniforms. One of the men sprouts a great black moustache.*]

MAJOR BROUNST [*He of the moustache; going to* VASCO, *hand outstretched.*]: Major Brounst. Confess we threw you off the scent! You took me for a woman . . . you even winked! This is Lieutenant Hans and Lieutenant Latour of the Field Intelligence Service. [*They all shake hands.*]

VASCO: I am Vasco . . .

BROUNST: Ssh! No names here! You shall be . . . Joachin the Idiot! just as I am Carmen, and these chaps, Giselle and Mimi. [VASCO *is unable to take his eyes off the Major's moustache.*] Ha! This moustache bothers you? But just consider! With this, they are *sure* to take me for a woman . . . [*Triumphantly.*] . . . a woman disguised as a man! One has to be subtle in our line of work. [*To* LATOUR.] Stop flirting with Joachin the Idiot! He is a colleague. Lieuten—I mean, Mademoiselle Mimi. [*To* VASCO.] Good. We've been expecting you since yesterday. You are from Colonel Piper's staff?

VASCO: Oh, no!

BROUNST [*With a smile full of innuendo.*]: All right . . . all right! Let us put it that you are . . . a "friend" . . . of Colonel Piper.

VASCO: I am friendly to everyone, but I don't even know Colonel Piper.

BROUNST [*Admiringly, to* HANS *and* LATOUR.]: Marvelous! There's the true Secret Service! [*In a low voice to* VASCO.] You have a message on you?

VASCO: Just greetings to Monsieur Bertrand . . .

BROUNST [*In an ecstasy of admiration; to the two lieutenants.*]: Fantastic! Notice his technique. One must live the role every moment, every word! [*He taps* VASCO *on the shoulder.*] At ease, Joachin. And we shall figure the best way to get you through

this cursed outpost. [*He turns to* LATOUR.] Pull up your skirt,
Mademoiselle Mimi . . . your sword belt is showing! And keep
facing front . . . it conceals your pistol. [*To* VASCO.] My God,
what a business! But it works. No later than yesterday Lieutenant
Latour bewitched an enemy dragoon who was prowling around
these parts.

VASCO: I don't know how you do it . . . dressing up like women . . .
risking your lives . . .

BROUNST: On the subject of courage, Joachin, you don't need to
envy anybody. [VASCO *looks at him inquiringly;* BROUNST *gestures
toward the horizon.*] There's a devil of a lot of duck hunting out
there where you're headed.

VASCO: They hunt ducks here? Isn't that something!

BROUNST [*Gazing at* VASCO *almost reverently.*]: Extraordinary!

LATOUR: Shouldn't we reconnoitre . . . to plan a route for Joachin?

BROUNST: Yes, yes . . . we will consider it, lieutenant. [*To* VASCO.]
Have a drink, while you're waiting, to keep your strength up.

VASCO: I'd rather have an apple. [*He opens his basket and takes
out an apple.*]

BROUNST [*Pointing to* VASCO's *umbrella.*]: We'd better also consider
the question of that umbrella. Should he take it with him?

VASCO: I feel much more at home under an umbrella.

BROUNST: Just the same, it makes a fine target.

VASCO [*Busily eating.*]: You'll finish by scaring me!

BROUNST [*Thinking* VASCO *is joking.*]: Ha . . . ha . . . ha . . . !

VASCO [*It's catching.*]: Ha . . . ha . . . ha . . . !

HANS: Major, there's also the problem of the basket. If Joachin
has to run, it might get in his way.

BROUNST [*Hefting the basket.*]: It's light as a thread!

VASCO: I've eaten everything in it. [*He laughs.* BROUNST *laughs; the
Lieutenants laugh.*]

BROUNST [*Roaring with laughter.*]: Ah, it's good fun to be out in
the country on a clear day, with friends . . . isn't it!

LATOUR [*Suddenly sobering.*]: Shall we get at it, Major?

BROUNST [*Sobering.*]: Yes, let's go. Are you ready, Mimi? [BROUNST
pulls out two pistols and hands one to LATOUR, *who has meanwhile adjusted his skirt, pulled a fan from one of his boots and
tried it, and then fluffed his wig out lightly.*] Stick this in your
back. [*To* VASCO; *pointing to* LATOUG.] We're going to do some
spying for you . . . just us two girls.

HANS: Be careful, Major, in the area near the cherry trees. The fire is very accurate there.

[BROUNST *and* LATOUR *exit. A moment later an imitation of a woman's voice singing is heard:* "I am a charming maiden . . . my breasts like blossoms bloom . . . "]

HANS: That's Mimi. She sings. [*He laughs; then, consolingly.*] They'll bring back valuable information for you. [*Grimly.*] They'd better! Everybody who's tried to get through—some brave lads among them—have fallen. [VASCO *is staring uneasily at him.*] Soho! It *is* bothering you!

VASCO: Yes . . . [*He hesitates, then points a finger.*] Your hair is so very badly cut! Please forgive me, but it isn't so much a coiffure as a ragout.

HANS [*Can't get over* VASCO's *thinking of such trifles in the face of danger.*]: What a thing to be thinking about!

VASCO: I speak as a man who knows. [*He points.*] That cluster there is awfully tangled. A goat would be more elegant . . . or a pineapple!

HANS: Imagine!

VASCO: A roll, to be well done, must be round and smooth as the inside of a trumpet . . .

HANS: Incredible!

VASCO: I could fix it . . . just for the pleasure of doing it. [*He indicates the basket.*] Sit down.

HANS [*Sitting.*]: But it's such a funny idea.

VASCO [*Taking his scissors from his pocket.*]: The weak point of this coiffure is the cluster. We must re*duce* it . . . [*He wields the scissors.*] tskk . . . tskk . . . [*He steps back to get the effect.*] . . . then re-*do* it. [*He takes another whack with the scissors.*] Tskk . . .

HANS: Not so fast! This hair isn't mine, you know!

VASCO: But it's on your head, isn't it? So why not a little more charm? . . . tskk . . . tskk . . .

HANS: That's what I keep saying to myself . . . second lieutenant Hans, got up like a floozy! I'm glad that someone else understands. To have to fight a war under these conditions . . . !

VASCO: Don't move around so much . . . the scissors are right by your ear.

HANS: I hear them. I hear them.

VASCO: I'm going to trim off the bangs . . . tskk . . . they cover your forehead . . . your intelligence . . . tskk . . .

HANS: It's all the Major's fault. He dresses us like some country cousin that he's remembered · from childhood. [*Muttering angrily.*] If we lose the war, it'll be because of this cousin!

VASCO: Careful, I'm near the other ear.

HANS: I'd rather have one less ear, and be free to say what I think about my equipment.

VASCO [*Wielding his scissors.*]: Tskk . . . tskk . . . tskkk . . .

HANS [*Still grumbling.*]: You see that hut, Joachin? [*With infinite scorn.*] Well, that is headquarters! For the Intelligence Service. Where is the military honor in *that*?

VASCO: Tskk . . . tskk . . . tskk . . .

HANS: Between us, it's all the Major's fault. He can't think of anything but "the Intelligence".

[*Some gunshots are heard in the distance.* HANS *rises abruptly and goes to listen.* VASCO *waits for him tranquilly, scissors in hand.* HANS *comes back and seats himself on the basket.*]

VASCO [*Going back to his work.*]: My, they waste a lot of powder down there shooting ducks!

[HANS *pushes away the scissors with his hand, and looks hard at* VASCO. *For the first time it crosses his mind that maybe* VASCO *isn't kidding.*]

HANS: You really believe that they are hunting ducks down there?

VASCO [*Thinks a bit, then shrugs.*]: I don't really know anything about it. But in any case, I have a very good reason for going there. I am going to dress the hair of Armando III.

HANS [*Relieved, roars with laughter.*]: Ha . . . ha . . . ha . . . ! You've an answer for everything! [*A pause.*] How goes the cluster?

VASCO: Wait . . . ! There, I've finished. [*He steps back to look at his work.*] It needs . . . something. [*He looks around, sees a flower and picks it.*] This little red flower in your hair will be very becoming.

HANS [*Jumping up.*]: Oh, no you don't! Not on my head . . . a blood colored flower! You forget I'm a soldier.

VASCO [*Raised eyebrows.*]: All right. I'll keep it for myself. [*He sticks the flower in the pocket of his vest.*]

HANS [*Watches him; then, in a low voice.*]: Right . . . over . . . his heart!

[MAJOR BROUNST *and* LATOUR *enter, returning from their inspection.*]

BROUNST: Here we are . . . back again! And everything seems fine for you, Joachin. The road is clear. [*He pantomimes to* HANS *that the news is very bad . . . terrible! While* LATOUR *picks up the glad message to* VASCO.]

LATOUR: Aside from a couple of scarecrows waving in the wind, and a lizard that surprised the Major on the rocks, the paths look perfectly clear . . . [*Slightly apologetic.*] Of course, it was only our eyes that travelled over them. [*He turns to* HANS, *and indicates that everything is hopeless.*]

BROUNST [*Joyously.*]: The blue sky is beautiful . . . and to sum it up, very encouraging!

LATOUR [*To* HANS.]: He'd do better to travel at night.

HANS: Night? That's a pretty grim prospect!

VASCO: Because of bats?

BROUNST: Ha . . . ha . . . ha . . . ! And devils!

VASCO: Ladies . . . gentlemen . . . make up your minds. Should I go by day or by night?

BROUNST: He's right. Let us make up our minds! [*Giving orders.*] First Lieutenant Latour. [LATOUR *snaps to attention.*] Second Lieutenant Hans. [HANS *snaps to attention.*] I, Major Brounst, Post Commander by order of General Mirador, decide as follows . . . [*In a much less military voice.*] . . . that you should leave . . . whenever you think best! [*Returning to his formal voice.*] And these are my recommendations: first . . . [*Fervently.*] . . . good luck! Second . . .

[*The noise of crackling branches is heard offstage.* BROUNST *and his men listen, then, dragging* VASCO *with them, run hide behind the hedgerow.* CESAR *enters, the dog,* FIDELE, *under one arm, while the other hand holds a whistle of the same type as* VASCO's. MARGUERITE *is moving timorously at his side.*]

CESAR [*Looking around, he catches sight of the hut.*]: I can read Post One, without my glasses!

MARGUERITE: This must be it, father.

CESAR: This silence bothers me. They are watching us, my girl.

Marguerite: Whistle, father!

Cesar [*Trying vainly to blow it.*]: It's stopped up.

Brounst [*In a terrible voice from behind the hedge.*]: Who goes there?

Marguerite: Blow, father, blow! I beg you!

Cesar [*Still trying desperately to blow the wrong end.*]: It's stopped up . . . !

Marguerite: They'll kill us, father . . . tell them who you are!

Cesar: Cesar!

Brounst [*Raising his head over the hedge.*]: Which one?

Cesar [*Indignantly.*]: What do you mean, which one! ME!

[*The three faces and three menacing pistols appear over the hedge. At this moment,* cesar *twists the whistle into the right position, and having started to blow, can't stop.* brounst *and the two* lieutenants *come out from behind the hedge, and help* cesar *remove the whistle from his lips. When calm is once more restored.*]

Brounst: Why couldn't you blow sooner? [*Holding up thumb and forefinger.*] You were that far from being the victim of the kind of military error that can never be corrected!

Cesar [*Staring at* brounst.]: Who is this monster, Marguerite?

Brounst: Major Brounst. [*He bows to* marguerite.] What a pity we have to be women.

Cesar: My daughter is a real girl . . . not a fake like you.

Hans [*Threateningly to* cesar.]: What wind blows you here?

Brounst: Search him, from head to foot . . . [*Twirling his moustache.*]: I will take care of the girl.

Cesar [*Holding out the whistle.*]: And this whistle, sir? [*Taking a paper from his pocket.*] And this letter, madame? [*Full of assurance now.*] Oho . . . ho . . . ho! You'd better walk softly with me!

[brounst *reads the letter, muttering from time to time, "Yes . . . yes . . ." while* latour *gives a coquettish glance at* cesar, *which he returns with a frowningly distrustful look.*]

Brounst: Captain Nidelbroun . . . yes . . . yes . . . [*To* cesar.] Do you known Captain Nidelbroun?

Cesar [*A little uncertainly.*] Well . . . of course.

BROUNST: He speaks only of your daughter. You're just in the post script. [*Glancing again at the letter*.] It seems that you're a philosopher?

CESAR: I am a student of war.

BROUNST: Under whom?

CESAR: My own observations.

BROUNST [*Gruffly, after a moment's thought*.]: Not bad. Let us pass on to your daughter. She is looking for her fiance, who is a soldier? [*To* MARGUERITE.] You're very wise, mademoiselle, to love a soldier.

CESAR: We have come to see my son-in-law and talk to him.

BROUNST: Son-in-law? According to Captain Nidelbroun the lady is only engaged to him. Lies, already!

CESAR: You talk to me of lies? And why are you dressed like that?

BROUNST: It's our duty to move about, unperceived.

CESAR [*Admiringly*.]: Ohhooooooo . . . !

BROUNST: *That* is the Secret Service, sir! The enemy is below, watching us through their field glasses . . . we have to fool them. Just the other day, we were out gathering information; three enemy spies were dressed as trees that day, and came creeping along, leaf by leaf, to spy on us. Well . . . when we all met down there on the plain . . .

CESAR [*Divining*]: . . . you were so well disguised, that neither of you recognized the other!

BROUNST: Bravo! That's just how successful the operation was on both sides. For them, and for us, we were just three ladies under the trees . . . nothing more.

CESAR: Noooooo!

BROUNST [*Modestly*.]: That's the Secret Service for you, my friend. But to get back to your daughter. [*To* MARGUERITE.] Come here, little one, and acquaint Major Brounst frankly with all the facts. In one sense, Captain Nidelbroun's letter is quite clear. He writes of a soldier in a very dangerous situation . . . a very fool for courage!

CESAR [*With great pride*.]: Our son-in-law is like that.

BROUNST: . . . But as to his branch of service, or his rank, the silence of a tomb. He may be with the Wing Brigade, because there's some vague mention here . . . [*He taps the letter*.] . . . of a haircut. I must say that the information he gives is not

much help in finding one soldier in the enormous stew pot of
war. Captain Nidelbroun did not have his wits about him when
he wrote this letter.

MARGUERITE: It was very early in the morning . . . and I was
crying . . .

BROUNST: Poor child!

HANS [*Like an echo.*]: Poor child!

BROUNST [*To himself.*]: But I wonder why they were directed to
Post One. There are no soldiers here in the strictest sense of
the word. [MARGUERITE *seats herself on* VASCO's *basket, looking
very depressed.*] Don't be discouraged, mademoiselle. We'll find
him for you. [*To* CESAR.] How was he dressed?

CESAR [*After a short hesitation.*]: In black . . . with gold on the
cuffs.

BROUNST: Aha! A lieutenant. [*To* MARGUERITE.] We'll get there
yet!

CESAR [*Getting warmed up.*]: A plume on his hat, and a silver
chain under his chin to hold the hat on.

BROUNST: Then he's a drum major! [*To himself.*] Well, why not?
The girls go crazy about them.

CESAR: His trousers have a red stripe on each side.

BROUNST [*Exploding.*]: Now he's a captain! I don't get it!

CESAR: I don't either, sir . . . I don't either! This girl is crazy!
[*He rushes to* MARGUERITE.] You hussy, Marguerite! Strumpet!

HANS: Be calm, be calm! Poor, unhappy father.

LATOUR [*To* BROUNST.]: Don't get irritated, Major.

[VASCO *raises his head over the hedge, then ducks down again.*]

BROUNST: How long has this lad been in the army?

CESAR: For several days.

BROUNST: I understand less than ever! In any case, you certainly won't find this phenomenon here with us.

LATOUR: A new recruit . . . he's probably at the training camp.

BROUNST [*To* HANS.]: Get me a pen and paper, lieutenant. [*To*
CESAR, *who is still carrying Fidele.*] Your dog is very charming.
How old is he?

CESAR: Three years when he died, and now, six.

BROUNST: Nice doggie . . . [HANS *hands him pen and paper. He
sits on a box to write.*] I'll write a few words for you to my colleague, Major Fonsagrive, who handles recruits.

LATOUR: The camp is ten leagues from here, as you follow the river. Through peaceful countryside. That's where you should have started.

CESAR: Thank you. [*He sits on* VASCO's *basket. To* BROUNST.] Don't forget to note at the end of your letter that I am a philosopher.

BROUNST: Surely sir. Your visit is an honor for us. [*He finishes writing.*] I hope I've been more clear than Captain Nidelbroun. [*He blows on the letter to dry the ink and hands it to* CESAR.]

CESAR [*Putting the letter in his pocket.*]: Thank you. I will always have a touching memory of Post One and the heroic ladies that we met here.

BROUNST [*To* MARGUERITE.]: Don't worry any more, mademoiselle. Your fiance is, if I may say so, practically in your father's pocket, with that letter to Major Fonsagrive.

CESAR [*Who has been exploring the inside of* VASCO's *basket.*]: Alas! There isn't anything in this basket.

[VASCO's *head pops up again. He eyes his basket uneasily, and then ducks down again.*]

BROUNST: If you like apples, follow me.

MARGUERITE [*Softly.*]: Father, let us go . . .

BROUNST [*Continuing; he points offstage.*]: There's an apple tree just beyond there. And to do it up brown, we'll open a bottle of wine. [*With a gesture to* HANS.] Lieutenant! [HANS *goes into the hut for the wine.*]

LATOUR [*Indicating where the* MAJOR *has pointed.*]: It's dangerous in that direction, Major.

CESAR: Oh? I don't like fruit that well!

BROUNST: There's no risk. We three will surround you, and you'll simply look like a father going for a walk with his daughters.

[HANS *returns with the wine.*]

CESAR: All right. [*Putting Fidele down near the drum.*] But don't let's get separated.

MARGUERITE [*Going to* CESAR.]: Please, father . . .

CESAR [*Taking the bottle from* HANS.]: No, no, Marguerite. This is men's work. And women must wait . . . [*His eye falling on* LATOUR's *skirt.*] . . . that is to say . . . women's work, and daughters must wait.

MARGUERITE [*Pleading.*]: Let us go to that camp . . . that he said . . . [*Pointing to the Major.*]

CESAR [*Reasonably.*]: We can't march on an empty stomach, my girl. That's elementary tactics. As a student of war I know about these things.

[*The men surround him and they start off.*]

BROUNST [*To* CESAR, *as they leave.*]: You're going to see an interesting view. This hill overlooks the whole war, practically. [*They go out, leaving* MARGUERITE *alone.* VASCO *comes out of his hiding place and heads for his basket. He opens his umbrella to see if it's in good shape, and is getting ready to leave, when he hears the men returning. He hides quickly behind the hedge. Neither he nor* MARGUERITE *have seen each other. Reentering, followed by the others.*] We made a mistake; we should have taken the other path.

CESAR: How marvelous, Major, to know where you're going out here . . . specially for apples! [*He notices* VASCO's *basket, slips his arm under the handle, and takes it with him.*]

MARGUERITE [*Looking around sadly.*]: I'm alone with Fidele . . . and a drum. The tables of night are covered with shadow . . . I can hear Fidele talking to the drum . . . and my own heart beating . . . but I don't even know the face of my love. My father has gone to drink wine, and left me alone . . . The stars are overhead, and will not stop . . . the moon-mill is in the trees . . . and I seek the face of my love. Those who think me mad to run after a shadow, what do they hold in their arms when the beloved is with them, if not the dream of their love! What have they more than I . . . alone with Fidele, and a drum . . . [VASCO *comes out of his hiding place. Startled.*] Where did you come from, shadow?

VASCO: I'm looking for my basket. I have to leave.

MARGUERITE: Your basket is on my father's arm. He will bring it back to you . . . [*She smiles.*] . . . provided it isn't a rooster. Are you really a soldier?

VASCO: Heaven forbid! [*Then a doubt strikes him.*] Are you *really* a girl? [*By way of apology.*] Everything around here seems to be false . . . even to calling me Joachin.

MARGUERITE [*Coquettishly.*]: Look at me. [VASCO *looks at her; then smiles; she smiles back.*]

VASCO: In any case, you are *really* very pretty.

MARGUERITE: You still haven't told me how you sprang from the earth?

VASCO: I was behind that hedge with the lieutenants when you arrived with your father, and I kept thinking, she's going to die because her father doesn't know how to whistle.

MARGUERITE: But my father did whistle.

VASCO: And I breathed again. [*Earnestly.*] I had to take several breaths. [*A silence.*]

MARGUERITE: I am looking for my fiance.

VASCO: Is he a soldier?

MARGUERITE [*Scornfully.*]: Just a soldier? You're joking. He is a famous military figure. Mirador calls him "his pigeon".

VASCO [*Softly.*]: Beware, mademoiselle . . . pigeons sometimes get roasted.

MARGUERITE [*Following her thoughts.*]: To a good heart, add all the courages, and it will be him! My father loves him as dearly as I . . . [*Dreamily.*] The first time I saw him, I was at my window. We live in a very pretty mansion, father and I, with our dogs . . . they're so lively and warm and moist . . . [*Explaining.*] . . . from the dew on the lawns. [*Back to her dream.*] He was on a horse. His horse was blowing smoke from his nostrils, and reared up on his hind legs when he was excited . . . [VASCO *is listening, enthralled.*] He made a little sign with his hand . . . [*She waves her hand.*] . . . and I quickly closed my window . . . so as not to look on anything else for the rest of that day . . .

VASCO [*Low.*]: Oh!

MARGUERITE: Yes. [*Then, a little guilty and unhappy.*] Well . . . maybe I'm lying just a little bit. [*Taking courage again.*] But it's true! He spent the next day, and several days after that, riding by, and waving . . . [*She waves.*] . . . without a word. And then, I threw him a flower!

VASCO [*His eyes lowered.*]: Which he wore over his heart.

MARGUERITE: No. [*She hesitates.*] His horse ate it. [*A pause.*] And I understood . . . that he loved me!

VASCO: Oh!

MARGUERITE: Then, my father—who is very serious minded—said, "That's enough, Marguerite, enough! You will marry him." I asked nothing better than that. [*In a sad voice.*] But he has gone off to war. And I have not seen him since. [*A hesitation.*]

I have never seen him, in truth.   ·

VASCO [*Softly.*]: How you must love him.

MARGUERITE: And now he is fighting . . . fighting . . .

VASCO: Suppose he is torn and dirty? His chest bare . . . spattered with blood?

MARGUERITE: I love him even more like that! [*She looks anxious.*]

VASCO [*Wishing to reassure her.*]: We mustn't exaggerate . . . there may be nothing at all wrong. Why, I'll bet right at this moment he's smoking his pipe.

MARGUERITE [*Letting her arms fall.*]: He hasn't time for that. [*With great confidence.*] He is a hero!

[CESAR *and the* MAJOR *enter, followed by the* LIEUTENANTS *who carry the basket.* CESAR *has an apple in his hand.*]

CESAR: In the case of a bomb, Major, I throw it like this . . . [*He demonstrates, but does not let go of the apple.*]

BROUNST [*Taking an apple out of the basket which the men have set down.*]: No, no! [*He strikes a stance.*] Like this . . . [*He winds up like a windmill.*] . . . and passing it over the head . . .

CESAR [*Fiercely, grabbing a second apple.*]: And with two hands you can blow up everything! Look, Marguerite, I have become a bomber! [*To* BROUNST.] Have another bomb, Major?

MAJOR [*Not answering, having just discovered* VASCO.]: Joachin! Not gone yet?

HANS [*Going to* VASCO.]: You'd better hurry, Joachin; it's almost night.

LATOUR [*Putting his hand on* VASCO'S *shoulder.*] : I hope everything goes well.

BROUNST [*To* VASCO, *who stands by his umbrella and basket.*]: Take the umbrella if you want to. [*He points to a path.*] And go that way.

VASCO: Alright . . . goodbye. [*He takes a few steps, umbrella under his arm and basket in hand.*]

BROUNST: Stop! We'll sound out the road for you, Joachin. Investigate the state of munitions, so to speak.

[HANS *picks up a stone and throws it in the direction of the path the Major has indicated. They all stand listening, as the stone goes rattling down the unseen slope; plink, plink, plank, plunk!*

On the last plunk, as it lands, there is a sudden and terrifying rattle of gunfire.]

Hans: A fire from hell down there!

[*For the first time,* vasco *seems uneasy.*]

Brounst: Don't move. [*To* latour.] Try on this side, lieutenant.

[latour *throws a stone in another direction. Everyone follows with great anxiety the course of this stone . . . plink, plink, plank, plunk. And again, on the final plunk, and even more frightening explosion of shots.* brounst *and the* lieutenants *whip off their wigs and surround* vasco, cesar *and* marguerite, *pistols pointed.*]

Vasco [*After a quavery moment*]: What should I do?
Cesar [*Categorically*]: Hide!
Brounst [*Upset*]: Let me think. [*To himself.*] The situation is as follows: it is dangerous!
Cesar: By heaven!
Marguerite: Wait. Maybe I'll bring him luck. [*She picks up a stone and throws it in another direction. They listen with bated breath.*]
The Stone: Plink! Plank! Plank! Plunk!

[*Complete silence. Everyone breathes again.*]

Brounst [*Embracing* vasco.]: Forward, march!

[vasco *takes his umbrella and basket and starts.*]

Vasco [*Stopping as he passes* marguerite]: Thank you. [*In a low voice*]: And I hope you find your fiance . . . a-horse or a-foot . . . but well. [*He exits.*]

[marguerite *watches him leave, then seems to feel a shiver of presentiment. She turns away, and as she does so, her foot strikes against the scissors* vasco *has dropped. She picks them up.*]

Hans: Oh! He forgot his scissors.
Marguerite [*Suddenly realizing, cries out.*]: Vasco! Vasco! It was Vasco! [*She tries desperately to run after him, but the others restrain her . . .*]

Curtain

Scene Four

*A barren plain. The light is concentrated Stage Left, to show
a clump of bushes, and a few feet beyond, one solitary scraggly
bush.*

*vasco strolls on from Left, stops, puts down his umbrella and
basket, and reaches into the basket to take out an apple.*

*In back of him, an enemy soldier with a mean looking face
pokes his head out of the clump of bushes, and slowly lifts
his gun to take aim.*

Vasco [*About to take a bite, looks at the apple in disgust. There
is a worm.*]: Oh no, you don't, my friend! [*He tosses the apple
over his shoulders, where it falls . . . right into the clump of
bushes. The* soldier *claps his hands over his ears, and ducks
down awaiting the explosion. vasco notices the scraggly bush.
He goes to it, shakes his head, and laughs.*] Poor little thing, you
look awful! [*Head cocked, he studies it a moment. The* enemy
soldier *slowly raises his head and looks at vasco. He raises his
gun, and is about to take aim again when vasco reaches into his
pocket . . .*] My good scissors . . . I must have left them at Post
One. [*He shrugs and whips out a pair from another pocket,
clicking them purposefully in the air . . . tskk . . . tskkk . . . The*
soldier *freezes, staring. vasco proceeds to trim the bush into the
form of a marvelous coiffure. The* soldier *slowly lowers his gun,
intrigued.*

*Curls, a pompadour piled high, then some flowers stuck
in for lips and eyes, and our bush is transformed! vasco works
quickly and deftly like an artist. He stands back to look at his
work . . . laughs delightedly . . . makes a deep bow . . . then
picks up his umbrella and basket and moves on.*

The soldier *comes out of his hiding place, and in absolute
fascination is revolving around the bush, as the lights fade out*

on left stage and up on stage right, to a strange little strain
of music.
   Another part of the plain. A clump of rocks to one side.
   VASCO enters, puts his basket on the ground and sits on it. He
seems tired . . . and lost in thought.]

VASCO: Funny how often I think of her . . . that pretty girl back
   at Post One. [He laughs.] Between her and Giselle and Mimi,
   she was by far the prettiest! [An ugly looking soldier rears up
   from behind the rocks. He carries a large and wicked sabre.
   VASCO takes out his mirror.] How brave he must be . . . her
   fiance. Handsome . . . and strong. [He studies himself in the
   mirror.] Her eyes are like hazelnuts, with tears àll around
   them . . .

   [The SOLDIER has started to creep toward VASCO's unsuspecting
   back, the sabre held out. But suddenly a beam of reflected sunlight from the mirror jumps full in his eyes. He tries to brush
   it away with his hand, but VASCO has started combing his hair,
   and as the mirror moves with the motions of his combing, the
   beam of sunlight plays like a dragonfly over the face of the
   soldier. He dodges, he twists, but in the end, the beam gets him.
   Slowly his arms drop to his side like wilting leaves, his movements take on a somnambulistic quality, and he finally stands
   dazed . . . in a word, hypnotized. VASCO rises and takes a step
   forward, studying his hairdo, the soldier takes a step forward.
   VASCO bends to the right, the soldier bends to the right. Finally,
   with a sigh, VASCO puts the mirror away.]
VASCO: Ah well . . . I'd better get on with my journey. [He looks
   around a little worried.] I wonder how far it is to the bridge
   with a plank missing?
SOLDIER [In a trancelike voice.]: Sixty-three kilometers and seven-
   eighths.
VASCO [Jumping.]: Oh! Excuse me, you startled me. I didn't know
   there was anyone around.
SOLDIER: There are. Indeed there are! [Same trancelike tone.]
VASCO: I beg your pardon? [No response. Puzzled, but polite.]
   Which way did you say to the bridge?
SOLDIER [Raises his arm and points off.]: North.
VASCO: Oh. Thank you very much . . . [He starts off, then stops
   and looks back at the soldier, still standing with his arm rigidly

outstretched. VASCO *stares for a moment, then shrugs innocently, and goes off.*

The lights dim slightly, then come up again on another part of the plain. Three chestnut trees are in view.]

FIRST TREE: Attention! Enemy scout!

SECOND TREE [*Passing it along.*]: Enemy scout . . .

THIRD TREE: Enemy scout . . .

FIRST TREE: Don't wiggle your branches!

SECOND TREE [*Passing it along.*]: Don't wiggle your branches!

THIRD TREE [*Forgetting there's no one beyond him.*]: Don't wiggle your branches!

FIRST AND SECOND TREES [*To the* THIRD.]: Ssshhhh!

[VASCO *enters. He puts down his basket and feels around inside of it.*]

VASCO: Nothing more to eat. Apples gone, bread gone! Nothing left but a whistle. Can you eat a whistle? [*He looks at his umbrella.*] And this umbrella certainly hasn't been much use. For the three days I've been walking, I seem to have been in the shade most of the time. [*He moves away, looking around.*] And I haven't seen hide nor hair of the river or a pond. So what could he be trout fishing *in*? [*The trees have stealthily followed him. He glances overhead.*] I don't understand why I never seem to get far from these chestnut trees? Am I going in circles? [*He takes the letter from his pocket.*] How will I ever deliver this letter to Monsieur Bertrand!

FIRST TREE: To *General* Bertrand.

VASCO [*Without thinking.*]: What general? I don't know any generals.

SECOND TREE [*In an awesome voice.*]: You will . . . you will . . .

VASCO [*Jumping.*]: But that wasn't me talking! Who answered me? [*He reads the address again from the letter, to see if it will bring a response.*] This letter is for Monsieur Bertrand . . . [*He listens, and not hearing anyone, lets out a sigh of relief.*]

THIRD TREE: For General Bertrand.

VASCO [*Jumping up.*]: Who is there? [*He looks around, then runs around all the trees, finding no one; and decides on one last test. He takes the envelope and reads.*] This letter is for . . . [*He reads the name without any sound, moving his lips only.*]

ALL THREE TREES: GENERAL BERTRAND, STUPID!

[VASCO *takes flight, but is followed and surrounded by the trees.*]

VASCO: Dear God! How do you talk to a tree?
FIRST TREE: Trees? [*They laugh uproariously.*] Sergeant Paraz!
SECOND TREE: Sergeant Alexander!
THIRD TREE: Sergeant Caquot! And off with your hat when you talk to the Sergeants, spy!

[*A branch of one of the trees snatches* VASCO's *hat and throws it on the ground. Another tree steps on it.*]

VASCO: Kind Chestnut Trees, war . . . is war. But I haven't anything to do with it.
FIRST TREE: Oh la, la, la, la!
SECOND TREE: For three days we've been right at your heels . . . and we've SEEN EVERYTHING.
THIRD TREE: What are you doing here . . . inside our lines?
VASCO: Through no desire of my own, I'm looking for . . . [*He hesitates.*] Monsieur Bertrand.
THE THREE TREES: GENERAL BERTRAND, STUPID!
VASCO: Please let me see you, Sergeants. With all respect, I keep confusing you with chestnut trees, and it frightens me.
FIRST TREE: Off with your branches, and face him!

[PARAZ, ALEXANDER *and* CAQUOT *in the blink of an eye, step out of their disguises.*]

VASCO [*Admiring and fearful.*]: Thank you.
PARAZ: You have fallen into our trap . . . [*He brings his hand up to his nose.*] . . . up to here.
VASCO: It's quite true. I can't move a foot, sergeants.
ALEXANDER [*Proudly.*]: With our bare branches, we have captured you!
CAQUOT: I'd better report to Barberis . . . and don't lose sight of this viper. [*He gives* VASCO *a swipe.*] That is only a sample, as you'll see when you meet Lieutenant Barberis and his bludgeon. [*To the two* SERGEANTS.] Between us, even though he is my own lieutenant, Barberis scares even me! [*He heads for a tall, enormously thick tree, and gives a code knock on the trunk. A trap door opens, and he enters.*]
VASCO: Please, help me, sergeants. I don't understand the reason for your anger.

Paraz: Say, the enemy sure knew what they were doing when they got this fellow up to look like an angel. Look at him. Soft talker like a baby . . . the eyes of Red Ridinghood who believes in the wolf . . . and the basket and umbrella for Absolute Innocence.

Alexander: Naw . . . he's too innocent. It smells bad.

Vasco [*With a surge of courage.*]: That's not true!

Alexander: Militarily speaking, ninny!

Paraz: A piece of white bread would look like lamb's droppings beside him!

Alexander: Well, wait'll he sees the jam that Barberis will spread!

Vasco [*Mopping his brow.*]: I was a lot less hot under the chestnut trees.

Alexander [*Suddenly.*]: What if this fellow's armed?

Paraz [*Whirls, drawing his pistol, and thunders.*]: Up with your hands! And your feet! [*vasco tries to comply; the result looks like a new kind of dance step. alexander searches him, takes out the whistle, which he gives to paraz.*]

Paraz: A little flute, eh? That's for my son. [*He puts it in his pocket.*]

Alexander [*Pulling out the mirror.*]: A mirror! [*He admires himself in it.*] This is for my daughter.

Vasco [*With a smile.*]: I'm pleased that you're pleased, gentlemen.

[*At this point,* caquot *appears.*]

Caquot: Follow me, Spy! [*To the* sergeants.] Barberis wants you to go on patrol as a pair of palm trees.

Paraz: Palm trees! God, they're awfully tall! It's dangerous.

Alexander: Aw, Caquot!

Vasco [*Trying to be helpful.*]: You could climb one on top of the other to make up the height, sergeants . . .

Caquot [*Swiping a kick at* vasco.]: Forward, march!

[*And as they move toward the tree, the lights fade out. The lights come up to disclose* vasco *standing in front of* lieutenant barberis, *who is seated at a table, writing.* caquot *is standing right, bareheaded. The room is austere: two stools, a window, and the bench on which* barberis *is seated writing* vasco's *deposition.*

barberis *is young, cold-eyed, wears gold rimmed glasses; he is slightly round shouldered.*]

BARBERIS [*Stops his writing, and reads in an expressionless voice.*]: You say that the green leaves were pleasant, and it was, so to speak, thanks to the coolness of their shade that you were led on this far, quite aside from the various songs of the feathered creatures which delighted you?

CAQUOT [*Proudly.*]: That was me, Lieutenant, caroling in my branches.

VASCO: Yes, your honor, sir . . . I was under the spell of the trees.

BARBERIS: And so, being a true lover of the woodlands, you strolled across this bare plain infested by war! And you claim that, being absent minded from birth, you noticed nothing? Neither the "snout of a gun" nor "the silver gleam of a sabre"? Those are your own words.

VASCO: I did not see anything of the war, your honor, sir.

BARBERIS: But the war saw a lot of you! [*He eyes* VASCO *coldly, then prepares to write again.*] Name? [VASCO *looks vaguely at him.*]

CAQUOT: Your name!

VASCO [*Jumping.*]: Joachin.

BARBERIS [*Looking fixedly at* VASCO.]: Is that all?

VASCO [*Hesitates, then.*]: Joachin the Idiot . . .

BARBERIS: Good. That agrees with what the sergeant overheard.

VASCO: But . . . I am not . . .

BARBERIS [*Cutting in.*]: . . . you are not an idiot, I know.

VASCO: That isn't what I was going to say . . . I . . .

CAQUOT [*Thunderingly.*]: Shut up, when you're talking to the Lieutenant.

BARBERIS: Where do you come from?

VASCO: From Sosso, Seigneur Officer.

CAQUOT: Where is Sosso?

VASCO [*Indicating with a wave of the hand.*]: Over that way.

BARBERIS: And what do you do at Sosso?

VASCO: I live in my house. [BARBERIS *shrugs his shoulders.*]

CAQUOT: The Lieutenant means, what is your profession?

VASCO [*Beginning to be suspicious of these questions; in spite of himself, however, he imitates with his hand the motion of his scissors.*]: I water the flowers . . . [*Realizing what gesture he is doing.*] . . . with scissors, that is.

CAQUOT: He cuts flowers, Lieutenant.

VASCO [*With rising fear.*]: Yes, I cut flowers . . . with water . . .

[*All tangled up.*] I water scissors with flowers . . . I mean . . . I was on my balcony, Sergeant . . .

CAQUOT [*To* BARBERIS, *twirling his moustache.*]: This fellow's all twisted up. I'd be happy to straighten him out, Lieutenant.

BARBERIS: No. [*To* VASCO.] Who gave you this letter?

VASCO: A man that I met in the courtyard of a barracks . . . he was very pleasant . . . he treated me like an old friend.

BARBERIS [*Butter wouldn't melt in his mouth.*]: And what did he say . . . this man you "met" in the barracks?

VASCO: That he was too old to carry out his social obligations, and that he would count on me to deliver his respects to . . . [*He hesitates;* CAQUOT *shoots him a murderous glance. Hoping to avoid the* SERGEANT's *anger.*] . . . to General Bertrand.

BARBERIS: And how did you know that this letter is addressed to General Bertrand, since the envelope says "For *Monsieur* Bertrand"?

VASCO: Sergeant Caquot told me.

BARBERIS [*Beginning to get irritated, drums with his fingers on the table.*]: Very well. The man who gave you this paper, was he a soldier?

VASCO: I don't know. He had a big nose. [*A pause.*] But when he leaned over, I saw on his collar, a cannon . . . a tiny little cannon . . . [*He smiles.*] . . . that couldn't do harm to anyone.

BARBERIS [*Pointing his finger, suddenly, to trap* VASCO.]: And what were you doing in a barracks?

VASCO [*Uneasily.*]: I came there with a lieutenant to . . . [*He makes the scissors gesture.*]

CAQUOT: To cut some flowers?

VASCO: Yes . . .

CAQUOT: It's the first time I've heard that one!

VASCO: And to find out the way to the house of Monsieur Armando III.

BARBERIS [*Leaping to his feet.*]: And what have you to do with him?

VASCO [*Nervously*]: Why . . . the flowers . . . [*Again the scissors.*] . . . were for him.

BARBERIS [*Sarcastically.*]: Just because you love him I suppose. Because you love Mirador's horse!

VASCO [*Frightened.*]: Oh, yes. I love him. [*Then it penetrates.*] A HORSE?

BARBERIS: And did you see this horse that you're so fond of?

VASCO: No . . . that is . . . pardon me, but are you sure? Is he russet? The color of autumn leaves?

BARBERIS [Slamming his hand on the table.]: Enough of this! Sergeant! Go find my bludgeon. We'll open this fellow up!

CAQUOT: At once, Lieutenant.

[VASCO *makes a dive for* CAQUOT *and grabs him by the coat tails.*]

VASCO: Sergeant Caquot, please don't leave me alone with Barberis! We can go look for the bludgeon together . . . [*With a look toward* BARBERIS.] . . . and I know a lot of things which I will tell only to you . . . if the Seigneur Officer permits?

BARBERIS [*Looks at* CAQUOT, *thinks, then says to* VASCO.]: Agreed. Go ahead. Talk.

[VASCO *returns to his position opposite* BARBERIS, *addressing him, but at the end of each sentence looking at the* SERGEANT, *and adding the word "sergeant".*]

VASCO [*Thinking.*]: At Post One . . . there is an apple tree.

CAQUOT: Big? Thick?

VASCO: Yes. You could fit in it very well, Sergeant.

BARBERIS [*Writing.*]: That's interesting.

VASCO: The apple tree is behind the hut . . . and wait! The apples are red, Sergeant!

CAQUOT: He's not such a fool after all.

BARBERIS: Was there anything else that struck you?

VASCO: Three ladies!

BARBERIS: We know that. [*In a detached voice.*] And let it be said in passing, that Major Brounst really is an old woman.

VASCO: In spite of . . . [*Finger over his lip to suggest a moustache.*]

BARBERIS: In spite of!

CAQUOT [*Vehemently in the face of* VASCO's *skeptic look.*]: I've seen him through my field glasses without his skirt, and I tell you that even from a distance . . .

BARBERIS [*Striking the table with his fist.*]: We don't talk about women here! [*To* VASCO.] Go on.

VASCO [*Searches his mind; then.*]: I've finished.

CAQUOT [*Pointing a stern finger at the letter.*]: What about this letter for General Bertrand?

BARBERIS [*Annoyed.*]: We'll get back to that in a minute, sergeant. At the present we're on Post One. [*To* VASCO.] I'm listening.

VASCO: What more can I say? I was just at Post One for a minute with the three ladies . . . [*Then suddenly his face lights up.*] Ah! Marguerite . . .

BARBERIS: Who's that?

VASCO: A real young lady . . . that I met with her father, a philosopher.

BARBERIS [*Suddenly very interested.*]: Hold on! [*He searches feverishly through his papers on the table.*] Is his name Cesar?

VASCO: Yes.

BARBERIS: I could hug you for that. Go on. [CAQUOT *pats him encouragingly.*]

VASCO [*Delighted.*]: I'll tell you all about it, Seigneur Officer. Marguerite . . . [*He sighs.*] I met her up there. And since that day, my heart has opened up . . . well, half way.

CAQUOT [*Trying to be amiable.*]: The heart is a very important organ. One bullet through it . . . [*He shakes his head to indicate that it's serious.*]

VASCO [*Softly.*]: Or else . . . love. And it's done for. [*To the* LIEUTENANT.] Excuse me . . . I've never been so moved by a memory.

BARBERIS: Good! Go on.

VASCO: She was sitting near a drum, watching her tears and the night fall. That's why she took me for a spirit when I approached. "What are you doing here, shadow? . . . and who are you?" [*After a moment.*] What is the beauty of a flower . . . what is the beauty of a young girl? That's the mystery of life, Sergeant.

[BARBERIS *drums on the table with his fingers.*]

CAQUOT [*Seeing the* LIEUTENANT'*s impatience.*]: We don't talk about women here!

BARBERIS [*Glancing at a paper on his table.*]: This young woman whose charm you evoke so tenderly, is, as a matter of fact, engaged to someone, according to the information I have here.

VASCO: That is why my heart opened only halfway. Actually, it was this fiance that . . .

BARBERIS [*An involuntary cry of satisfaction.*]: Ah!

VASCO: . . . she was searching for at Post One.

BARBERIS [*Coming to* VASCO, *and in an amiable voice.*]: And did you meet him there, this fiance?

Vasco: Does this interest you?

Barberis: Very much.

Vasco: Well, don't even bother to try, Seigneur Officer. He can not be found. Not Marguerite, nor Major Brounst, nor the others know where he hides himself, or where he goes. Poor Marguerite . . .

Barberis [*Through clenched teeth.*]: It is absolutely imperative to intercept this man and hang him! He is an emissary of Mirador's.

Vasco: Ah, I understand. [*To* caquot.] Come here. [*To the two men, after looking right and left to be sure no one is listening.*] You are right to beware of him. He is a terror! Marguerite told me . . . Mirador has decorated him . . . Keep your eyes wide open, or you're lost!

Barberis [*Thoughtfully.*]: Are you able to give us a description? [*Tensely.*] We don't know anything but his name: Vasco, a Neopolitan hairdresser.

Vasco [*Jumping.*]: Vasco? Impossible! Because Vasco is . . . is . . . [*His breath fails him; he beats on his breast to indicate that it is he, but suddenly realizes his danger.*] . . . NOT ME! Isn't that right, Sergeant?

[*The* lieutenant *shrugs disdainfully.*]

Caquot: This is no time for jokes, Joachin.

Vasco [*Fervently.*]: Thank you, sergeant . . . oh, thank you!

Barberis: Do you know what he looks like?

Vasco: No . . . no . . . Vasco . . . no one has seen him!

Barberis [*Furiously.*]: He is probably at this very moment within our lines! [*Seizing* vasco's *jacket.*] Failing accurate information, at least give us Marguerite's romantic words about him.

Vasco [*Quivering.*]: But love is blind . . . it might be mistaken . . . [*He decides to try to throw them off the scent.*] Wait a minute . . . I think I remember . . .

Caquot: Is he big or little?

Vasco: Tall, sergeant . . . palm tree size. [*He jumps onto the stool.*] As tall as this, in comparison to me! [barberis *walks to the window, thinking.* vasco *stands on his stool, looking first at the* lieutenant, *then at* caquot.] Should I come down? Or stay here?

[barberis *signals to* caquot *to come close; then whispers a few words in his ear.*]

CAQUOT: Right now? Good . . . very good. At your orders, Lieutenant.

[BARBERIS *exits.*]

CAQUOT [*Going to* VASCO *with a big smile, stretching out his hand to help him off the stool.*]: Hup! Sit down, and don't think about a thing any more! Pretend you're my son. You're a sergeant and I'm a sergeant and we talk together . . . about everything! Just between you and me, Barberis is not a bad fellow. If it had been me, I'd have taken you by the throat . . . [*He makes the gesture of strangling someone.*] . . . and made you spit it out. But, you are my son, so no more of that . . . [*He jumps up, suddenly.*] I forgot the wine! [CAQUOT *goes to the window. Putting two fingers to his lips, he whistles. From outside the window a bottle of wine and two glasses is handed up. He comes back to the table and fills his own glass first, taking a long swig.*] I drink before you do because my thirst is greater. [*He puts his glass down, and fills one for* VASCO.] Now, we're ready . . . good health!

VASCO: I'll drink to that!

CAQUOT: To both of us! [*They drink.*] You like biscuits? [*He pulls a package out of his pocket.*] They're my passion. Take two! [*He takes a big swallow of wine.*] There's nothing like wine to free the mind.

VASCO: I feel better. [*He laughs a little; then suddenly turns to* CAQUOT *with pleading eyes.*] To tell you the truth, sergeant, I'm terribly scared of being here.

CAQUOT: Joachin! [*He throws his arms around* VASCO, *but over his shoulder, his face is seen to have a wicked gleam.*] Relax! There . . . just imagine you're in a swing. Open up your heart to me. [*He takes a swig of wine.*]

VASCO: Easy, Sergeant! or you'll soon be drunk.

CAQUOT: And whose fault is it, if it isn't yours? You grieve me. I accuse you of distrusting me. [*He beats his chest.*] Poor Caquot! Listen . . . [*He tries to pour some wine, but the bottle is empty. To himself.*] The bottle's empty, and we haven't made any progress at all. [*He goes to the window and whistles, another bottle is handed up. He returns and sits near* VASCO. *Then suddenly, in a mysterious voice.*] Don't you know . . . where the powder magazine is? [VASCO, *terrified, opens his mouth wide.*]

The location! of the gunpowder supply . . . theirs! Just slip me a word. [*He indicates a paper on the table.*] Or make an X on the map. [*He looks breathlessly at* VASCO.]

VASCO: How can you ask me such a question! I'm sweating.

CAQUOT: Didn't you hear any talk? Tongues wag freely in the farmyards . . . [VASCO *looks blank.*] . . . or maybe you saw, here or there, little caves . . . guarded by sentries? That's where they sometimes hide the kegs of the stuff that makes the world go BOOOOOOM!

[VASCO *covers his ears so as not to hear the explosion. Then:*]

VASCO: I did see some caves . . .

CAQUOT [*Encouragingly.*]: Of course he saw some caves . . .

VASCO: . . . with little waterfalls . . . like a bit of tinkling music . . .

CAQUOT [*Furious.*]: MMmmmmmmm. Very humid places . . . caves! [*To himself.*] He's no soldier, this moron. Oh, well . . . [*He takes a drink.*] Take your consolation where you may. [*He leans again toward* VASCO, *confidentially.*] I suppose their cannons are disguised as cows. Did you by any chance, see any over there . . . while you were crossing the fields?

VASCO: Oh, yes . . . lots.

CAQUOT [*Rubbing his hands with satisfaction.*]: Here we go!

VASCO: They were eating grass . . . like real cows.

CAQUOT [*He takes a drink.*]: I'll never find my way out of this! [*He rises, takes a few steps, and as he passes in back of* VASCO *makes a gesture of wanting to strangle him. Then, carried away, he shouts.*] Vasco! Tell me about Vasco!

VASCO [*The wine is giving him volume, if nothing else, so he shouts.*]: It's not me . . . it's him!

CAQUOT: Tell me what he's like! [*Pleading.*] They'll make me a master sergeant.

VASCO: Ask Marguerite. She's the one that knows him . . . not me. [*Staggering to his feet, menacingly.*] In any case, Caquot, if he were suddenly to open that door . . . [*Stressing each syllable.*] . . . and ap-pear be-fore you . . . [*Rapidly.*] . . . you'd take off like a salamander!

CAQUOT [*Convinced.*]: At least! [*He picks up his glass.*] But who is this man that all the reports talk about, and nobody's ever, ever seen!

VASCO: Except Marguerite.

CAQUOT: Do you think she has seen him?

VASCO [*Amazed.*]: Why, he is her fiance, sergeant!

CAQUOT [*Shrugging.*]: I know these women. [*He describes a circle with his finger at his temple.*] Crazy in the head . . . [*He laughs lewdly.*] . . . as well as other places!

VASCO: Not Marguerite!

CAQUOT: Are you trying to contradict me? I've had plenty of women, let me tell you. I'm a soldier!

VASCO: That's very possible. [*He starts to pour some wine, but finds the bottle empty. He goes to the window, and imitating* CAQUOT, *puts two fingers in his mouth, but only a little peep comes out. Outside the window, a tiny bottle of wine appears. He looks at it in surprise.*]

CAQUOT: You have to blow louder than that. [*As* VASCO *returns to the table.*] Very seldom do women fall in love from seeing you, take it from me!

VASCO: How funny.

CAQUOT: Don't you know the story of the colonel and the waitress?

VASCO: No.

CAQUOT: Well, I'll tell it to you. A waitress fell in love with a colonel that she'd *never even seen*!

VASCO [*A thought seems to be stirring.*]: A colonel . . . that she'd never even seen . . . [*After a pause, to* CAQUOT.] And then?

CAQUOT: That's all. [*After a pause.*] She used to batter our ears with her "Colonel Bronzo . . . who was off fighting in the other hemisphere." It's true, he was very brave.

VASCO: And . . . ?

CAQUOT: She died of old age waiting for him, without ever having seen a hair of his moustache! Holy Bronzo! [*To himself.*] Women . . . they make such a flutter about courage. Half the battle is already won if you have it.

VASCO: Are you sure that his name is Vasco . . . Marguerite's fiance?

CAQUOT [*Pointing to the papers on the table, categorically.*]: It's in the official records. [VASCO *rises, a half dreamy, half ecstatic look on his face.* CAQUOT *takes another drink.*] Women! With just a touch of courage, you can swallow them up like a nougat.

VASCO [*To himself.*]: She has heard about me . . . surely. Holy Bronzo!

CAQUOT [*Going on with his thoughts.*]: War is an aphrodisiac for working girls and soldiers.

VASCO [*Following his own thoughts.*]: Marguerite loves me . . . but how can I become brave? [*They each take a drink, a long one, and then suddenly become aware of the other.*]

CAQUOT:	VASCO:
You were saying . . .	What did you say?

[*There is a brief pause, then* VASCO *assumes a terrifying expression. He points his finger at* CAQUOT, *as* BARBERIS *once did to him.*]

VASCO: On your feet, Sergeant! [CAQUOT *looks at him astonished, then rises heavily.*] Eyes front!

CAQUOT: I don't think I can manage it, boy. [VASCO'S *courage suddenly dissolves. He runs to* CAQUOT *and pushes him gently onto the stool.*]

VASCO: Sit down, Sergeant . . . I beg you!

CAQUOT [*With an air of surprise, then nastily.*]: You remind me of Lieutenant Tchiribeli, a dirty hypocrite. Gentle . . . and mean.

VASCO [*A prey to conflicting pulls.*]: No . . . wait. You *shall* be a master sergeant! [*He runs to the window, blows two very loud whistles, and holds out both hands. Two bottles appear at the window. After filling both glasses.*] This letter I carried . . . is it really for General Bertrand?

CAQUOT: Of course.

VASCO: Well, Master Sergeant, I will complete the information it contains. But first, I have to read it.

CAQUOT: It's totally unimportant . . . Bertrand was captured yesterday. [*Wagging his finger playfully.*] We didn't tell you that. [*Disdainfully.*] He's no Colonel Bronzo!

VASCO: That's too bad. [*He paces a bit.*] Holy Bronzo. Then how can I make myself like him?

CAQUOT: There are only one or two Bronzo's in a century!

VASCO [*Thinking.*]: But if General Bertrand has been captured, then you have conquered. What more do you need?

CAQUOT: Come, now, Joachin . . . Mirador has more than one general!

VASCO [*Abruptly.*]: Then go call Barberis. And all those officers I saw from the window. I have pockets full of letters for generals! [*He prances and caracoles an instant like a Spanish dancer.*]

CAQUOT [*Half rises, then sits down again.*]: Liar! We searched you.

VASCO [*Pointing to his head.*]: In here.

CAQUOT [*Rising.*]: For true? Are you ready to . . . talk?

VASCO: But wait . . . ! What would make them happy?

CAQUOT: What?

VASCO: Happy. To know. I have to prepare the answers, so bring me up to date.

CAQUOT [*Suddenly distrustful.*]: You're not trying to pull me around by the nose, are you, lad?

VASCO: At ease . . . Sergeant.

CAQUOT: You're not calling me "Master Sergeant" any more?

VASCO [*Categorically.*]: When you become one. [*Then in a persuasive tone.*] After all, I have to know what they want to hear, if I'm to help you . . . right?

CAQUOT [*Thinks frowning, a moment, then.*]: All right . . . it's a deal! [*They each take a big drink, then hitch their stools closer, confidentially.*] Above everything else, tell them about the defenses of Command Twelve. That's all we hear these days . . . Command Twelve. [*His hand on* VASCO'S *shoulder.*] It is accurate information that wins wars! [*Shaking his finger under* VASCO'S *nose.*] Very important, number Twelve!

VASCO: Who is in command there?

CAQUOT: Of our forces?

VASCO: No, ours.

CAQUOT [*Distrustfully.*]: You don't know?

VASCO [*Shaking his finger at* CAQUOT.]: Not yet . . . MASTER Sergeant.

CAQUOT: Well . . . it's Septembre.

VASCO [*Amazed.*]: Lieutenant Septembre? Why, he's the one who . . .

CAQUOT: . . . was aide-de-camp to Mirador. I know. But he's been rewarded now . . . some special mission that he's accomplished . . . so, if you please, he's COLONEL Septembre as of this time, and cock of the roost at Command Twelve.

VASCO: Good. All right for Number Twelve. What else?

CAQUOT: The rivers. They're very anxious to get hold of a map of the rivers. They make a big fuss over this business of water.

VASCO: What are you talking about? Anybody can see a river!

CAQUOT [*Pityingly.*]: My boy! In summer they often get over-
heated and dry up. And troops without water get hydrophobia.
Now can't you just see us all running around barking and baying?

VASCO: Sapristi! [*He goes to the end of the table for the bottle
of wine.*] I will tell them . . .

[*He falls silent, for* BARBERIS *comes in.* CAQUOT *staggers to his
feet.* BARBERIS *moves slowly to the table, and looks coldly at
the wine bottles.*]

CAQUOT [*Finally blurting out.*]: It's been hard work, Lieutenant,
but it's done! You will have your information.

BARBERIS [*With a smile of satisfaction.*]: Go lie down and rest . . .
[*Patting* CAQUOT's *shoulder.*] . . . Master Sergeant!

[VASCO *smiles at* CAQUOT. CAQUOT *beams back, and exits.*]

BARBERIS: So you've finally decided to talk?

VASCO [*Suddenly seized again by fear.*]: Me?

BARBERIS [*Coldly.*]: Yes.

VASCO [*Pulling himself together, firmly.*]: Yes.

BARBERIS: I won't be ungrateful, you know. In any event, you can
count on my silence.

VASCO: It's all the same to me. I'm not so fond of Colonel
Septembre. [BARBERIS *looks surprised, and interested.*] Yes, I
know him very well. [*He lowers his eyes, and stares at the floor.*]
I used to clean his pipe.

BARBERIS: Look at me.

VASCO [*Looks at him, then cries out.*]: I want everybody to know
it was me!

BARBERIS: Ha! Revenge? Very good.

VASCO: I've been as close to him as two riders on the same horse.
I have all the plans of Post Twelve at my fingertips . . .

BARBERIS: Wait! This is very important. Several officers are coming
to hear you . . . but don't be afraid. [*He takes a few steps to
leave, then turns and comes back to* VASCO.] One word . . . for
we never know how things will turn out . . . [*He looks* VASCO
right in the eye.] If your statements are rash, or false . . . I warn
you! you will be returned to Post One with a riddled body and
our compliments. Is that clear? [BARBERIS *turns and walks out
quickly.*]

[VASCO *walks up and down, a prey to panic.*]

VASCO: Every man for himself, now. If I were a bird . . . how nice it would be . . . [*He paces.*] Why lie? I'm very pleased with myself. If Marguerite could see me, how proud she would be of her fiance. [*He takes a drink of wine.*] One against all! That's me. It's fun to be brave. Yes, I must admit, fear is very depressing . . . [*Suddenly he dissolves.*] Why did I leave my house, my Sosso, my village! What do I care about Colonel Bronzo? For one thing, he's dead. [*He takes another drink of wine.*] If Major Brounst could see me now . . . [*He pats himself on the shoulder.*] "Brave Vasco, you'll trick the enemy, all right!" If wars "are won with accurate information," then with false information, they ought to be lost . . . the problem is to mess up their plans, but what should I say? [*Suddenly.*] Maybe if I prayed . . . Oh blessed Virgin who is in Heaven, I, in this room . . . [*He stops.*] What a fool I am! The Virgin isn't a saint of wars . . . for the fields, maybe . . . and my shaving brush . . . but not for war! [*He drinks again.*] Holy Bronzo! Now there was a brave fellow! [*Suddenly he calms down, his features firm. We see that he has made a great decision. He sits on a stool, crosses his arms, and in a voice with no weakness in it.*] I have decided. I await Barberis. I know what I am going to say to him . . . and Septembre, *my* Colonel Septembre, *will win!* [*After a pause.*] And Marguerite will know that it is thanks to her fiance Vasco . . . [*A pause.*] Holy Vasco! Now there was a brave fellow . . . !

[*The lights fade out. A roll of drums is heard. Then in a half light downstage,* BARBERIS *enters. With his back to the audience, he draws himself up.*]

BARBERIS [*Calling loudly.*]: Atten—SHUN! The Colonels!

[*The lights come up upstage, and we see in a sort of halo, five colonels in varying but splendid uniforms, seated at the table. An enormous military map is overflowing the table.* VASCO *moves toward the colonels, fascinated, and looks at them in admiration and fear. One colonel, seated in the middle, rises and invites* VASCO *with a gesture to lean over the map, and speak.*]

Curtain

Epilogue

The same clearing as the first scene.

The crows are lined up in the trees. MARGUERITE *is kneeling before a body covered with a white cloth; nearby stands the dog, Fidele.* CESAR *is looking at his daughter.*

It is dark, in spite of the lantern which hangs from the shaft of the cart.

Two SOLDIERS, *guns over their shoulders, appear on the scene. Seeing* CESAR'S *form, they stop.*

FIRST SOLDIER [*Pointing his gun.*]: Who goes there? Woodman or soldier?

CESAR [*In a tragic voice, moving toward them.*]: Have you a spade or a shovel to bury a Christian?

FIRST SOLDIER: We're not in the Engineers, old fellow. [*He laughs, then says to the* SECOND SOLDIER.] Anyway, a Christian doesn't need anything but a place in heaven.

CESAR [*Gesturing at them.*]: Go away . . . beaten turntails!

FIRST SOLDIER [*Haughtily.*]: We belong to the regiment of Colonel Septembre!

SECOND SOLDIER: Doesn't that mean anything to you, old fool?

FIRST SOLDIER: Beaten! Us! We're going to Sosso to order a Victory Parade!

SECOND SOLDIER [*Cutting a caper.*]: And a feast . . . with pullets . . . and fruits . . . and wine!

FIRST SOLDIER: Say, Frichoune . . . you're pretty pleased with yourself! Because you're the first to announce the victory?

SECOND SOLDIER: The first! Hell's fires! You'll be the first . . . [*Grumbling, he moves on.*]

FIRST SOLDIER [*Moving with him.*]: Oho! So you don't like being under my orders!

SECOND SOLDIER: I didn't say that! But it *is* you that'll be first to speak at headquarters.

FIRST SOLDIER [*Stopping.*]: Listen, Frichoune, I'm gonna do you a favor. *You'll* be the first to speak!

SECOND SOLDIER: Honest?

FIRST SOLDIER: Yep. You'll say, "This is Corporal Aldo!" . . . and then I'll carry on.

SECOND SOLDIER: Awww . . .

FIRST SOLDIER: I'll say, "Excellency . . . " that's what you call Mirador . . . "Excellency, Colonel Septembre has smashed the enemy, thanks to a BARBER FROM SOSSO NAMED VASCO!" A hero, let me tell you! [*They start moving again, but the* SECOND SOLDIER *still grumbles at not being the one to announce the victory.*] Listen, you're nothing but a plain foot-soldier. It's a pretty good break for you to be *right behind* the corporal that announces the victory!

SECOND SOLDIER [*Stubbornly.*]: It isn't the same thing.

FIRST SOLDIER: Well . . . you can *think* first. Me, I'll *talk*!

[*A crow croaks mournfully.*]

SECOND SOLDIER [*Stopping just short of the wings.*]: That crow . . . is he thinking or talking?

FIRST SOLDIER: He's thinking! Now, on your way, Frichoune! [*He boots him off.*]

[*A soft light has begun to shine on the kneeling* MARGUERITE. CESAR *goes to her. Only her sobs and the rustle of the crows is heard for a moment.*]

CESAR [*Low.*]: Wait for who? For what? Nobody's going to come. For two nights you've been here . . . two long nights in the wind . . . your old father watching with you, weeping with you, Marguerite. And the spring and the green fields around . . . but not a single nightingale, Marguerite. [MARGUERITE *weeps.*] This approach is too sad. [*To* MARGUERITE.] Get up, child . . . stop this grieving. [*To himself.*] Not a candle for the death of a Christian. Not a drop of holy water for the resurrection of the flesh! Don't cry any more, Marguerite . . . let your fiancee sleep. Let us go away, my child. [*A pause, then despairingly.*] No one will come! [*Slowly.*] Let us go to Sosso. There is a grand fete there, at

Sosso. You heard the soldiers. We will walk by his house, and
look at it as if it were our own . . . "hello, Vasco" . . .

MARGUERITE [*In a tiny voice.*]: "Hello . . . "

CESAR [*Drying his tears.*]: This melancholy mood . . .

MARGUERITE: Right at the point of my dream, he fell asleep . . .

CESAR: Enough, Marguerite . . . enough! To get into such a state
for a . . . a vision. It *was* a dream, wasn't it? You didn't deceive
me? And anyway, who was it that wanted to go off to war when
he'd just got engaged . . . you or him? [*To himself.*] I don't like
soldiers, even when they're dead. Most people die just before
their death, or just at the moment of death. But soldiers . . . a
long time before.

[*A voice is heard calling from offstage.*]

DRUM MAJOR KRANZ: Gregory! Come on Gregory! [*He enters,
fat and puffing for breath. He is followed by* GREGORY, *young
and stupid-looking, and carrying an enormous drum in a canvas
cover on his back.*] At last, a lantern! Let's have a look at our
drum, you clumsy. [GREGORY *raises his hands as though to say
he's not responsible for what has happened.*] You may very well
raise your hands to Heaven, Gregory . . . but who was it that
rolled around on the ground with this poor drum, like an ass
with his pack!

GREGORY [*Nearly blubbering.*]: One little slip on a path like this
one, is not unreasonable!

KRANZ: Yes, yes, yes! Speak for yourself! But we'd better check it.
Try the poor old tub. [GREGORY *takes the drumstick and beats
three times.*]

DRUM: Boum . . . boum . . . boummm . . .

[GREGORY *looks at* KRANZ *to see what the latter thinks.* KRANZ
gestures to try again.]

DRUM: Boum . . . boum . . . b o
                                   u
                               mmm . . .

CESAR [*Appearing.*]: I liked the first boums better.

KRANZ [*Not at all surprised by this apparition.*]: This old woods-
man out of the night is right. [*He makes a sign to* GREGORY *to
continue.* GREGORY *does three more boums.*]

CESAR: There is a falling off of the vibrations in the boums . . .
You see, I am a scientist.

KRANZ: Did you hear that, Gregory? Look into it!

GREGORY [*Whining.*]: I'm no musician, to go around repairing
drums!

KRANZ: All right, all right, we'll look into it later. But how am I
to play my new Victory March with the drum in this condition?

CESAR [*Admiringly.*]: You write music?

KRANZ [*Complacently.*]: "A Hymn to a Hero" . . . subtitled "The
Barber of Sosso". We will play it in honor of Colonel Septembre,
who has apparently pierced through . . . [*He trails off uncertainly.*]

CESAR [*Interestedly.*]: Through what?

KRANZ: Well, I actually haven't the faintest idea. But it's very
important. And now, onward, good Gregory, to the victory
procession! [*He calls to* CESAR *as they leave.*] If you come to
Sosso, my dear forester, I invite you to sit at the Music table,
between the first fife and the cymbals. That's the choice spot.

CESAR [*Forlornly, as they disappear.*]: Thank you. [*A crow croaks;
then another.* CESAR *looks up at them sadly.*] Excuse us . . . be
patient! [*He starts to move toward* MARGUERITE, *then turns, and
in the voice of a prophet.*] We will not leave, crows, we will not
leave! Neither I nor my daughter, until we have given him the
place of a flower seed in the earth . . . until we have recited all
the prayers to confound demons. Look at me, crows, look at me!
Tonight I am my daughter's spouse in grief. And you, birds of
absence and of horror, will not touch our bread! [*After a
moment.*] They are motionless as evil shadows. Not a child
nearby to frighten them . . . nor even a white dove to chase them
away. [*He calls out.*] Soldiers! Soldiers! Crows! [MARGUERITE *rises
and throws herself into his arms.*] My angel, Marguerite! He
didn't even wear a uniform when they brought him back . . . his
little hat upon his chest, poor fellow. You are right to weep,
Marguerite . . . you are right. Come child, come and rest. [*He
seats her at the foot of a tree near* VASCO's *body.*] Where is the
lantern so I may look at you when you dream, child . . . and
when you live . . . [*The light is beginning to change. Dawn is
breaking. There is the rustling of feathers as the crows stir
around in the trees.* SEPTEMBRE *appears. The crows set up a
deafening noise.* SEPTEMBRE *stops.* CESAR *takes a few steps*

toward him. In a strange voice.] Are you looking for the house
of Vasco, Lieutenant? [SEPTEMBRE *doesn't move; looks impassively at* CESAR. *Again* CESAR *says:*] Are you looking for the house
of Vasco? [SEPTEMBRE *doesn't answer.*]

MARGUERITE [*Her eyes lost, in the voice of a sleepwalker.*]: My
father will tell you where it is . . . I know about other things.

CESAR [*Breaking out of his rigidity, goes to* SEPTEMBRE.]: In front
of Post One . . . they left him, as they retreated, his body riddled
with bullets. Hans and Latour helped to bring him here . . .

SEPTEMBRE [*Calmly.*]: I know.

CESAR: Since then, my child hasn't spoken . . . as though she had,
herself, become one with the earth! [*Haggardly.*] She had a
dream . . . and I didn't believe her. Liar, Marguerite! [*He points
to* VASCO's *body.*] Go, now, see if a dream is nothing.!

[SEPTEMBRE *moves toward* VASCO. *He kneels and pulls the cover
back to look at his face. Slowly he takes off his hat and puts it
down on the ground.*]

SEPTEMBRE [*Softly.*]: Blood of a dream . . . A price to pay for the
marching years from the innocence of youth to that foolishness
of men which passes for maturity. [*Suddenly he draws the cover
over* VASCO *and rises; passionately.*] I am not the face of Destiny,
Marguerite . . . but only of the world of men! In me are all the
fragments, good and bad . . . and even . . . a trace . . . of the
dream. [MARGUERITE *does not look at him. She stares . . . seeing
nothing. He goes to* CESAR.] Take your daughter, Cesar . . . wait
for me in Sosso.

CESAR [*Pointing to the crows.*]: Look!

SEPTEMBRE: I will not leave him . . . rest easy.

CESAR [*To* MARGUERITE.]: Say your farewells, child, and we will go.
The lieutenant will stay with him. [MARGUERITE *kneels.* CESAR
turns to SEPTEMBRE.] Don't you wish to pray with us? [SEPTEMBRE
*slowly turns his back, as though he wishes to avoid at any price,
sharing in their prayers.* CESAR *kneels.*] In the name of the Father
. . . and of the Son . . .

MARGUERITE [*Gravely.*]: In the name of the Father . . .

CESAR: Let those ancient servants who lead souls to God, open
the gates of Jerusalem to this boy, dead . . . like a bird beating
at the shelter of the air . . .

MARGUERITE: In the name of the Son . . . [*With infinite tender-*

ness, looking at VASCO.] What makes him so lazy he won't even smile . . .

CESAR [*Smiling and weeping.*]: Fidele is nearby, scratching at his fleas. [*A pause.*] Lord, listen to my child . . .

MARGUERITE: I say nothing, Lord, except that I have dreamed, as you did, when you wrote the Book of the Sea . . .

SEPTEMBRE [*His back still turned; bitterly.*]: . . . and of the Sands, with letters traced in fresh blood. The Book of Glory!

CESAR [*Rising, without looking at* SEPTEMBRE.]: Glory? . . . and what does that word mean when a person is no more? When he hasn't even a bit of bread in his mouth for remembrance!

[CESAR *and* MARGUERITE *start off slowly.* SEPTEMBRE *stands bare headed, pistol in hand hanging down at his side. Suddenly he takes a few steps as though to join them.*]

SEPTEMBRE [*In a fierce voice, distorted with bitterness.*]: Don't forget, Cesar and Marguerite! The Victory parade at Sosso! [MARGUERITE *stops, and like a sleeper awakened, looks slowly around, bewildered, till her glance meets* SEPTEMBRE'*s. He looks at her a long moment, then says softly, gently.*] Victory, Marguerite . . . victory at Sosso.

[*She stares at him a moment more, then turns and goes off with her father.*]

The Curtain Falls

THE CAGE

A Play in Three Acts

Mario Fratti

translated by
Marguerita Carra *and* Louise Warner

Characters

(In order of appearance)

Cristiano - a sensitive young man whose contempt and hostility towards his fellow man is a cover-up for his deep fears and insecurity

First Delivery Boy - sarcastic

Second Delivery Boy - a dull slow-witted fellow who follows his friend blindly

The Mother - a widow; quiet but strong

Nella - Cristiano's sister in her twenties; obedient, passive

Sergio - Nella's fiance - in his thirties; simple but simpatico

Pietro - Cristiano's older brother; bitter, strong, violent

Chiara - Pietro's wife; a real woman; confident, realistic

From the newspapers:

... "During a search, a man of 30 was found in a cage. A thorough investigation proved that this unusual isolation was voluntary."

Act One

SCENE: *At center stage a large circular cage isolates* CRISTIANO, *surrounded by his bed, a chair and a table on which is a set of the Rizzoli edition of Chekhov's works.*

In the background, Left, there is a curtain which conceals a bed; in the Center, a window and a sink; at Right, a second curtain conceals another double bed.

Downstage, not far from the cage is a table with chairs. The door at Right leads to the outside. The door is half open.

Two delivery boys in white jackets enter cautiously. The door creaks, but CRISTIANO, *a nervous young man, morbidly sensitive, doesn't turn.*

FIRST BOY [*Carrying a tray of pastries.*]: May we come in? [*There is no answer. The boys enter. The first whispers to his companion, who is carrying two bottles of champagne and weight-lifting equipment.*] He's pretending not to hear us. [*Points to* CRISTIANO *scornfully.*] He's always like this—lost when his mother's not around and won't have a thing to do with anyone. He's crazy—full of complexes. He's got weak hands. He's afraid of sex, can't cope with life and thinks the world's a jungle. He's sick up here. [*Taps head.*] Let's have some fun. Remember, now. [*Indicating the champagne bottles, the pastries and the weights.*] We'll attract his attention. This will force him to speak and then I'll introduce you. All you have to do is work the date of your birth into the conversation: make it January 17th.
SECOND BOY: But I . . .
FIRST BOY [*Interrupting.*]: He won't ask you for a birth certificate! This way the trap will spring by itself. Do as I do. We'll have fun. [*He steps forward quietly, followed by the* SECOND BOY. *They*

set everything down on the table very noisily. CRISTIANO *is
startled but does not turn. Coming up behind him.*] Good
morning, Professor. [*There is no reaction.*] Professor, good morning. [*Still no reaction. He walks around the cage and plants
himself in front of him.*] Did you sleep well, Professor?

CRISTIANO [*Finally forced to speak.*]: How many times do I have
to tell you that I am not a Professor?

FIRST BOY: Because you didn't get your degree? But you read all
day long! That's what counts. You lacked only a few months,
I remember . . .

CRISTIANO: Three years.

FIRST BOY: But you took a lot of exams.

CRISTIANO: Five.

FIRST BOY: So did what's his name . . . [*Searching.*] that philosopher who discovered Aesthetics . . . B. Croce. He only took a few
exams and never got a degree. Wouldn't you have given him
the title of professor? And what about D'Annunzio, who in his
advanced studies of the Classics flunked in Italian? I read about
it in the Sunday *Courier*. Listen to me, school is unimportant.
It isn't the degree that stamps real genius. It's all a question of
memory and will. You want to hear of a case? Once, during the
war, I was helping my captain with a crossword puzzle. He didn't
know the author of *Francesca da Rimini*. S.P.* I knew it and
told him. So what good is school? Anyway, if you'd prefer it, I'll
call you "Maestro." [*After a pause, with no reply forthcoming.*]
Where's your mother, Maestro?

CRISTIANO: The Signora.

FIRST BOY: Yes, the Signora. She ordered champagne and pastries.
[*Pointing to the table.*] So *we* brought them. What's the
occasion?

CRISTIANO [*Cutting him off.*]: She'll be here soon.

FIRST BOY: We'll wait . . . Allow me to . . . [*Signals his friend to
come over.*] . . . introduce Hercules. He works with us—when
he's not at the gym. He's an athlete. [*He motions to him to
shake hands, egging him on.*]

SECOND BOY [*Slipping his hand through the bars.*]: I'm honored.

[CRISTIANO, *who has tried to ignore all this, finding himself
cornered, gives his hand listlessly.*]

* "S.P." = Silvio Pellico, author of *Francesca da Rimini*.

CRISTIANO [*Hardly audible.*]: Pleased. [*He tries not to show his displeasure at the vigorous handshake.*]

FIRST BOY: Did you see the size of that hand? And those muscles? A real giant. He was in the semifinals of the weight-lifting contest. He almost won a medal for the city—just think . . . Show him the photograph, Hercules. [*The* SECOND BOY *looks through his wallet and takes out a photograph. He holds it out to* CRISTIANO, *who is forced to take it.*] This is the result of determination and drive. [*Slapping him on the back.*] Like you . . . strong-willed, stubborn. You see? He was skinny . . . No offense, Maestro . . . like you. Even thinner. [*For the first time* CRISTIANO *shows some interest. He returns the photograph.*]

CRISTIANO: A remarkable transformation. How many years did it take?

FIRST BOY [*Before his companion can reply.*]: A few months. Tell him Hercules. Tell the Maestro.

SECOND BOY [*Mechanically, as if he is repeating a lesson.*]: At school I always lost. I tried in the gym. I was quick on my feet, but I didn't have any strength. I could hit ten times, twenty times, [*All the while shadow boxing.*] but my opponent was still on his feet. But one blow from him was enough to flatten me out. I had to start again from the beginning. With my hands. [*By this time* CRISTIANO *is really interested.*] Alfredo helped me. You probably know him, Maestro. He's the goalie of the local team. He needed strong hands, so he improved himself with these. [*He pulls two iron weights from the rest of the equipment, and lifts them several times with great ease.*] See Maestro? It's nothing; after a few months your fingers get strong and there's power in your fist. Do you want to try? [CRISTIANO *shrinks away.*] Go ahead, try it. It's easy. [CRISTIANO *takes the heavy weight, clumsily tries to repeat the exercise but is unsuccessful. The weight falls to the floor with a crash.*]

FIRST BOY [*At once.*]: I was there the first time he tried. [*Pointing to Hercules.*] Exactly the same thing happened—it almost fell on his foot. [*Eagerly.*] Can you leave them here Hercules? The bar, too. Then he can do a little weight lifting himself.

CRISTIANO: No, thanks, I . . .

SECOND BOY: Please do, Maestro. I have more weights at home. I'm practically a collector. I'll gladly leave them with you. No obligations. [*He pushes everything into the cage.*]

CRISTIANO [*Uncomfortable.*]: Thank you. If I have time . . .

[*An embarrassed pause follows.* CRISTIANO *picks up one of the green books on the table.*]

FIRST BOY [*Picking up the conversation.*]: And in a few months, Maestro . . . [*Making a muscle, with a wink toward his friend.*] . . . we'll see you with muscles almost as big as Hercules's. [CRISTIANO *shrinks at the thought.*] When were you born, Maestro?

CRISTIANO: 1936.

FIRST BOY [*Hypocritically.*]: Look! what a coincidence?! Same as Hercules. [*Encouraging Hercules.*] Tell him.

SECOND BOY: That's right, Maestro. I was born on the 17th of January, 1936.

CRISTIANO [*Turning slowly.*]: The seventeenth of January. Strange. When we were talking about hands I thought for a moment . . . Do you know who was born on the seventeenth of January in 1860?

SECOND BOY [*Looking at his friend.*] Yes. [*With wrong pronunciation.*] Chekhov—the one who wrote *The Wedding* and *The Orchard of the Three Sisters.* He told me. [*Pointing to his friend.*]

FIRST BOY [*Annoyed.*]: We've talked about it, yes. I told him about your passion for Chekhov . . . that we discuss him now and then . . . how his brother considered him a loafer . . .

CRISTIANO [*Won over by the subject, happy for the opportunity to show off his knowledge.*]: Michael Pavlovich, his brother and biographer, states in his *Memoirs* "The least of all men capable of manual labor." [*Explaining excitedly.*] He couldn't make use of his hands. He renounced his profession—he received his medical degree in 1884—he was afraid to touch the wounds of the world, the diseased that surrounded him. [*With emotion.*] The greatest writer of all time.

FIRST BOY: By the way, about those frames of mind that you keep finding in his stories . . . I asked my friends . . . You're right. Even in our life almost everybody . . . Two people had sent, when they were children, letters asking protection and help. Only writing on the envelope "To my uncle" or to "Grandpa" . . . with no exact address.

CRISTIANO [*Learnedly, interrupting him.*]: "The Letter," page 32 of the French edition.

FIRST BOY [*Continuing.*]: All of them had daydreamed before the mirror, building up misfortunes, imagining catastrophes or living golden dreams.

CRISTIANO [*Pedantically.*]: "The Mirror. [*By heart, with ecstasy.*]: "Something falls from Nelle's hand and hits the floor. Startled, she leaps up and opens her eyes wide. She sees that one mirror is lying at her feet, the other is on the table as it was before. She looks at herself in the mirror and sees a pale, tear-stained face." Volume four, 12th story, page 8.

FIRST BOY [*To* SECOND BOY.]: You, too?

SECOND BOY [*Absentminded.*]: I, what?

FIRST BOY: In front of a mirror—have you ever daydreamed? "I'll become the champion." "I'll enter the Olympics. . . ."

SECOND BOY: Of course.

FIRST BOY: Chekhov is one who foretells everything. The Professor [*Correcting himself.*] I mean the Maestro asks me . . . "Do you know anyone that's done this, behaved like this, thought like this?" I find them for him. He tells me which story, which page. A fabulous writer, a magician.

CRISTIANO [*Fully involved.*]: He suffered deeply from men's mediocrity, corruption, their envy and servility. He dissects them with a surgical knife. He sees through, unmasks and exposes them. For instance, if you had an examination, in school, how did you behave? I mean from the time you left your house until you arrived at school. Be careful, now . . . from house to school. Think about it.

FIRST BOY [*After due reflection.*]: I'd drop by the church, say a few prayers, put a few coins in the poor box.

CRISTIANO [*With undisguised satisfaction, to the* SECOND BOY.]: And what about you?

SECOND BOY [*Imitating.*]: I'd drop by the church, say a few prayers, put a few coins in the poor box.

CRISTIANO [*Triumphantly.*]: "A Classical Student." [*By heart.*] "He kissed all the icons, gave two kopecks to a poor man . . ." Sixth chapter, first volume, page thirty-five. You see? He reads into your soul; he gets you down on your knees. It's cowardly to turn to God only in moments of need. You've all done it.

[*Pleased with the result of his questioning.*] Has it ever happened to you, for example, when you're out with a girl, to curse her, as she talks, because later that evening you'll have to escort her all the way home?

FIRST BOY: Yes.

SECOND BOY: Many times.

CRISTIANO [*Triumphantly.*]: "Verochka." Twenty-third chapter, volume four, page 163. [*Carried away with his enthusiasm.*] And more than that—when your father caught you smoking for the first time, what did he say to you?

FIRST BOY: He slapped me.

SECOND BOY: He slapped me.

CRISTIANO [*Annoyed.*]: He must have said something to you afterwards? He must have said that . . . [*He focuses on the* FIRST BOY, *trying, with gestures, to draw out the answer that he wants.*]

FIRST BOY: Yes . . . "It is harmful" . . .

[CRISTIANO *now fixes his attention on the* SECOND BOY.]

SECOND BOY: That cigarettes would weaken you, and would make you impotent when you're still a young man . . .

CRISTIANO [*With satisfaction.*]: That it was bad for your health. [*Reciting.*] " . . . The young Prince became ill and died of consumption when he was only twenty years old . . . " "At Home." Twenty-first chapter, volume four, translated "Defense de Fumer" in the French edition.

SECOND BOY [*Pretending to be sincere.*]: You're amazing! A specialist . . .

CRISTIANO [*Pleased.*]: We live in a world which demands specialists. In the past we knew nothing about everything. Today it's just the reverse.

FIRST BOY [*Feigning sincerity.*]: The reverse.

SECOND BOY [*Admiringly.*]: You should be on "Double or Nothing!"

FIRST BOY: If he were not so shy.

CRISTIANO [*Ignoring this reference to shyness.*]: In his isolation Antoscia's writings show enough vision for ten . . . He suffered for ten . . . he wept for a hundred. [*Caressing his table.*] Even chained to a table it's possible to live intensely . . . to create.

SECOND BOY [*Turning to his companion, with sincerity.*]: Who's Antoscia?

FIRST BOY [*Reprovingly.*]: Chekhov.

CRISTIANO [*Patiently, explaining.*] Antoscia Chekhonté is the nickname given to him by his instructor in religion at the school he attended.

SECOND BOY [*With renewed admiration.*]: What a man this Antoscia was! And did he really write all those plays? I've only seen the one about three sisters who were unhappy because they were forced to sell the cherries which they loved . . .

CRISTIANO [*Fatherly.*]: Those are two different plays. One is about three sisters. The other is about a cherry orchard.

SECOND BOY: Maybe you're right. But they are alike. Such sad, tired people. They talk and walk around and talk some more. They never know what they want. In one of the two plays, the last scene impressed me the most, where they forgot the servant in the house. He was an old man who was devoted to them and they locked up the house with him in it.

FIRST BOY [*Cutting him off.*]: By the way, Maestro, just ask him about his choice of women in those "locked houses." [CRISTIANO *ignores him.*] I'll ask him myself. Allow me, Maestro? [*To his companion, without waiting for* CRISTIANO's *permission.*] You did go to those houses when they were open, didn't you?

SECOND BOY: Of course.

FIRST BOY: We all used to go. [*He looks at* CRISTIANO *from the corner of his eye, who, in return, avoids him. Then, to his friend.*] You go in . . . you look around . . . you make your choice. Whom do you choose?

SECOND BOY: A blonde.

FIRST BOY: What type of blonde?

SECOND BOY: Young.

FIRST BOY [*Impatiently.*]: Fat, thin, pale?

SECOND BOY: Fat. Even if you think of their dirty profession—of all the others they've had—a fat one can still excite you.

FIRST BOY: You don't understand a thing. I, he, we would pick a . . .

CRISTIANO [*Correcting him.*]: The student Vassiliev.

FIRST BOY: The student Vassi . . . he would pick a thin, pale one.

SECOND BOY: Why?

CRISTIANO [*Quoting from memory; with delicacy.*]: " . . . his attention was arrested by a pale face, a little sleepy and tired. She was dark, no longer a young girl, dressed in a spangled gown.

She was sitting in a chair looking at the floor and lost in her thoughts."*

SECOND BOY: It's a question of taste.

CRISTIANO [*Patiently.*]: He would choose a tired, sad person. One who thinks . . . The best of us prefer thinkers . . . intimate suffering. The best of us always choose, prefer meditation—a suffered life. Antoscia is always like this. His best protagonists are tormented. They analyze and dissect themselves. He makes them judges of sorrow and pain. And there is poetry in every one of his descriptions. In the death of an animal, of a child, in the reflection that such deaths stir in the souls of all those around . . .

FIRST BOY [*Pointing to his friend.*]: He lost a child. [*To his friend.*] What did you feel?

SECOND BOY [*Surprised. Trying to hide his embarrassment.*]: A great sorrow . . . very great . [*It is apparent that he does not like to jest with this subject. It is bad luck to talk about the death of a child.*]

CRISTIANO [*Interested.*]: How old was he?

SECOND BOY [*In a low voice.*]: Six, almost six years old.

CRISTIANO: Did you want to talk about it afterwards, did you feel the need to talk?

SECOND BOY [*Embarrassed.*]: I wanted the others to talk about it.

CRISTIANO [*Avidly interested.*]: Go on—tell me all about it.

SECOND BOY: He seemed alive to me when they talked about him— I could see him through their eyes. Instead . . .

CRISTIANO: Instead?

SECOND BOY [*Encouraged by his friend to tell the whole story.*]: I remember, you had found me the job just that day and I would have lost it if you hadn't forced me to go. On the way you were trying to give me some advice about the job, but all I talked about was the child. I tried to talk about him to everyone I met, even to the customers. They would give me a few words of sympathy and then forget all about it. It was terrible . . . They buried him this way . . . they buried him forever.

CRISTIANO [*Excited by a similar event which he has already enjoyed in the pages of Chekhov.*]: Even this, you see, your own feeling, so personal, so difficult, even this he has described. In a beautiful short story, "Anguish." The cab driver, Jona, has

* "The Student Vassiliev."

lost his son, a young man—The situation doesn't change—He tries to talk about it to his customers . . . [*The word "customers," used earlier by the* SECOND BOY, *makes* CRISTIANO *look with suspicion at the* FIRST BOY. *Slowly.*] It seems to me that I had already discussed this story with you.

FIRST BOY [*Embarrassed.*]: Yes, this is the only thing I hadn't asked him. An unusual case. I just didn't think of him . . . It slipped my mind.

CRISTIANO [*Diffident, to* SECOND BOY.]: How old were you when you got married?

SECOND BOY [*Trying to repeat without error.*]: Six—six years ago.

CRISTIANO: You don't even wear a wedding ring.

SECOND BOY: It was an agreement, it was a pact between me and my wife, who was already expecting. [*Pantomimes a pregnant woman.*] "I'll marry you but I won't wear a wedding ring." I have it at home, though. [*With an attempt at humor.*] I haven't pawned it yet.

[*There is an embarrassed pause.* CRISTIANO's *diffidence has chilled the atmosphere.*]

FIRST BOY [*Attempting to clear the air.*]: Let's see, that story about the man who was bored . . . I don't remember . . . the one who doesn't know how to spend his time . . . Oh, yes! [*To* SECOND BOY.] Have you ever tried to read signs upside down?

SECOND BOY: Sure I have.

FIRST BOY: You see? He even wrote about this. Isn't that true, Maestro? "The Story of a Bored Man." [*A silence.*]

CRISTIANO [*Won over.*]: "A Boring Story."

SECOND BOY: Well, if it's boring, why did he write it?

CRISTIANO [*Again fatherly and didactic.*]: He announces his intention, he says it right at the beginning, to stress the boredom which characterizes man's life. Antoscia is loved above all for having written about the emptiness of life, drawing attention to its mediocrity and its futility

SECOND BOY: I know. Ugly women do that too. They admit they are ugly to arouse sympathy and to have you notice how modest they are. They want to attract your interest by hinting great depths and lasting values. [*Encouraged along by his friend.*] You, Maestro, excuse me . . . what kind do you prefer? [CRISTIANO *is above all this. He pretends to read.*] You said before you chose the thoughtful ones who were shy and weary. Tell us, do you like ugly ones, too? I know they can be surprising sometimes. [*Appraisingly.*] They're more passionate, they give more of themselves and better . . . maybe because they don't want to lose you.

FIRST BOY: I, Maestro, was hinting to you that there is someone who . . . she's not beautiful, but . . . she'd even come here. [CRISTIANO *begins to show his nervousness. He hurriedly turns pages. He would like to escape this torture. To the* SECOND BOY.] You know her. Rosanna.

SECOND BOY: Sure. And she's not even expensive. She has a good head, too. I find her reading all the time. [*To his friend.*] Why don't you bring her to him? When his mother's out, I mean the Signora—of course.

FIRST BOY [*Hypocritically.*]: He doesn't want me to.

SECOND BOY: Have you shown him her picture?

FIRST BOY: Yes. Maybe he doesn't like her.

SECOND BOY [*To* CRISTIANO.]: Or do you think the price is too high? She might not even charge an intellectual.

CRISTIANO [*Exploding.*]: That's enough! [*Mastering himself.*] That's all for now, please! I must study.

FIRST BOY [*After looking him over and getting serious.*]: You've read those books a hundred times. That's all you do all day long. A little small talk is good for you once in a while. [*Hypocritically.*] We're your friends and we want to help you.

SECOND BOY: It's none of my business—but how do you manage? Don't you ever go out? [*Pointing to his friend.*] He's told me that . . .

CRISTIANO [*Jumping to his feet; shouting.*]: Get out! Get out! Get out! That's enough! What more do you want? [*Pointing to the pastries, champagne, etc.*] You've brought it—now go!

FIRST BOY [*Arrogantly.*]: And the money? We're waiting for the old lady.

SECOND BOY [*Sure of himself.*]: Quiet, mama's pet, relax. As soon as we get paid we'll go.

CRISTIANO [*Exasperated.*]: She's coming, she's coming! [*Desperately calling his mother, who can't be far away.*] Mamma! Mamma! [*No reply.*] Do me a favor. She's in the next apartment. Up those steps. [*He motions to them to go and find her.*]

FIRST BOY [*Sitting.*]: You go yourself, Maestro.

CRISTIANO [*Beside himself.*]: Slaves! Lackeys! Do you know what "He" would call you? "Slaves in frock coats."

SECOND BOY [*Scornfully.*]: Stop quoting. Find your own words. Where is the frock coat? [*Indicating his own shabby white jacket.*] This is only a lousy jacket. And we had to pay for them out of our own pockets.

[*The* MOTHER *enters with champagne glasses. Alarmed, as she quickly senses that her son is upset. The two boys rise.*]

MOTHER: Cristiano, what have they done to you? Why are you so excited? [*She puts the glasses down, goes over to soothe him.*] I can't leave for a moment. [*Looking at the two boys reprovingly.*] What have they done to you?

FIRST BOY [*Uneasily.*]: Nothing, Signora. We were talking . . .

CRISTIANO [*Looking daggers at him, but to stop any embarrassing explanations.*]: Nothing, Mamma.

FIRST BOY [*Who is eager to get out.*]: We brought the champagne and the pastries . . . Nineteen hundred lire.

MOTHER [*Hunts for money, puts down 2,000 lire.*]: Here, now go!

BOTH BOYS: Thank you, Signora . . . thank you. Goodbye, Maestro.

CRISTIANO: Get out!

[*They exit.*]

MOTHER [*Turning to soothe her son.*]: Calm yourself, Cristiano . . . They're just peasants, coarse, uncivilized . . . maybe they offended you without meaning to.

CRISTIANO [*Gripping the bars.*]: No, no, they *knew* what they were saying!

MOTHER: What?

[*He doesn't answer. The* MOTHER *prefers not to insist. She begins to set the table, carefully arranging the glasses and pastries for a small party.*]

MOTHER: Don't take it so hard, Cristiano . . . you should be used to it, by now . . . All—the few who have occasion to come here— are inquisitive and ask questions. [CRISTIANO *turns to his book. He is glum.*] It's three years now since . . . and a handsome young man like you! It's all right to want to study . . . it's all right to want to be alone, but . . . [*Pause; the* MOTHER *looks at him with grief.*] Three years ago, if you had gone to visit a friend and had found him living as you are, you would have been surprised and you would have asked . . . maybe with tact, maybe with curiosity, or scornfully.

CRISTIANO: Now, you too!

MOTHER [*Not heeding him.*]: It depends on a person's education. You would have found just the right words to use because you're educated . . . well read . . . the others aren't. [*She stops short, not daring to start another discussion.*] Your sister's fiancé, for example . . .

CRISTIANO [*Looking up.*]: Well?

MOTHER: He's a laborer . . . One can't expect . . .

CRISTIANO: Expect what?

MOTHER [*Falteringly.*]: Perhaps, without meaning to, he could offend you.

CRISTIANO [*Pointing to the chair nearest the cage.*]: Make him sit here. I'll bash his face in.

MOTHER [*Upset.*]: Please, Cristiano . . . You'll ruin your sister's happiness . . . Please! She'll die! Be patient. I don't think he'll ask any questions, but . . .

CRISTIANO [*Suspiciously.*]: Why won't he ask any questions?

MOTHER: Because . . . he's a fine boy . . . he's made a good impression on me . . .

CRISTIANO: What have you told him?

MOTHER [*Alarmed.*]: I . . . nothing, nothing . . . I've only seen him on the street, once . . . This will be his first visit here . . . we kept postponing . . .

CRISTIANO [*Interrupting.*]: Because of me.

MOTHER: No. He was just an apprentice. He was waiting . . . not because of you . . . In fact . . .

CRISTIANO: In fact?

MOTHER [*Slowly.*]: Your sister loves you. She's counting on you. I beg you . . . for her sake . . .

CRISTIANO: I'm not a child.

MOTHER [*After a pause.*]: I've promised her . . . [*There is a pause. She fears* CRISTIANO's *reaction.*]

CRISTIANO: What?

MOTHER [*Timidly.*]: To signal her if . . .

CRISTIANO: If?

MOTHER [*Entreatingly.*]: If you come out of the cage.

CRISTIANO [*With finality.*]: No. No. No.

MOTHER [*Imploringly.*]: Only for half an hour, I beg you. You can sit there, in the corner. You don't have to leave the room. It's the same for you.

CRISTIANO: I'm not a hypocrite. I'd feel dirty if I did a thing like that. For you it's easy. You're all dishonest from habit. But I'm not. [*With derision.*] The champagne, the pastries, the borrowed glasses, all because someone is coming to relieve you of another mouth to feed.

MOTHER: Don't talk like this, please. If you really don't want to . . . [*Making another attempt.*] It was only for your sister's sake. Just for half an hour . . . [*No answer; she goes toward the window. After a pause, hopefully.*] May I open the window?

CRISTIANO: No.

MOTHER [*Drying a tear.*]: All right, I understand. It's a question of principle . . . of character . . . you're a man, you've decided to shut yourself up for three, four, five years . . . How many? [*No answer.*] How many? [CRISTIANO *is bent over his book. Decisively.*] If you say four or five, I'll respect your wishes. If you don't answer, I'll open the cage. [*She pulls out a key and goes towards the cage.*]

CRISTIANO [*Very alarmed.*]: No, Mamma, no! [*He holds back her hands.*] I promise not to give you any more trouble . . . try to understand, Mamma . . .

[NELLA, *her pretty, young daughter, enters breathlessly, her fiancé supposedly following.*]

NELLA [*Anxiously, to her mother.*]: Well?

MOTHER [*With a despairing gesture.*]: He doesn't want to.

[*Without looking at her brother,* NELLA *goes out, dejected. She detains her fiancé outside, probably speaking to him.*]

CRISTIANO [*Nervously, not seeing them enter.*]: What's she telling him?

MOTHER [*Nervous also.*]: Nothing. What are you imagining? She's probably kissing him.

[NELLA *and* SERGIO *finally enter.* SERGIO *is a man about thirty. He's "simpatico" in the Italian meaning of the word. An ordinary worker, straight-forward and honest. Evidently forewarned, looks over the cage with definite curiosity.*]

SERGIO [*Taking the* MOTHER'*s hands in his.*]: "Mammetta," thank
you for this invitation. [*He gives her a kiss, then turns toward*
CRISTIANO.]

NELLA: This is my brother, Cristiano.

SERGIO: How do you do?

CRISTIANO: Pleased to meet you. [SERGIO *watches him for a few*
seconds. CRISTIANO "*escapes.*"]

[*They sit in embarrassed silence;* CRISTIANO *partially turned*
away from the rest.]

SERGIO [*Looking around.*]: This is a big room. You didn't do it
justice when you told me about it. There's space, plenty of
air . . .

MOTHER: This is it. [*Motioning to left.*] Pietro, my other son, and
his wife sleep there. [*Points right, then to daughter.*] We two
sleep over there . . .

[*There is a pause. The* MOTHER *looks at* CRISTIANO'*s bed, but*
says nothing.]

CRISTIANO [*Banging his hand on bed.*]: I sleep here.

SERGIO: There are only two little rooms in my house, just two by
four. [*Hugging his fiancé, who is close to him.*] You'll feel as if
you're in a cage. [*Pause.* CRISTIANO *stares at* SERGIO, *suspicious*
of a hidden meaning.]

NELLA [*Looking at* CRISTIANO, *fearing some kind of a reaction.*
She draws close to SERGIO.]: We'll be alone. That's what counts.

SERGIO [*Having caught his mistake, doesn't turn.*]: Mother will
use the smaller room, when she's in the house. We'll be alone
all the time. [*A pause. To* CRISTIANO.] When will your brother
be back? [CRISTIANO *nods toward his mother.*]

MOTHER: Pretty soon. [*Pointing again to the bed on the left.*]
Chiara is at her mother's.

SERGIO [*Gaily.*]: They're all alive, these mothers-in-law!

[*They all laugh.*]

MOTHER [*Lightly.*]: "A bad weed never dies."

[CRISTIANO *is nervous and on the defensive; he suspects double*
meaning in all allusions.]

SERGIO [*Caressing* NELLA.]: You'll love my mother. She's an angel.

And with yours—I hope I'll never have any occasion to quarrel.
[*Looking at* MOTHER *warmly.*] She seems gentle. What do you
say, Cristiano?

CRISTIANO [*Who is forced to answer.*]: She's a mother.

SERGIO [*To* MOTHER.]: Did you hear? "A Mother." He's given you
a compliment. Bravo, Cristiano.

MOTHER [*Picking up the tray.*]: Would you like a pastry?

SERGIO: Shouldn't we wait for the others?

MOTHER: There's plenty. [*She offers one to the guest, who passes
it, underhand, to* NELLA: *the* MOTHER *then passes one to* CRIS-
TIANO, *still fearing his touchiness. She turns to* SERGIO.] Finished,
already?

SERGIO [*Laughing.*]: It was such a small one! One bite. May I?
[*He takes another, eats it.* NELLA *takes hers, then kisses* SERGIO
on the neck and caresses him. CRISTIANO *is annoyed and pretends
not to see.*] Would you like a cigarette? [*Offers them to*
CRISTIANO.]

CRISTIANO: I don't smoke.

SERGIO: Do you mind if I offer one to your sister?

CRISTIANO: Ask Mamma.

MOTHER: When Pietro sees her smoking he slaps her. If you
want to risk it . . .

SERGIO [*Sure of himself.*]: We'll risk it. [*Lights* NELLA's *cigarette.*
CRISTIANO *signals to his* MOTHER *that he'd like another pastry.*
SERGIO *notices this.*] Anyhow, I see you like sweets.

CRISTIANO [*Peevishly.*]: You've had two already.

SERGIO: That's right.

[MOTHER *and daughter begin to be on the alert, fearful.*]

NELLA: I'm the one who ate two. He gave the first one to me.

[CRISTIANO *is annoyed, not having noticed the byplay.*]

SERGIO [*To* NELLA.]: Your brother doesn't miss a thing. He has the
gift of seeing and listening without giving himself away, but
something may escape him when . . .

CRISTIANO [*Impolitely.*]: Nothing escapes me. I already know all
about you.

SERGIO: Congratulations! Tell us.

CRISTIANO: Your fingers are yellow from nicotine. You smoke a
lot. You've been eyeing the champagne. You drink. You can

charm women. You know them. There's a newspaper in your pocket . . . [*He points to it.*] You're interested in politics.

SERGIO [*Pleasantly, though a bit disconcerted.*]: Good . . . I see you have a real talent for observation. But I don't think I lost much in their eyes.

CRISTIANO: That was not my intention.

SERGIO: You've pointed out two vices and two virtues.

CRISTIANO: Which are the virtues?

SERGIO: The last two. [*Pause.*] Don't you agree?

CRISTIANO: No.

SERGIO: It's a matter of opinion. [*A pause.*]

MOTHER [*Imprudently.*]: What do you think of my Cristiano?

CRISTIANO [*Violently, to his* MOTHER.]: What do you want to know? He'll tell her later and she'll tell you.

NELLA [*Reprovingly.*]: Cristiano . . .

SERGIO: Why do you say "later"? I have already formed my opinion.

CRISTIANO [*Sarcastically.*]: What is it?

SERGIO: I'm not a scholar like you, and less of an observer, but . . .

CRISTIANO: Speak up!

SERGIO: Mine are only general impressions. Compared to your sharp and intelligent deductions . . .

CRISTIANO: Go on!

SERGIO: Impressions, more than anything else . . .

CRISTIANO: What are they?

SERGIO [*To the* MOTHER.]: Your son is a determined young man.

CRISTIANO: Don't evade the issue.

SERGIO [*Cornered.*]: It might be better, before giving one's own impression, the first one, if . . .

CRISTIANO: I'll tell you what the first one is. Curiosity. [*He studies* SERGIO.]

SERGIO: Maybe.

CRISTIANO: I'll take care of that right away. [*Pointing to the bed.*] My pot is under the bed. Women? As before. One can live without them. How do priests manage? Without them.

NELLA [*Bursting into tears.*]: Mamma . . .

MOTHER [*Going toward cage.*]: Please, Cristiano . . .

CRISTIANO [*To the* MOTHER.]: Let me talk. [*To* SERGIO.] Are you satisfied? [*There is a tense pause.*]

SERGIO [*Caressing* NELLA *and succeeding in calming her.*]: I wanted to say, first of all, that you are . . . intelligent, morbidly sensitive . . . I will add, "Spiteful" . . . full of hatred for everyone . . . unjustified hatred . . . [*Emphasizing.*] No matter what they've done to you.

CRISTIANO: Who?

SERGIO [*Slowly, staring at him.*]: People.

[PIETRO *enters dressed in his work clothes. He is tired. He notices* NELLA *drying her tears before presenting her fiancé to him.*]

PIETRO [*Severely, looking at* CRISTIANO, *whom he suspects.*]: What happened?

[SERGIO *starts to shake his hand to distract him.*]

SERGIO: Ciao. It's a pleasure to meet you at last.

PIETRO: Ciao. [*He continues to stare at* CRISTIANO, *expecting an answer.*]

MOTHER [*Pointing to* CRISTIANO, *in confirmation.*]: Nothing . . . [*She makes a vague gesture.*]

PIETRO [*Kissing his sister's forehead, and inviting the guest to sit.*]: Don't pay any attention to him. [*He sits with his back to* CRISTIANO, *ignoring him.*] My sister has told me a lot about you. She's really in love. How much are you making?

SERGIO: Forty-two thousand lire.

NELLA [*Quickly.*]: We've already figured it out. Twelve for the rent, twenty-seven for food and three for emergencies.

PIETRO: And do you also have a mother to take care of?

SERGIO: She eats very little, poor thing. She's promised to pay for the electricity, water, and gas. A real saint.

PIETRO: You're lucky! [*Pointing to* NELLA.] Living like that she'll keep her figure.

SERGIO: As you know, young people today get employment through the church if they promise not to join our union. Imagine . . . !

PIETRO: Last month, at the factory we were able to squeeze out five lire more an hour. Everybody went on strike. Even the most obedient churchgoers.

SERGIO: That's the way it should always be. There is plenty of work. I'm hoping for a lot of overtime in the next few months.

PIETRO [*To* MOTHER.]: How about something to drink, mamma?

MOTHER: Aren't we going to wait for Chiara?

PIETRO [*Firmly.*]: No. [*While the* MOTHER *is opening the first bottle, to* SERGIO.] When do you plan to be married?

SERGIO [*As* NELLA *cuddles up to him.*]: Very soon. I'm over thirty. [*He kisses* NELLA.]: She won't want me any more if I wait too long.

NELLA [*Responding to the kiss while* CRISTIANO *watches them with condescendence.*]: Always.

PIETRO: In the beginning it's "always."

NELLA: Only in the beginning?

PIETRO: He and I understand each other.

NELLA [*Pretending reproof.*]: So! So you've already gotten together?

SERGIO: Between men of "virtue!" [*Looks at* CRISTIANO.]

PIETRO: A church wedding?

NELLA: Naturally.

SERGIO: It's back in style. To avoid trouble. [*To* CRISTIANO.] Will you come, too?

CRISTIANO: Just because I talked about priests? No. You know that.

PIETRO [*Very surprised.*]: Did you talk about priests? Really? You got him to talk to you? What did he say about them? He studied with them and for a while I thought he was a religious fanatic. He never opens up. He's a living question mark . . . [*Points to* CRISTIANO, *without looking.*]

SERGIO: You should talk to him more, try to help him. Maybe he's lonely.

PIETRO: And who locked him up in there? We know how many tears mamma has shed.

SERGIO: There must be a reason for it. You should find out what it is.

PIETRO: It would take the patience of a saint. Mamma still tries. She puts the key under his nose twice a day and begs him to come out. I don't. I've been ignoring him for months. I'm fed up with his nonsense.

CRISTIANO [*Grips the bars, roaring. To* SERGIO.]: Just leave me alone!

PIETRO: Don't mind him. He's harmless.

[CRISTIANO *utters menacing words, incomprehensible and indistinct; he is very agitated. The* MOTHER *goes over to console him.*]

SERGIO: You shouldn't talk to him like that.

PIETRO: I'll tell you why I do. [*In a low voice, seeing that* CRISTIANO *is not listening.*] Every time I insult him, and tell him that he's a useless clown and knows nothing about the world, etc., he usually shows signs of improvement . . . he asks for newspapers, comments on them out loud to show he's well informed on current events. To annoy me.

SERGIO: That might be the right cure.

PIETRO: I think it's the only one. I offend him just in the hope that he'll react and decide to be a man. [*To* MOTHER.] Nothing to drink? [*The* MOTHER *continues to calm* CRISTIANO.] Leave him with his "Antoscia."

[MOTHER *continues to soothe* CRISTIANO *for a moment, then returns to get the bottle.*]

SERGIO: Chekhov. Nella told me about this passion. He's an important writer.

PIETRO: That may be, but this is a fixation with him. You can ask him how many syllables there are to a page . . . you can ask anything you want to know from any volume . . . and he can tell you. He's a fanatic, and I'm not sure that those books aren't partly to blame for his condition. He's always quoting sad, sordid stories . . . cases of corruption and cruelty. A gallery of spineless men . . . crawling at the feet of overdecorated lackeys in uniforms.

SERGIO: It's better than nothing. Better than not reading at all.

PIETRO: He knows nothing else. Take politics. He doesn't even care who's president. And women . . . I'll go into that later. [*To the* MOTHER.] How about a drink?

MOTHER [*Timidly.*]: Aren't we going to wait for Chiara?

PIETRO [*Emphatically.*]: No. [*The* MOTHER *opens the champagne. They ad-lib. The cork pops.* NELLA *kisses* SERGIO. *She hands him a glass.* SERGIO *offers the glass to* CRISTIANO, *insists and succeeds in making him take it.*] This makes you forget the past . . . gives hope for the future!

ALL: To the future!

MOTHER: To my children.

PIETRO [*To the engaged couple.*]: To your happiness!

[*The toast is interrupted by the entrance of* CHIARA, *a seductive, voluptuous woman.* PIETRO, *ignoring* CHIARA's *presence, drinks. The others wait.*]

CHIARA [*Everyone looks at her as she moves with confidence toward* SERGIO; *offering him her hand.*]: I'm sorry I'm late. My best wishes. [SERGIO *offers her his glass.*] Thank you.

[PIETRO *fills another glass and gives it to* SERGIO.]

PIETRO [*To his wife.*]: Isn't she dead yet?
CHIARA: Who?
PIETRO: Didn't you go to your "sick old mother"? Isn't she dead yet?
CHIARA [*Simply.*]: No. She's holding on so she can enjoy your funeral.

[*There is a cold silence.*]

PIETRO [*Pouring a second glass, clinks it with force against his wife's glass.*]: To happiness . . . in marriage.
CHIARA [*Defiant; ignoring the champagne which* PIETRO *spilled.*]: To happiness!!

[*They all drink.*]

Curtain

Act Two

SCENE: *Same as ACT I. Early morning.*

At right the bed of the mother and daughter is unmade. They have already gone out. In the cage, motionless, CRISTIANO *seems to be asleep. From left is heard the sound of an alarm clock.* PIETRO *jumps out of bed, pulls the curtain which shows* CHIARA *still asleep. He opens the shutters and puts on his pants.*

PIETRO [*Half uncovering his wife.*]: Get my coffee!! [CHIARA *continues to sleep;* PIETRO *goes to wash. He, shouting, while drying himself.*] Coffee! [CHIARA *doesn't answer. He decides to heat*

the coffee himself. He goes to get his shoes, sees they are dirty,
looks at her angrily. He gives shoes a quick polish and puts
them on, muttering. Looks at her with hatred while he drinks
his coffee. Shaking her.] Wake up! Wake up! It's late . . .
[With his jacket over his arm, he starts to go out cursing her.
Then, feeling he's being too lenient, he goes back.] Just look at
you! Everyone's at work and you . . . *[Gestures as though to*
strike her.] My mother and my sister are already up and out
and you . . . *[Irritated, he rips the covers off.]* Get up! Get up!

*[*CHIARA, *half nude, sits on the edge of the bed looking at him*
sleepily, without understanding. PIETRO, *with some satisfaction,*
leaves, slamming the door and uttering indistinct threats.
CHIARA *falls back on the bed groping for the covers but can't*
find them. She stretches out with her face against the pillow,
half naked and with one arm hanging out. There is a pause.
She and CRISTIANO *both seem to be asleep.* CHIARA, *however,*
is aware that CRISTIANO *is watching her.]*

CHIARA *[Without raising her head.]*: Why are you spying on me?
CRISTIANO *[Pretending indignation.]*: Me?!? *[Another pause.]*
CHIARA: Haven't you ever seen a naked woman?
CRISTIANO *[After a pause.]*: Why does your husband hate you?
CHIARA *[Still half dozing.]*: All husbands hate their wives.
CRISTIANO: Why?
CHIARA *[With ambiguity.]*: Because we like being in bed.
CRISTIANO *[Timidly, entreatingly.]*: I'm sorry, I didn't understand
. . . For me it's important . . . Did you say . . . "bed" meaning . . . ?
CHIARA: I was joking.
CRISTIANO: Not really. It may be true. I've thought about it.
CHIARA: It's the man who takes the initiative. He trains her as
he likes.
CRISTIANO: And what if she was trained by someone else?
CHIARA *[Raising her head with a look toward him.]*: You're no fool!
You figured it out.
CRISTIANO: You . . . how were you "trained"? *[*CHIARA *gives him a*
long look with indefinable expression. CRISTIANO, *timidly, regret-*
fully.] Excuse me . . . But he's thrown it in your face so many
times . . . he calls your mother a slut and says that she gave you
too much freedom . . . *[Ashamed of all he has dared to say.]*
Forgive me.

CHIARA [*Bitterly.*]: It's true. To love "him" means to be in love. To have loved "another," *before,* means being a slut. Trouble is . . . in our country we can't make a mistake. Each woman is entitled to *one* man only for life.

CRISTIANO [*Disturbed.*]: You'll have to admit that for a man it's terrible to think of others caressing the body of the one you love . . . it's enough to drive you mad!

CHIARA: There must be one person in life, the first—the one we have believed in . . . It could be you, someone else, that doesn't matter. What does matter is who continues to love, who keeps the flame alive, not the one who has possessed, touched . . . No trace of that stays with us, Cristiano, believe me.

CRISTIANO: But if the other one . . . say that the other . . . [*Finds difficulty expressing himself.*]

CHIARA: What are you trying to say?

CRISTIANO: Living with that "first one." Many months, for example, a long time . . . he's had time to . . . everything . . .

CHIARA: Everything what?

CRISTIANO: It's terrible. You . . . you told Pietro?

CHIARA: Yes.

CRISTIANO: And he?

CHIARA: He had the good taste not to insist.

CRISTIANO: At first he must have wanted to know . . . the particulars . . . the details . . .

CHIARA: You're sick. There aren't any "details" as you say. Nothing but love exists, being comfortable together. I've been through this twice in my life. And now I'm not even "comfortable" with Pietro. [*Wide awake now, she stares at* CRISTIANO.] I'm a new woman, understand? A new woman, clean . . . ready to be born tomorrow, to love deeply for the first time. It is always the first time.

CRISTIANO: And the memory—the memory of how someone else . . . the way he . . . he was perhaps more . . .

CHIARA: More what?

CRISTIANO: More . . . you know what I mean . . . men are different. For example, I have less experience than others.

CHIARA [*Maternally.*]: Look, Cristiano, that's exactly your trouble. You put too much value on sex . . . [CRISTIANO *listens intently though timidly.*] Your brother and I don't get along for other reasons.

CRISTIANO: What are they?

CHIARA [*Listlessly.*]: We "trapped him," he says. I gave in to him right away and he had to marry me. I had a miscarriage twenty days after the wedding and NO man forgives that kind of miscarriage. If he had waited twenty days, he could have kept the freedom that he lost out of sentiment.

CRISTIANO: What about you?

CHIARA: I was his because I loved him . . . He was a strong, healthy man and he seemed kind . . . [*Sadly.*] What I lack now is only a caress, a kind word . . . He could win me back with a kiss on the forehead, on my hand . . . [*She looks at her hands.*] . . . They're ugly now, I know, but no more than they were yesterday. There was a time when he'd kiss them. You don't know what it means, to a woman, to be given a little kindness, a flower . . . I said "bed" before, only jokingly. What I meant more than anything else was my laziness. [*Looking at him.*] I didn't mean what *you* were thinking.

CRISTIANO [*Reflecting, slowly.*]: What you've just said is beautiful and it may be true. Hate can be born from other reasons. I wouldn't act like that with my wife.

CHIARA: I know.

CRISTIANO [*Surprised.*]: You know?

CHIARA: Your woman will be happy.

CRISTIANO [*Still very surprised.*]: Do you really think so? Why? What do you know about me?

CHIARA: It's just a feeling. A woman's intuition.

CRISTIANO [*Entreating her.*]: Please . . . be more specific . . . You know something. Maybe you've understood, you can help me . . .

CHIARA: How? [*A pause.*] Why don't you answer?

CRISTIANO [*Evasively.*]: What makes you think I would know how to make a woman happy?

CHIARA: Go out . . . love someone . . . she'll be grateful to you. [CRISTIANO, *frustrated by the suggestion of going out and facing "the others," bows his head.*] What are you doing in there? You're wasting away, growing old . . . You mustn't be afraid. There's a place for everyone in this world.

CRISTIANO [*Painfully.*]: Who would be able to understand and love me? Who?

CHIARA: The world is full of women. [CRISTIANO *drops his head again, frustrated. After a brief pause,* CHIARA, *reading his thoughts.*] They think as I do, Cristiano, all of them. Don't be afraid of a woman . . . All she'll ask of you is a little love so she can feel alive, and useful . . .

CRISTIANO [*Raising his head.*]: You . . . you're not loved. How do you put up with it?

CHIARA [*Putting on her old slippers.*]: You see. I'm waiting.

CRISTIANO: For what?

CHIARA: Like all women in a catholic country I'm waiting for a miracle.

CRISTIANO: What miracle?

CHIARA: Where divorce doesn't exist? . . . A death. . . .

CRISTIANO: What do you mean?

CHIARA: I was just joking. I'm waiting for love.

CRISTIANO: Hoping . . . that he? . . .

CHIARA: No.

CRISTIANO: What, then?

CHIARA [*Vaguely.*]: Love for a child, the warmth of someone near to us . . . [*Looking directly at him.*] Your friendship . . .

CRISTIANO [*Troubled.*]: You know, Chiara, I . . .

CHIARA: Finally, you said my name! This is the way one begins to love people. A person's name is something engraved, inseparable. If someone calls you by name, you feel alive . . . born, needed. [*Enjoying it.*] "Cristiano" . . . yours is beautiful. [*Scantily clad, she moves seductively toward the cage looking beautiful and languidly feline.*]

CRISTIANO [*Disturbed.*]: Chiara . . .

CHIARA [*Turning her back to him.*]: Thank you. You have made me feel alive twice today. Today I'll be happy and I owe it to you. [*She turns on the small radio; subtle background music is heard. She moves about the room, enticing in her transparent slip.* CRISTIANO's *eyes follow her.*]

CRISTIANO [*Insistently, as* CHIARA *begins to make the bed.*]: What makes you think that I could make a woman happy?

CHIARA: You're convinced of it yourself. That's a good beginning.

CRISTIANO: I think so. But *you* . . . What makes you think I could?

CHIARA [*Slowly.*]: Those who fear they'll not make a woman happy are always the best ones. [*Studying him.*] Last night you practiced with the weights until late. You were looking at your hands—

you have the will to succeed. But you need a different kind of practice . . . exercising your feelings, a humility which will let you feel equal to others—which is a privilege—the desire to understand them and to be understood . . . Even with your brains—[*Pointing to books.*]—forgetting them for a moment— you've already begun. [CRISTIANO *looks at her questioningly; he doesn't understand.*]

CHIARA: By talking with me you know me a little better . . . you understand me; perhaps you can even justify my . . .

CRISTIANO: If they were all like you!

CHIARA: We always say that—to everyone—to everyone we've allowed to speak—whose world we haven't rejected because of our own lack of esteem, our disgust, our laziness . . . What do you think of your sister?

CRISTIANO: She's not bad . . . Perhaps a little stupid.

CHIARA: What sort of conversation have you ever had with her?— "Bring me a glass of water"; "Did you wash my handkerchiefs?"; "Change the sheets"—I've talked to her seriously. I know her better than you do. She's a very sensitive girl—your blood. Hungry for love. But she's been able to get it. Her husband will be happy.

CRISTIANO: That peasant.

CHIARA: There, you see? This is your problem. Thinking you are superior to "peasants." Sergio may not be able to write letters correctly, but he knows how to live. To live, do you understand? An eighteen-year-old illiterate who has a child and loves him is more important than you who can quote ten books from memory but do not . . . [*She sees that she has offended him too cruelly and moderates her language.*] . . . than you who don't live among men . . . don't know how to find your own happiness . . . [*Moves toward him, strokes his hair.*] I'm sorry. [CRISTIANO *lifts his face to her, looking at her gratefully. He kisses her hand, which is close to his mouth.* CHIARA *is surprised and moved. She pulls her hand back and casually caresses it. There is a knock on the door.* CHIARA *puts on a housecoat and opens the door.* SERGIO *enters, jovial as usual, carrying his electrical kit and newspapers.*]

SERGIO: Good morning my little sister-in-law. [*He kisses her spontaneously on the cheek.*] Ciao, Cristiano. [*He offers his hand to* CRISTIANO *who, unhappy at the intrusion, takes it with-*

out enthusiasm.] I have to repair an installation nearby. They're still asleep, so I'll go there later. [*He sits.*] So, Cristiano, how are you?

CRISTIANO: Alright. Nella's not in.

SERGIO: I know. I went by the marketplace. [*Brief embarrassment.*]

CHIARA [*Her housecoat unfastened, she shuffles about the room.*]: Would you like some coffee?

SERGIO: Thank you. I never refuse it. [*Another short embarrassed silence. To* CRISTIANO, *with whom he now talks more familiarly.*] Did you read about yesterday's massacre? Here is the follow-up. [*Hands him paper, which* CRISTIANO *takes half-heartedly. To* CHIARA.] There's been a small raise in salaries. Pietro will bring you more money this month.

CHIARA [*Sarcastically.*]: We'll go on a spree!

SERGIO: You women are never content. Look at the way we fight for you.

CHIARA: A thousand more, a thousand less. Everything is going up.

SERGIO [*Ironically.*]: Except gas—

CHIARA: Good for those who have cars.

SERGIO: Patience, my little sister-in-law. The day of the ten-thousand-lire raise will come. [*To* CRISTIANO, *who has been glancing at the article.*] What do you say?

CRISTIANO: The same old thing. Four idealists get themselves killed in the name of "liberty." Again whites firing at blacks. It's far away. It's not our business.

SERGIO: We're one big family—the human race. When one small nucleus rebels, frees itself, we should be happy. We should feel ourselves one with them. What do you feel, what do you think, when you know they have become masters of their own destiny?

CRISTIANO: Nothing.

SERGIO: A little admiration, sympathy?

CRISTIANO: No.

[CHIARA, *without making it obvious, listens intently.*]

SERGIO: They're men like us. We've fought our wars for independence; they're fighting theirs. They're small victories on the road to progress. Every man is enriched by the victories of his brothers.

CRISTIANO: Every man lives his own life, alone. [*Reciting from memory an extract from Chekhov.*] "We have advanced on the road to personal perfection, but has this progress had a significant influence on the life around us? Has it, at least, brought advantage to someone? No."

[SERGIO *looks at him, surprised at the unexpected outburst; then looks at* CHIARA *who is preparing the coffee.*]

CHIARA [*With sarcasm.*]: Chekhov. Such and such a volume, such and such a story, page so and so.

CRISTIANO [*Being specific.*]: "My Life"—last story of the eleventh volume, page 27.

SERGIO [*Continuing.*]: It's true up to a certain point. You study, but you're not useful to anyone. I read, but I can be useful to someone. I have opportunities, I see people, I . . . communicate . . . [*Pause;* CRISTIANO *smiles condescendingly; he does not respond.*] A man is worth what he is able to give and every man is happy if he gives. In the end every man is author of his own life and of his own happiness.

CRISTIANO [*Quoting from memory.*]: "But what the devil kind of an author is he if it takes only a toothache or a mean mother-in-law to send his happiness out the window?" From "A Happy Man."

[SERGIO *looks at* CRISTIANO, *stunned; then at* CHIARA *who smiles maliciously.*]

CHIARA [*Throwing out her arms.*]: Chekhov. Such and such a story . . . [*With a gesture she invites* CRISTIANO *to name the page;* CRISTIANO *this time has the sense to be quiet.*]

SERGIO: And you, do you allow your happiness to be ruined by a toothache or a mother-in-law?

CRISTIANO: It's possible.

SERGIO [*To* CHIARA *with an eloquent gesture.*]: Would you say the screws are loose up there?

CHIARA [*Filling cups.*]: Not loose, just rusty. [*Brings coffee.*] He's a spoiled child. [*She stares at* CRISTIANO *until he avoids her look.*] At fourteen they should have pushed him out into the world among people to fight his way with the strongest. To fight for a piece of bread, for a woman. Now he would appreciate and know the value of a piece of bread, of possessing a woman. [*She drinks her coffee.*] Drink, you'll be able to argue better.

SERGIO: Thank you.

CRISTIANO: Thank you.

[*They drink while* CHIARA *draws curtain to bed at left, then to bed at right. She begins to heat some water.*]

SERGIO [*To* CRISTIANO.]: What a temperament! [CRISTIANO *looks at him in disapproval.*] She has a head on her shoulders, that one.

CHIARA [*Who has heard.*]: If I did, I wouldn't be here. [*The two look at her with interest.*]

CRISTIANO [*In a low voice.*]: Where would you be?

CHIARA [*Mysteriously.*]: Far, far away . . .

SERGIO: Alone?

CHIARA [*Who may be joking.*]: Does anyone with a head on her shoulders stay alone? [SERGIO, *finished with his coffee, takes his and* CRISTIANO's *cups to the sink.* CRISTIANO *is trembling.*]

[SERGIO *whispers a few words to* CHIARA. CRISTIANO *is impatient and nervous at not being able to hear what they are saying. It must be some compliment.*]

CHIARA [*Coquettish.*]: Thank you.

SERGIO [*Returns to his chair near cage. Pause.*]: Nella saw you reading yesterday.

CRISTIANO: I always read.

SERGIO: I mean the newspapers I sent to you.

CRISTIANO: So now she's become a spy. Where did you see her?

SERGIO: I told you, at the marketplace. They hadn't sold much. [*A pause.*] Didn't you find anything in the ads?

CRISTIANO: Ads don't interest me. [*Sarcastically.*] I nourished my mind with those headlines. Yesterday you said that man is "good, a marvelous creature" and that it's not true we are living in a jungle. [*Reads headlines from various newspapers.*]— "Caserta. Sells his fiancée in order to pay his debts."—"Paris. The Legion of Honor bestowed on a torturer of the Algerians."—"He worked in a factory with a broken arm. He's been denounced for theft."—"Homosexuals' den raided in Palermo."—"She elopes with a Latin Professor."—"Only those who have many children can find work because the boss gets an allowance for each." [*With emphasis.*]—"Young wife condemned to five year sentence for mutilating husband during honeymoon because of negligence and rejection."—"Student writes to his mother: 'I'm eating well.' Found dead from starvation."—[*Turning pages.*] And this other one [*Reads with disgust, shuddering.*]—"A

thirteen-year-old working girl, scalped. The 13-year-old Maria
Bucelli was left completely scalped by a machine called the
'Twister.' Her hair became caught in the gears, scalping her
completely." Not like the Indians in the movies, even her eyebrows and ears . . . This is your world, the "outside." A jungle
infested with beasts. [*Quoting from memory another extract.*]
"I don't understand men and I fear them. The sight of them
frightens me. I don't know for what divine purpose they suffer
and for what reason they live." [*Wearily, disheartened.*] "Fear."
It's fear what destroys men.

SERGIO [*Disconcerted by these frequent, sad quotations.*]: I don't
say you are wrong . . . On the whole you're right. There is suffering and fear "outside," but less all the time. This you've got to
recognize! And thanks to those who fight.

CRISTIANO [*Ignoring the last words.*]: "From early morning till
night they bend their backs. They become sick from doing
work beyond their strength. Throughout their lives they tremble
with fear for their sick and hungry children. Throughout their
lives they fear death and sickness. They fade early, grow old
quickly, and die in filth and stench. Their children growing up
begin the same round and thus centuries go by and millions of
men live worse than beasts: only to earn a piece of bread, but
always in a state of fear.*

[CHIARA, *in the meantime, has prepared a tub with water. She
sits down with her back to* SERGIO *and begins washing her legs.*
CRISTIANO *does not take his eyes off her.*]

SERGIO: I agree about the fears. All of Chekhov's world is like this
—sad, desperate. [*Following* CRISTIANO's *intense gaze, he looks
at* CHIARA's *legs.*] But as time goes by, everything changes. One
learns to fight; suffering and misery become less.

CRISTIANO [*Continues to stare at* CHIARA's *legs, fascinated.*]:
"Shrinking from the cold, he thought that such a wind had blown
in the days of Ruirik and in the time of Ivan the Terrible and
Peter. In their time there was exactly the same desperate poverty
and hunger." **

SERGIO [*Forcing himself to be patient.*]: Wonderful. You're a
genius. You even know who Ruirik is!

* "The House with the Mansard."
** "The Student."

CRISTIANO [*Still looking at* CHIARA.]: The footnote says that he was a Norman chief who died in 879.

SERGIO [*Sarcastically.*]: You even know the footnotes. I repeat— You're a genius. But what use do you make of all this knowledge?

CHIARA [*To whom* SERGIO *now turns.*]: If you were smart you'd cut it short by telling him that fifty years have passed since Chekhov's time. And what years! [SERGIO *too is now excited by* CHIARA'S *legs.* CRISTIANO *is jealous and resents the fact that* SERGIO *too is staring at them.*]

SERGIO: Our Union has advised us not to praise the Soviet Union all the time. We would be guilty of servility as those who always praise everything coming from America. [*Fascinated by and admiring* CHIARA'S *shapely legs.*] With all the blessings of God we have right here in Italy . . .

CHIARA [*Flattered.*]: Not so dumb these "peasants." [*She looks over at* CRISTIANO.]

CRISTIANO [*Who now has* SERGIO'S *attention.*]: The corruption is in Man. In our anguish, in our feelings of helplessness, and in our uselessness.

SERGIO: I've found a job for you. [*Pause.*]

CHIARA [*Drying her legs.*]: Really? What kind of a job?

SERGIO [*Turning to* CHIARA.]: Easy work, very pleasant.

CRISTIANO: Who asked you?

SERGIO: No one. I wanted to help you, to make you feel needed.

CHIARA: What kind of work?

SERGIO: Keeping the union library in order. Just the job for you.

CHIARA [*With enthusiasm.*]: Splendid! I'll come to you for advice and borrow books.

SERGIO: Exactly! You'll be advising people what to read. You could start with a couple of lectures on Chekhov. You know him by heart.

CRISTIANO: Would they understand? [*Embarrassed silence.*]

SERGIO [*Patiently.*]: Suppose they are all illiterates. You're a genius,—why don't you give them a little of your knowledge? In what way are they different from you? They have two eyes, two ears, a brain. You could improve them.

CRISTIANO [*Enraptured as usual by his quotations learned by memory.*]: No improvement is possible. " . . . As she walked the streets she spat blood and each one of those red spots reminded her of her life—an ugly, painful life—of the insults she had endured and would suffer again tomorrow, the following weeks . . . " * [*Explaining.*] This is a prostitute who goes to see her former "client," a dentist. He doesn't recognize her and thinks she's there to have a tooth extracted. She pays him with her last ruble for a needless extraction. She goes out—spitting blood in the streets and reflects upon her condition. But after a few hours we find her eating a meal offered her by a "young merchant from Kazan" . . . For all the efforts they make, the human race will never get better. The greatest "orgy of charity" would be useless, wasted. Men refuse the voice of poetry, art, beauty. I refuse all contact with them.

SERGIO [*Coldly.*]: Aside from "charity," which no one asks of you, of what use are professors, schools, books? . . . [*Pointing to* CRISTIANO'S *books.*]

CRISTIANO: Have you read Antoscia?

SERGIO: A little.

CRISTIANO: "A little" means nothing when you speak of books. He's too difficult a writer for you.

SERGIO [*Beginning to lose patience.*]: I'd have read him if we had him in the library. The cheapest edition costs 12,000 lire. I've never been able to spend that much for a book. I can't afford it.

CRISTIANO: Then why did you say "a little"? You're always lying. [*Quoting again from memory.*] "Everybody's interested in carefully hiding ignorance and discontent with life . . ." **

SERGIO [*Trying to control himself.*]: I've only read some short stories that were published in our newspaper.

CRISTIANO [*Hoping to embarrass him in front of* CHIARA.]: Which ones? [*Doubting that he may remember it.*] Tell us . . . if you remember it.

SERGIO [*Trying to remember.*]: "The Oysters." . . . [*Remembering.*] A child is begging for alms. He had never heard of oysters until he saw them in a store-window. Instead of begging for money he begs for oysters. A few rich rascals, to amuse themselves, stuff him with oysters until he bursts. They leave laughing . . . they had their amusement for the day.

CRISTIANO: Did your friends understand it?

SERGIO [*With anger.*]: And why not? More than you, who has his bowl of soup served faithfully! [*He regrets the insult, would like to retract it.*] I'm sorry.

CRISTIANO [*Pause, trying to gain ground.*]: Any others?

* "Oh my teeth."
** "The Teacher of Literature."

SERGIO [*Thinking.*]: "Sleepy." A young servant girl, after an exhausting day's work, must watch over a baby that doesn't stop crying. In desperation she kills the baby . . . falls on the dead body and is finally able to sleep.

CHIARA [*Upset.*]: Terrible. Will you read it to me, Cristiano?

CRISTIANO: Later. [*A painful silence.*]

SERGIO: Are you serious? About refusing the job?

CHIARA: How much would they pay him? [*Turning off the radio.*]

SERGIO: Not much. We'll see . . . [*They look at* CRISTIANO *waiting for his decision.*]

CRISTIANO [*Wringing his hands, confessing.*]: It isn't because of the money, whatever it amounts to; it isn't even a matter of giving time and effort uselessly, for a few lire . . . It's because I'd have to come in contact with others . . . with people who get their way by pushing you aside. They trample you down to impress their superiors . . . Avid, petty people, they disgust me with their mediocrity . . . Always asking stupid senseless questions . . . If the local team is ahead two points or one, if I've seen the latest TV show with the idol of the day, if Antoscia caused the revolution of 1917 . . . that's the most intelligent of their questions. And when they ask personal ones, about me . . . why? Why do they want to know? Why must they torment me? Do I ask anything of them? For instance they ask who I'm going to vote for; and all of them flatter you and watch you . . . pretending that their curiosity is in your interests . . . all of them . . . What do they want? Why persecute someone who wants only to live in peace, alone? [*In singsong fashion.*] And they ask about my secret life, the women I've had, the tricks I've played. Their hypocritical smiles, their implications . . . I can't survive out there in their midst . . . I don't know how to behave, how to endure it . . . You know all that, you know me . . . It's useless to fight; I'm not a fighter . . . They slaughter one another without mercy. I'm not strong. [*He inadvertently shows his hands.*] I would kill—if I were out there—to defend myself against their so called "sympathy," their hypocrisy, their derision . . . and so I'm waiting, I prefer . . . [*With despair.*] We're small, weak . . . useless . . . [*Rhetorically reciting from memory.*] "Death will sweep you from the face of the earth like water rats."*

* "The Bet."

SERGIO: And so what? If we would think about death all the time...

CRISTIANO: I do think about it . . . that's another reason for not coming out. I'm safer here . . . out there I'd be a misfit. I'd be beaten, destroyed . . . There's no hope for me out there.

SERGIO [*Completely losing patience.*]: Shoot yourself then! What kind of life is yours?· [*Regrets his outburst.*] I'm sorry, forgive me . . . I'm sorry for your poor old mother . . . I had promised her . . . Look, I even had a new key made for you. [*He passes the key through the bars and puts it on the table.*] She had really hoped . . . Truthfully, even I . . . [CRISTIANO *with contempt takes the key and throws it out of the cage across the room. Disappointed, they stare at him reprovingly.*] Goodbye, Chiara . . . [*He kisses* CHIARA *on the cheek as he did when he entered— taking her hands.*] and tell Nella that I'll be on time. [*Leaves without saying goodbye to* CRISTIANO; *a silence.* CHIARA *closes door after* SERGIO, *sits on bed and takes her housecoat off.*]

CHIARA: You behaved badly.

CRISTIANO: What about you? [CHIARA *looks at him questioningly, surprised by his tone and attitude.*] You looked like the "Sinner in an old Portrait"* . . . [*Morbidly.*] half naked, washing your legs . . . [*He contemplates her breasts.*]

CHIARA: I had my housecoat on.

CRISTIANO: Wide open.

CHIARA: As usual . . . After all, he had his back to me.

CRISTIANO: You let him kiss you.

CHIARA [*Teasingly.*]: Cristiano, it was a friendly kiss, nothing more. You're the one who's making something out of it. [*Coquettishly.*] More friendly than that kiss you gave me before . . . on my hand . . . [*She looks straight into his eyes,* CRISTIANO *feels uncomfortable.*] He's an impulsive young man, sincere . . .

CRISTIANO [*In desperation.*]: No, no, it's not true! This is your mistake. To believe in the sincerity of others.

CHIARA [*Calmly.*]: He seems sincere to me. What makes you think otherwise?

CRISTIANO [*Emphatically.*]: No one is sincere in this world! You're not when you "accept" your husband [*Pointing to the bed.*] He's not [*Pointing to door from which* SERGIO *left.*] when he preaches. Why do you think we have missionaries? Because they want to be leaders of a flock, no matter how small it may be . . .

* "The Lady with the Dog."

They pretend to love the weak, the ignorant. Why? Because they want to lead a fraction of humanity. No one is sincere in this world.

CHIARA [*Slowly.*]: He offered you a chance to become a "leader," in their library.

CRISTIANO: I don't care.

CHIARA: He ran the risk of being ousted by you. You're cultured, you've read more than he. He might lose his "leadership" by letting you in.

CRISTIANO: He knew perfectly well that I wouldn't accept.

CHIARA: You accuse him of bad faith, then.

CRISTIANO: Like everyone else.

CHIARA: Even your mother?

CRISTIANO: Yes . . . when she pretends to feel sorry for me. She has her outbursts which she checks with difficulty. I sense it . . . even though she's learned to control herself.

CHIARA [*Slowly studying him.*]: One question. According to you, can one lie out of pity, love?

CRISTIANO: No.

CHIARA: It takes courage to be sincere. Do you have it?

CRISTIANO: Yes.

CHIARA: With whom?

CRISTIANO: With everyone.

CHIARA: With us perhaps. The few people you know because you feel protected by those bars.

CRISTIANO: With everyone.

CHIARA: How commendable! You're the only one, then, who is sincere? [CRISTIANO *doesn't answer.*] Everyone else in this house lies?

CRISTIANO: Everyone, even your husband who despises you and then . . . [*Points to bed.*]

CHIARA [*Ignoring the allusion.*]: Even your sister?

CRISTIANO: Even my sister. You've seen her—she's more "feminine" when he's here! She deceives him with her play acting, by pretending she's in love.

CHIARA: Isn't she?

CRISTIANO [*Hesitantly.*]: I don't know . . .

CHIARA: How can *you* judge love? You don't know what it is. [*Almost to herself, with passion.*] It's a fever that consumes you, a desire to touch the one you love, to lose yourself in him, to belong to him, to be beautiful. Your sister wants to appear better in Sergio's eyes. Your sister is in love.

CRISTIANO: She just wants to get out of this house. She wants a change.

CHIARA: Even that is love. To escape from the present, which is "putrid," as you describe it, for a better life, in the future . . .

CRISTIANO: Even the "future" is putrid.

CHIARA: In your books.

CRISTIANO: These books confirm what I've seen out there.

CHIARA: How many years were you "out there," among men?

CRISTIANO: Long enough for me to know them. I'm afraid of them. I'm afraid of myself . . . because . . . [*Excitedly.*] I could kill, yes . . . I would kill those who lie, flatter, ridicule.

CHIARA [*Again to herself, fascinated by the idea.*]: "To kill" . . .

CRISTIANO [*Tormenting himself.*]: Yes. I feel I have the strength, the will. Why do you think I locked myself behind these bars? Because I even hate all of you . . . [*Wringing his hands.*] I could even kill all of you. To control oneself is a superhuman effort. These bars help me. [*With bowed head he withdraws into himself.*]

CHIARA [*Again to herself.*]: "To kill" . . .

CRISTIANO: Yes. Man is the dirtiest of animals. He lives from hand to mouth, crawling, vile. He forgets dignity, dedication, love. [*Reciting.*] "But in no way could he remember either his baby or the willow tree" . . . *

CHIARA [*Reprimanding him.*]: Those words, as usual, aren't yours.

CRISTIANO: A baby, imagine, an infant, forgotten! It's true. [*He taps the book.*] It's written here. How can you forget the birth of a son? Your own son, your own flesh and blood?

CHIARA: How sentimental you are! You'd even know how to love a son, maybe . . .

CRISTIANO [*Ignoring what she says he goes on.*]: In "Rothschild's Fiddle" a dying wife recalls her dead son. The father doesn't remember ever having had him. He remembers nothing, imagine!

CHIARA: Maybe he was numbed by misery. Today no one forgets his son. Today one loves with more intensity. The years that go by are not in vain.

CRISTIANO [*Accusingly.*]: . . . "All these amateur theatrical and literary evenings are invented only to make it easier to get a rich

* "Rothschild's Fiddle."

merchant to take on a girl as his mistress . . . " "At A Country House"—a story written sixty years ago. Has anything changed? Women still hunt for money, only for money. From the same story—"a slip of a girl of twelve is scheming to get a lover." Does that remind you of anything? It seems like yesterday's newspaper—where they talk about "Lolitas" . . . or the day before yesterday . . . [*Reading an article from a newspaper.*] "In England brassieres are sold to ten-year-olds. It is considered advisable to prevent them from having complexes." Has anything changed? Is the world any cleaner today than it was sixty years ago, than yesterday?

CHIARA [*After a pause, maternally.*]: What have they done to you, Cristiano?

CRISTIANO: Nothing. [*He points to the stage, meaning the family, then he slowly includes the audience, the world.*] You are all hoping for something, waiting for some kind of revelation. There is no revelation, or if it suits you, there is. I couldn't care less. [*Accusingly.*] You've flattered me, rejected me, robbed me, scorned me. It was nothing to you, it meant everything to me. I lived amongst you holding my breath, not to disturb you. I allowed you to hate, to love, to torture. I asked nothing. Only to watch you with eyes full of horror. You dragged me down to your level by involving me. I felt hate, disgust. Everything has a price, if one lives among you. Even the most sacred things: a smile, a caress . . . for a thousand lire you're loved indifferently; for two thousand with a little more interest. If you promise ten thousand, they seem sincere. And you tremble with joy, with ecstasy. Afterwards . . . you realize that it had no meaning, that none of it was true, not a single caress was sincere. Then you want to tear off their masks, straighten their backs that are bent with servility, avidity, and lies. You want to spit on them, to kill . . . [*With anguish.*] Have I the right to trample on worms? No. These bars keep me safe.

CHIARA [*She has finished dressing, while listening with interest; she sits now near the cage.*]: What have you done, Cristiano, to make yourself be loved?

CRISTIANO: I've waited in silence, watching with eyes of love.

CHIARA: What have you done, Cristiano, to deserve their confidence?

CRISTIANO [*Slight pause.*]: They haven't given me the chance.

CHIARA: What about the last one—to work at the library? You're
the one who refuses contacts. Who knows you in this city?
Your mother, perhaps, who's watched you grow up. Maybe I . . .
[*Pause.* CRISTIANO *looks at her with humility, hopefully.*] Today
more than yesterday because you have talked to me with an
open heart about yourself. You've moved me. You make me
feel deeply . . . real emotion . . . sympathy.

CRISTIANO [*Disappointed.*]: I don't know what to do with sympathy.

CHIARA: It's the first of all sentiments. You feel it for someone
who reveals himself, for someone you respect. I respect you,
Cristiano. I've been watching you for months, I know how much
good there is in you. Treasures! You are a good man, better than
most, better than anyone here. [CRISTIANO *listens breathlessly.*]
The only one who has any idea of understanding, of the true
intensity of a love, or a hate. You know what I suffer in this
prison! I, too, am in chains. You understand what it means not
to be loved, to be alone, a prisoner within real or imaginary bars.
You are the only one who knows. *And even though you've done
nothing for me,* I feel your sympathy and understanding! We
live only once, Cristiano. This is woman's real tragedy . . . being
a prisoner of circumstances, realizing that her beauty is fading
and her youth disappearing, and yet, to lack the courage to
escape, to dare . . . [*Deliberately, suggestively.*] not to find anyone who'll help her to escape . . . [*She does not take her eyes
away from him.*]

CRISTIANO [*Quoting with rapture.*]: "Life is given us only
once . . . "* You're right. These are also Lipa's words, a gentle
creature to whom . . .

CHIARA [*Interrupting him.*]: They do exist, then, these gentle
creatures? It isn't true, then, that we live in a sewer, that they
all lie, that no one loves or gives?

CRISTIANO [*Disturbed.*]: . . . I don't think so . . . Maybe . . . [*Enraptured.*] There is one . . . there is one who even killed for love.

CHIARA [*With passion, suggestively.*]: That is real love. Who kills
for love deserves adoration.

CRISTIANO: Not this one. Her name is Masha. She had murdered
for her Matvei. He didn't understand! He turned against her
at the trial, condemned her . . . He didn't understand. Afterwards

* "In the Ravine."

he brought tea and sugar to her cell. She rejected him. He couldn't understand her hatred for the inhumanity of those gifts.

CHIARA: A woman appreciates sacrifice and rewards true love. A woman never forgets the man who kills for her, a man who loves her to that point.

CRISTIANO: It's true . . . Men are less appreciative, they feel less. Listen . . . [*He picks up a book.*] . . . One of the most beautiful pages he wrote, listen . . . the story of a woman who loves, who knows how to love. [*Looking for the page.*] "The Huntsman" . . . [*He turns some pages until he finds the passage he wants.*]— "Yegor put his cap on the back of his head and, calling his dog, went on his way. His wife stood still looking after him. Her eyes were full of sadness and tender affection. Her gaze flitted over her husband's tall, lean figure and caressed and fondled it. He, as though he felt that gaze, stopped and looked around . . . He did not speak, but from his face, from his shrugged shoulders, she could see that he wanted to say something to her. She went up to him timidly and looked at him with imploring eyes. 'Take it,' he said, turning around. He gave her a crumpled ruble note and walked quickly away.—Goodbye, Yegor, she said mechanically, taking the ruble. He walked down the long road, straight as a taut strap. She stood, pale as a statue, her eyes watching every step he took. But then the red of his shirt melted into the dark color of his trousers, his steps could not be seen, and the dog could not be distinguished from the boots. Nothing could be seen but the cap, and—suddenly—he turned off sharply into the clearing and the cap vanished in the greenness.—Goodbye, Yegor, she whispered, and stood on tiptoe to see the white cap once more." *

[*They are both very moved by the story.*]

CHIARA: Beautiful! Think how much tenderness a woman like that could give to a man who deserves it.

CRISTIANO: To someone who deserves it . . .

CHIARA [*Suggestively.*]: To someone who *could prove* it. A woman like that, modest, devoted, sincere, perhaps exists . . . For you. [*There is a long tender kiss.*]

[*The MOTHER enters, with a bottle of wine. She is shocked to*

* "The Huntsman."

find CHIARA and CRISTIANO *in an embrace. She drops the bottle, which crashes on the floor breaking into pieces. Horrified, she makes the sign of the cross.*]

CRISTIANO [*After a pause of shame and guilt,* CRISTIANO *finds a way out; he offers his mother the "gift" of coming out; he points to the key which he threw away before.*] The key, Mamma . . . Sergio brought me the key . . . it's over there . . .

[*He points to it timidly but hopefully; the* MOTHER, *paralyzed and stunned from the shock, stares at them painfully. She refuses to grant* CRISTIANO *his newborn desire. She refuses to let him out, now.*]

Curtain

Act Three

. . . A few days later

SCENE: *The* MOTHER, *with her back to the audience, is working at the sink. She is silent and morose, bent over from the weight of the misfortune that has poisoned her family.* CHIARA, *sitting on the bed, is turning the pages of one of* CRISTIANO's *books.* CRISTIANO, *clutching the bars of the cage, tries to get his* MOTHER *to answer him; from time to time he looks at* CHIARA *with tenderness.*

CRISTIANO [*Timidly, to his mother who does not answer.*]: Do you think, Mamma, that the time I've spent in this cage has been useful to me? . . . I think so . . . I needed many many months to think, to talk to myself calmly . . . To be confined helps, it makes you think . . . I have had the good fortune to have you and my books . . . all the advantages of isolation and none of the disadvantages . . . Why does society isolate an individual? To give him time to meditate, to collect himself . . . If he can be destructive, he should be isolated. I was on the verge of becoming dangerous . . . I understood it myself . . . that's my strength . . . I locked myself up to keep from hurting some-one. Do you remember, Mamma, when I would come home from my walks? [*She does not reply.*] I wrung my hands . . . I had won, yes; I had succeeded in controlling myself, in not killing . . . I would walk alone, minding my own business . . . Everyone laughed at my hurried steps . . . almost a flight . . . What right had they? I wanted to cry out! . . . Obscene propo-sitions and insinuations, dirty looks . . . the world was dirty . . . It still is, Mamma, I realize that, but I'm stronger now. I am stronger, Mamma; will I succeed? [*He is tormented, waiting for an answer.*] Don't you think I have profited from these years? You kept begging me, Mamma . . . I was accustomed to your pleading . . . I thought you were on their side . . . on the side of those blind corrupt creatures who persecuted me, only me . . . Then I realized, thanks to you, Mamma . . . they do it to every-one . . . "Homo homini lupus" . . . they are wolves, Mamma . . . they rob and cheat whenever they can . . . you know, they even try to cheat you but you endure . . . If you can, Mamma, why can't I? [*A silence follows; the fact that his* MOTHER *doesn't answer saddens and disturbs him. He feels uneasy and looks to* CHIARA *for sympathy and consolation.*]

CHIARA [*To* CRISTIANO, *after a pause.*]: Cristiano, do you remember "The Post"? [CRISTIANO *nods.*] One of the characters talks and talks while the other keeps silent never answering. Do you re-member the last sentence? [*Pointing ironically to the* MOTHER, *who works in silence.* CHIARA *reading.*] "With whom is she angry? Men, misery or the autumn nights?" [*A tense pause; then sar-castically.*] With whom are you angry, Mamma? The autumn nights? When did you have your last? . . . When Nella was conceived?

[*The* MOTHER *looks reproachfully at* CRISTIANO *for permitting her to speak this way.* CHIARA, *wisely, does not continue and returns to her book. A heavy silence.* CHIARA *thumbing through various books, while the* MOTHER, *who has finished doing the dishes, dries her hands and takes off her apron, which she places momentarily near* CHIARA. CHIARA *takes advantage of this op-portunity to take the key from the apron pocket, then goes back to her book pretending to read. The* MOTHER *goes over to make up the bed at stage right.*]

CHIARA [*Reading.*]: Listen . . . how beautiful. [*Slowly, savoring the words.*] "But no matter how much he thought and how much he wrinkled his brow, he could not find in his past a single exclamation point" . . . * How well it describes in a few words the life of a poor man. Will there be any exclamation points in your life, Cristiano? [CHIARA *takes advantage of the moment when the* MOTHER'*s back is turned to show* CRISTIANO, *the key to the cage.*]

CRISTIANO [*His eyes brightening.*]: Yes.

MOTHER [*Without turning.*]: Help me with the bed.

CHIARA [*Harshly.*]: I've helped you for ten years. I've had enough. [*Continues reading.*] Here he seems to be talking about you . . . "The fear instilled since infancy of appearing sentimental and ridiculous" ** . . . [*She points to a flower in a vase which is on the table. Evidently it is a gift from* CRISTIANO; *they look at it smiling.*] Do you still feel that way?

CRISTIANO [*Moved by so much attention.*]: No.

MOTHER [*She has finished making the bed and puts a pair of shoes besides* CHIARA.]: Leave him alone. Clean your husband's shoes.

CHIARA [*Aggressively.*]: How many times have you begged me to be "polite" to Cristiano, to be "tolerant"? Now I'm doing it of my own accord. He's loaned me books and I'm reading them with interest and "politeness." [*Defiant.*] Do you mind? Everyone should read these books. There's art and poetry here. Cristiano deserves more than any of you. He's sensitive, good, he's better than all of you.

[*There is no reaction. The* MOTHER, *having finished her work, is ready to go out. Instead she fusses about, unable to decide whether or not to leave them alone. She takes now her apron and hangs it up.*]

CHIARA [*Hoping the* MOTHER *will leave soon.*]: Is there anything you want me to tell Nella?

MOTHER: No. [*She walks around, waiting for* NELLA *to come home;*

---

* "The Exclamation Point."
** "A Stranger's Tale."

CHIARA *and* CRISTIANO *become more and more nervous antici-
pating the hour when they'll be left alone.* NELLA *enters and
without speaking kisses her* MOTHER; *she seats herself between*
CHIARA *and* CRISTIANO *facing the audience, and begins to knit a
sweater.* MOTHER *exits.*]

CHIARA [*Irritated.*]: The changing of the Guard.

CRISTIANO [*Gently, after a brief pause.*]: Are the papers ready?

NELLA [*Bored, expressionless.*]: They're ready.

CRISTIANO: Did it cost much?

NELLA: No. The real expense will be the decorations in the church.

CRISTIANO: Do without them.

NELLA [*Surprised.*]: This is the first time you and Sergio are in
agreement about something. [*Brief pause.*]

CRISTIANO: Is the bedroom ready?

NELLA: Almost.

CRISTIANO: Has the date been set?

NELLA: When his boss gets back from his vacation. In October.

CRISTIANO: It's a nice month. [*Pause.*] It will be difficult for
Mamma . . . without you . . .

NELLA [*Directed at him, sarcastically.*]: With you . . .

CRISTIANO: What do you mean?

NELLA: You've given her so many worries.

CRISTIANO: What kind of worries?

NELLA: You know very well.

CRISTIANO [*After a pause.*]: Do you think she would be happy
if . . . [*Gestures of leaving the cage.*]

NELLA [*Placidly.*]: I think so.

CRISTIANO: You say it without enthusiasm. Why do you only
"think so"?

NELLA: It's *my* opinion.

CRISTIANO: She doesn't ask me any more.

NELLA: She's probably tired of begging you.

CRISTIANO: Only since . . . [NELLA *doesn't react as* CRISTIANO *would
like her to.*] Why just lately?

NELLA: I don't know. Maybe she's given up the struggle; she's
very tired.

CRISTIANO: She used to plead with me from morning till night . . .

NELLA: That's exactly the reason. [*Brief pause.*]

CRISTIANO: Don't you find her a little changed?

NELLA: No.

CRISTIANO: She doesn't talk so much. She didn't say a thing, not a word, before you came in.

NELLA: She's probably worn out. Poor Mamma.

CRISTIANO: I know she's tired. You ought to help her a little more. [*There is a silence; no reaction from* NELLA.] You just sit there lately . . .

NELLA: I'm preparing my trousseau.

CRISTIANO: You could do that at the market while she's selling. [*Silence.*] She needs company, someone to encourage her when business is bad. She needs some support . . .

NELLA: You begin.

CRISTIANO: Begin what?

NELLA: To encourage her, to support her . . .

CRISTIANO [*Nervously.*]: I? Am I a problem to her? She shouldn't worry about me. Who is less trouble than I, shut up in here, reading all day? [NELLA *looks at him, ironically.*] Why do you look at me that way? Don't you agree?

NELLA: Of course.

CRISTIANO: I'm the only one who minds his own business. *My* business, do you understand?

NELLA: I understand. [*Long pause.*]

CRISTIANO [*Trying to control his nervousness.*]: Won't it be necessary for you and Mamma to be working together any more?

NELLA: No. In many stands there is only one person selling. One of us will be enough.

CRISTIANO: And when two or three customers are there at the same time?

NELLA: They'll wait.

CRISTIANO: And what if they steal something?

NELLA: It can't be helped. Mamma says—if they do, it's because they need it. We count it as charity.

CRISTIANO: So it's charity now! Are we rich all of a sudden?

NELLA: You've never lacked anything.

CRISTIANO: What kind of talk is this? So now, even you begrudge me a bowl of soup? [*Losing his temper, threatening.*] You'll regret this, you'll regret this! . . .

CHIARA [*Not raising her eyes from the book.*]: Be calm, Cristiano.

[NELLA's *overbearing presence, her indifference as she continues to knit, begins to gnaw at* CRISTIANO.]

CRISTIANO: Don't you have anything to do?

NELLA [*Holding up the sweater she's knitting.*]: This.

CRISTIANO: . . . I mean outside?

NELLA: Outside, no. [*Silence.*]

CRISTIANO: Tell me the truth, Mamma makes you stay here, doesn't she? What did she tell you?

NELLA: Nothing.

CRISTIANO: What do you think, then, of this change?

NELLA: Nothing.

CRISTIANO: Hypocrite. You never leave me alone any more. Why?

NELLA: We never left you alone.

CRISTIANO: I mean . . . [*Hesitates, controls himself.*] Did I ever say anything when you were flirting with him? Did I ever watch you, persecute you? [NELLA *is reminded by the reference to* SERGIO; *opens her handbag and hands* CRISTIANO *a newspaper.*]

NELLA: It's today's.

CRISTIANO [*Grabbing it and throwing it over his shoulder angrily.*]: Lies, lies, all lies! They're all hypocrites, like you! Such great concern for the unemployed, the suicides, and yet . . . Listen to this from yesterday's paper. [*He looks for the newspaper, finds the page and reads aloud with scorn and anger. Proof of his morbid sensitivity.*] "Notes on Fishing" . . . "A fishing hook that is deeply embedded and has lodged itself in the body cavity has certainly caused damage to organs that are vital and highly sensitive. It is a mistake to suppose the fish can continue to live. Once the hook has been removed, the fish is mortally injured and will suffer an interminable agony that will affect its flavor. If the fish has swallowed the hook and is killed immediately, there is no need to fear that its flavor will be impaired. What renders him unfit to eat is a long agony. Large fish die quickly when struck with a small hammer just above the eyes . . . " [*To* CHIARA, *then to* NELLA.] There you have them! The champions of humanity! A refined technique of sadism. Not even animals are respected . . . Here is where they betray themselves, here is where they show their true nature: cruelty! [*To* NELLA.] That's your man, he is of that breed: false, hypocritical, always lying . . . When he pretends to be moved, when he's preaching, when he's with you. He talks of love, he promises to respect you and then . . . [*Morbidly.*] Does he really respect you, tell me, does he? What do you do downstairs, for hours, and Mamma . . . tolerates it pretending not to know, while your brother drains the bottle of wine bought for your "fiancé." How disgusting! Hypocrisy and filth are everywhere; in the world and in everyone's mind. [*Persisting.*] What do you do, down there? Do Chiara and I come down to watch you, to annoy you? We are the only two who aren't hypocrites and liars. We know perfectly well what you are doing. We don't pretend to ignore it by drinking and fiddling around. It's I who advise Mamma to . . . [*Repenting what he said.*] Nothing, we say nothing. We let you go your way, talk as you please . . . [*A brief pause, he looks at* NELLA *with hatred.*] What if Chiara and I want to talk now?

NELLA [*Calmly.*]: Talk.

CRISTIANO: I mean alone, about our personal affairs?

NELLA: I won't listen to you, I've work to do. It won't be the first time you've talked together in front of me.

CRISTIANO: That was before. Before, I didn't know her. I thought she was like all the rest of you, with your mentality and dullness. One can only talk about "food, drink and sleep" with people like this and it doesn't matter who's around. But when you discover new worlds together, when two souls feel as one about the same things—about the same poem . . . you wouldn't understand.

NELLA: All the more reason for you to ignore me.

CRISTIANO [*Furiously.*]: Give me the key, Chiara! [*Raising her eyes,* NELLA *watches him closely.*]

CHIARA [*Trying to prevent him from going on, from talking too much.*]: What key? You know your mother won't part with it any more. [*Pointing to* NELLA.] Maybe she has one, the one Sergio had made.

NELLA: Would you really come out? [*A silence; she walks towards the cage.*] Have you asked Mamma for it?

CRISTIANO [*Ready to strike.*]: It's I who decides. I don't need anyone's permission. Come closer! [NELLA *hesitates.*] Closer! [NELLA *decides not to; ignoring* CRISTIANO, *she sits down again.*] You're afraid, you stupid little worm, you're afraid! . . . You know that . . . You know that I hate all of you . . . You're all stupid, blind, dirty . . . What do you see of the world?

NELLA [*With calm.*]: More than you.

CRISTIANO: What do you really "see," when walking? Do you feel the poetry of the sky, do you delight over the awesomeness of nature? . . . Do you realize that one page can fill you with more joy or suffering than ten years of living? Do you realize that a single page can be the synthesis of an entire lifetime? Of the very best of life? That it can be rich with reflections unknown to you, with details that you will never perceive? What do you know of the poetry of existence, of the understanding between two souls?

CHIARA [*Reading.*]: "I am surrounded by vulgarity and more vulgarity, wearisome insignificant people, pots of sour cream, jugs of milk, cockroaches and . . . [*Looking at* NELLA.] stupid women . . . " *

NELLA [*Undisturbed.*]: Your disciple preaches nonsense. Like you. She really understands you. She sees pots of sour cream, milk and cockroaches even if there aren't any. [*Sarcastically.*] Yes, that's poetry all right!

CRISTIANO [*Scornfully.*]: You and your peasant will never understand! No, never. Man is blind, putrid, incurable . . . nothing will save you . . . I hate you, I despise you, and I thank these bars that separate me from you. I've chosen them because I'm afraid, afraid to live among beasts . . . Nothing is sacred to you . . . nothing . . . neither man's need for silence nor his need for warmth . . . I've tried to educate you, I've read to you . . . but not even the birth of a sentiment, the flowering of a love, have you understood or respected . . . You're capable only of animal appetites, that's all . . . Your only desire is to escape from light, from what is clean . . . you wallow in mud and ignorance . . . [*Shaking the bars.*] Oh bars, how I thank you! You've kept me from carrying out justice, you enabled me to . . . [*Looking tenderly at* CHIARA.] appreciate the value of waiting—to escape despair—to feel reborn with hope.

[*The sound of* PIETRO'*s heavy footsteps at right.* NELLA *quickly puts away her knitting and goes to the sink, pretending to be busy, not wanting to give the impression that she is there to watch* CHIARA *and* CRISTIANO, CRISTIANO *and* CHIARA *follow her movements with surprise and fear.* PIETRO *enters slowly, rolling a cigarette; he ignores them; stops by the cage still rolling the cigarette in silence. He goes closer to* CHIARA, *wets his cigarette and lights it with his last match, throwing the empty box at* CHIARA'*s feet. There is a tense silence while* CRISTIANO

* "The Teacher of Literature."

and CHIARA *remain rigid, caught by the oppressive silence that terrorizes the guilty.* NELLA, *pretending to be busy in the kitchen, doesn't dare to turn around.* PIETRO, *with impenetrable expression, goes quietly towards her; then stops to stare at her.*]

NELLA [*After resisting for a moment, she gives up and turns around.*]: Ciao, Pietro.

PIETRO: Ciao. [*Another heavy silence.*]

NELLA [*Very uneasy and timid.*]: I didn't see you. [*She avoids his eyes.*]

PIETRO [*Motionless.*]: I believe you.

NELLA [*Justifying herself.*]: . . . Just doing a few chores . . . I'm almost through.

PIETRO [*Still motionless.*]: I see. [*Another pause.*]

NELLA [*Very timidly.*]: Only the glasses . . . [*She lines them up to her right.*]

PIETRO: I see.

NELLA: I'll dry them and . . .

PIETRO [*Mumbling an assent.*]: Uh huh . . . [CHIARA *and* CRISTIANO *are very tense; they suspect that* PIETRO *knows something.*]

NELLA: I must go now . . . I promised Mamma I'd meet her soon . . .

PIETRO [*Sarcastically.*]: With so much to do . . .

NELLA: Yes . . .

PIETRO [*More aggressively.*]: What for example?

NELLA [*Uneasily, and on the defensive now.*]: In a house . . .

PIETRO: Little "chores" for me?

NELLA: No.

PIETRO: Little "chores" for Chiara?

NELLA: No.

PIETRO [*Still sarcastically.*]: Our bed?

NELLA: No . . .

PIETRO: Then, what?

NELLA: Nothing much.

PIETRO: So you stay home, for . . . "nothing much"? [CHIARA *and* CRISTIANO *are startled; with questioning looks towards one another.*]

NELLA [*Embarrassed.*]: Just finishing up before going . . . [*Points unintentionally to her bed.*]

PIETRO [*Insistently.*]: Your bed?

NELLA: No . . .

PIETRO: Who made it?

NELLA: Mamma, I guess.

PIETRO: And the dishes?

NELLA: I don't know. Maybe Mamma . . .

PIETRO: What did *you* do, then?

NELLA [*Vaguely.*]: I was drying them, putting things away, preparing for tonight.

PIETRO: Things Mamma usually does by herself, before going off to the market . . . *Alone.*

NELLA: She left a few minutes ago . . . I'm going to her right now.

PIETRO: Before, you always left together.

NELLA [*Hurrying to leave*]: I'll catch up with her, I told you.

PIETRO [*He now reveals the real reason for his silence and sarcasm.*]: The older you get the worse you behave! Congratulations! You don't love Mamma. At least you don't show it. [*Points to* CHIARA, *to whom the reproaches are directed.*] That *she* doesn't worry about her is understandable. But you . . . Do you know how old Mamma is?

[CRISTIANO *and* CHIARA *relax their vigilant fear of* PIETRO'S *suspicions, not attaching much weight to his attack on* CHIARA'S *laziness.*]

NELLA [*Humbly.*]: I know.

PIETRO: Why do you neglect her, then? Do you or don't you realize that she's tired, that she shouldn't do a thing, not a thing? Have you looked at her face, these last few days? And you leave her alone, wasting your time on foolishness. There's someone *here* who can do the housework—who will learn to do it. [*Pointing to* CHIARA.] She's been lying around long enough. Soon you'll be leaving this house. Let her take the initiative, the responsibility, the satisfaction of keeping the house in order. [*Sarcastically.*] She's promised to get up early, do the washing and so on . . . She'll become a real wife, she'll learn . . . [*To* NELLA.] You are already, with a mother like ours as an example . . . She, she can't be blamed, coming from that kind of family. Here she found two naive women, in you and Mamma. So tomorrow she begins . . . Even today . . . *She* starts doing it alone. Right, Chiara? And you, Nella, don't you touch a fork, a glass, a dish any more. I forbid it . . . You stay with Mamma—that's all.

NELLA: All right.

PIETRO: That goes for the two of you. [*To* CHIARA.] Do you understand?

CHIARA [*Annoyed.*]: I understand.

PIETRO: I don't want any arguing—none of that; "You're supposed to do that," "I'm supposed to do this" . . . None of that! Mamma is getting on in years—it's enough that she goes to work every day. Even that's too much. Nella's getting married and this house isn't her responsibility any longer. [*With emphasis.*] You're not to do a thing!

NELLA [*Trying to end the "lecture."*]: What about some coffee?

PIETRO: Go to Mamma. Hurry! [*Pointing to* CHIARA.] Let her ask me.

NELLA [*To all three.*]: Goodbye. [*She goes out.*]

[PIETRO *takes a long look at* CHIARA *who tries to ignore him; then she rises nervously, to prepare the coffee; she looks to see how much there is in the pot.*]

CHIARA [*To* CRISTIANO.]: You too?

CRISTIANO: Yes.

PIETRO [*Noticing that there is just a little coffee left.*]: Fill up my cup first. [CHIARA *starts to fill the cups at the sink.*] Do it here. [CHIARA *is forced to fill the cups at the table, in front of* PIETRO. *She leaves a full cup on the table for* PIETRO; *hands a half-filled cup to* CRISTIANO.]

CHIARA: I'll make you some more later.

CRISTIANO: Thank you [PIETRO *watches them with contempt.* CHIARA *takes* CRISTIANO's *empty cup, waits for* PIETRO *to finish his coffee.* PIETRO *drinks slowly and* CHIARA *loses her patience. She takes only* CRISTIANO's *cup to the sink.*]

PIETRO [*As soon as* CHIARA *returns to her bed,* PIETRO *holds up his cup.*]: Here! [*After a moment's hesitation* CHIARA *takes it.* PIETRO *speaks to* CRISTIANO, *who is gripping the bars.*] Aren't you reading today?

CRISTIANO: No.

PIETRO [*With sarcasm*]: Wonderful! It's good for your health. [*Taking a regular cigarette since the one he made doesn't draw, he looks for matches, but remembers he used his last one.*] You want one? [CRISTIANO, *surprised at the unusual offer, shakes his head.*] If you took it—we'd get a light right away. [*Without*

turning, he reaches out his hand for a match, which CHIARA
*doesn't bring. She—who has just sat down pretends not to
see him.*]

PIETRO [*Screaming*]: Matches! [CHIARA *looks at him with hatred,
gives in and brings him a match. As she turns to leave.*] My
slippers! [CHIARA *brings them from under the bed handing them
to* PIETRO.] Put them on! [CHIARA, *controlling herself, starts
to kneel.*]

CRISTIANO [*Exploding.*]: Don't! [PIETRO *looks at him with surprise.*]

PIETRO: What's the matter, little brother?

CRISTIANO [*Furious*]: That's no way to treat a woman.

PIETRO [*To* CHIARA *in a husbandly tone.*]: My slippers. [CHIARA
looks at CRISTIANO; *feeling insufficiently defended, she kneels
down to remove* PIETRO's *shoes.*] These tigers, you don't know
them.

CRISTIANO: You don't treat a wife that way.

PIETRO: Give them a finger and they'll take an arm. With a "type"
like me she hardly obeys. With a type like you . . . If you ever
have the courage to marry—you'll end up wearing the apron.

CRISTIANO: She hates you.

PIETRO: Love and hate are two sides of the same coin. Someone
said it—maybe your Antoscia. [*Sarcastically.*] What page? . . .
Or some other writer, it doesn't matter. [*Pointing to* CHIARA,
who's rising.] You see how she chafes at the bit? What's important is not to let her bite my hand. [CHIARA *returns to her bed,
sits down and tries to read.*]

CRISTIANO: A woman is sacred. She's a human being and should
be treated with love and respect.

PIETRO [*Sarcastically.*]: You know her well!

CRISTIANO: What do we all need at times? A kind word, a smile,
a flower . . .

PIETRO [*Taking the flower out of the vase and throwing it away.*]:
Here's one. [CHIARA, *hurt, picks it up, caresses and kisses it,
then puts it in water.* PIETRO *is surprised by her action.*] Look!
Did you see that! You're right Cristiano, she loves flowers.
Had I fallen she wouldn't even have turned around to look. But
when a flower falls . . . It's true, a woman is an inexhaustible
source of surprises. I've lived with her ten years and I never saw
her caress a flower, or with a flower . . . [*To* CRISTIANO.] By the
way, who bought *that* one? [*There is a moment of confusion;*

CRISTIANO *and* CHIARA *suspect again that* PIETRO *is aware of something.*] I bet it was Sergio—he has a way with women, that boy. Better than I. He won't suffer much with Nella. [*Looking at* CHIARA, *instinctively.*] Nella is modest and honest. She demands little, she accepts the plain life she's accustomed to. She's obedient, and her past is crystal clean. [*Short pause.*] A daughter turns out well when she's brought up by a mother like ours. She has nothing to be ashamed of.

CRISTIANO: And when Mamma leaves them alone downstairs?

PIETRO: They're getting married.

CRISTIANO: And if he died tomorrow? Electrocuted by his own gadgets? Would she still be a "respectable" girl?

PIETRO [*Pointing to* CRISTIANO'*s hands, which are gripping the bars*]: You do well to touch iron—You wouldn't wish that boy any harm, I hope?

CRISTIANO: You still haven't answered my question.

PIETRO [*After a moment's hesitation.*]: She would be. She's pure gold. Sergio has chosen well. [*Stares at* CHIARA, *who is reading.*] You see, I—maybe it's not even her fault—I was used to a different kind of woman . . . living with Mamma and Nella . . . [*Pointing to* CHIARA.] Can you imagine that one gentle like Mamma, or active like Nella? . . . Can you imagine her—"old"? I can't. Even in her old age she'll be a tigress . . . a tigress thirsty for life, experiences, born to rebel. Did you see?—When she picked up the flower—do you think she really loves flowers? She put it in water only to spite me. You don't know this kind of women. They have a fever in their blood . . . To be endured by one of them, you have to give them everything: comfort, adoration and all of yourself every minute. You have to be their slave . . . A slave, do you understand? . . . You have to be available, ready and obedient . . . Only under these conditions she might tolerate you . . .

CRISTIANO [*Suffering.*]: No, you don't know her. You'll never understand her.

PIETRO [*Sarcastically.*]: You're right, you've slept with her. [*Now to* CHIARA.] He's suffering. Aren't you making the coffee you promised him?

CHIARA [*To both of them.*]: You really want some?

PIETRO: I don't. [CRISTIANO *shakes his head,* CHIARA *continues reading.*] See how lazy she is? She doesn't even keep her promises.

Not even a promise made to her crazy little brother-in-law.
[*To* CHIARA.] Don't you like him a little? Poor thing, he's so good,
so kind. Did you see? He even takes your side. He says I don't
understand you . . . He's cultured, refined, beautiful . . . [*Brief
pause;* PIETRO *glances quickly to see her reaction.*] Would you
"try it" with a maniac? [CRISTIANO *strikes* PIETRO; *taken by complete surprise,* PIETRO *jumps up from his chair ready to retaliate,
to strike back; controls himself with effort.* CRISTIANO, *for the
first time, shows no fear; the brothers confront each other.*
CHIARA *observes them. She has waited for this violence, instigated
by her and upon which her future depends. After a few
seconds* PIETRO *overcomes his anger, his hand covering his face,
slowly and calmly speaking to* CRISTIANO.] Maybe I deserved it
. . . I want to help you. I won't fight.
CHIARA: Because you're a coward.
PIETRO [*Hurt, quickly turning to her.*]: You know why I won't
fight. [*A pause.*] You know why I insult him.
CRISTIANO: Why?
PIETRO: Ask her.
CRISTIANO: Why?
CHIARA: I don't know what you're talking about.
PIETRO [*Sneeringly.*]: We "suffer" for you when we're in bed
together whooping it up . . . We laugh, yes, [*With a forced
smile.*] we laugh at you. "She doesn't know what I'm talking
about . . ."
CHIARA [*With desperation, trembling that her plan is collapsing*]:
I don't! It's not true, Cristiano!
PIETRO: I admit at times she defends you. I tell her that I insult
you to make a man out of you. She says I got too far. Maybe I
did today, but you reacted. It's to my credit that you reacted.
If I didn't defend myself, it was to give you a little courage.
To make you hope that in *this* world there are all kinds who
for one reason or another would take it from you. I didn't
defend myself to make you feel stronger. Besides I'll let you
cut a good figure in her eyes. After all, she *is* a woman. Maybe
now you'll find the courage to face one, to go to bed with one.
Not one like her. She's insufferable! You deserve one with a
better disposition. [*He approaches* CHIARA; *he's visibly forcing
himself to keep control.*] Always like the cat in heat. [CHIARA
pretends to read.] Even if she doesn't give that impression.

She could deceive a saint. With me she became a football fan; she knew every detail of the game. With you she reads short stories. Pretending to enjoy them. With somebody else . . . [*Insinuating.*] Is there somebody else in your life? [CHIARA *is very nervous still pretending to read: she does not answer.* PIETRO *knocks the book out of her hands and sends it flying across the room.*] Answer me!

CHIARA [*Screaming.*]: That's enough . . . Stop it! [*She jumps off the bed.*]

PIETRO: It's a delicate subject. Are you ashamed?

CHIARA: And you? Letting someone strike you? Aren't you ashamed of lying, and insinuating? . . .

PIETRO: It's my duty to help him a little, poor devil. I'm his brother. To encourage him, I took the slap. But now that he's ready to come out do you want him to fall into the arms of someone like you? It's my duty to tell him, to put him on his guard.

CHIARA [*Hitting him ineffectively on the chest.*]: Coward, coward, coward! [CHIARA *tries to push him towards the cage.* PIETRO, *however, is solidly planted in the middle of the room embracing her by force.*]

PIETRO [*Holding her tightly.*]: Do you want me to calm you? . . . You have a right to it, I admit. I've neglected you a little lately. Or are you embarrassed? [CHIARA *manages to break away from him; to* CRISTIANO.] Women are always like this . . . reluctant, coy, pretending not to want it. Take it from me. If you run across someone who makes a fuss like this, don't let it discourage you. Give it to her anyway. [*To* CHIARA, *who's trying to escape from him.*] Come, let's show him how it's done . . . it's a brotherly duty. Come . . . [*He tries to push her towards the bed but doesn't succeed; to* CRISTIANO.] Have you ever heard her say "enough," in bed? Has she ever refused it? You're always awake; you hear us. You *know* . . . Never! Today is the first time. Maybe because . . . [*Recalling.*] I understand; she's reluctant to give in to a husband who didn't strike back . . . [*To* CHIARA.] Now is the time to show him what a good sister-in-law you are.

CHIARA [*Struggling.*] Cristiano!

PIETRO: He too may get it one day, out there. We must let him hope that "she" will still want him, even after . . . [*To* CRISTIANO.] Strange animals, women . . . Capricious . . . [*To* CHIARA *who has escaped from him.*] Come here . . . [CHIARA *protects herself from*

PIETRO *with a chair.*] Come here, baby, come here . . . let's not disappoint him, come . . . let's help him, come . . . Afterwards, he'll come out with courage, shouting with joy . . . Have you the key to the cage? I know where Mamma keeps it. In her housecoat . . . [*He's about to go for the key;* CHIARA *tries to stop him; she holds the chair with her back to the apron, which is hanging on the wall and protects herself from him with the chair. A pause. They are tense again.* PIETRO *might find out there is no key in the apron.*] Later, you're right, after we . . . If he's encouraged and wants it. [*To* CRISTIANO, *pointing to* CHIARA *and the key.*] You want? . . .

CRISTIANO: You bully! Insulting a woman . . .

PIETRO [*Interrupting sharply, points at him.*]: From one woman, meaning *you,* I took it. From another I won't take it. She has no complexes. [*Trying to catch her.*] Am I right, baby? Am I? Or . . . maybe she has—that life is escaping her, it's too short, that she's missing the excitement and thrills that she wants. That's her complex. [*To* CRISTIANO.] Not yours . . . [*To* CHIARA.] Are you this way with the other one . . . ? [*Confidentially to* CRISTIANO.] You know, Cristiano, I'm not cutting a good figure, but you're my brother after all . . . Do you think she goes to her mother's in the afternoon? [CHIARA *rushes at him hitting him with her fists and trying to prevent him from going on.* PIETRO *protects himself with difficulty.*]

CHIARA: Shut your dirty mouth!

PIETRO: Calm yourself, calm yourself. What a temper! You see, Cristiano, could you tame someone like this? As I was saying before—I have to tell you something about this bitch . . . [CHIARA *attacks desperately.*] Calm yourself, calm . . .

CHIARA: Liar! Liar!

PIETRO: I had her followed . . . Every other day she meets . . . [*While he is being pushed by* CHIARA *towards the cage.*] Calm down, calm down, now . . . you see, Cristiano . . . she doesn't want you to know about . . . [CHIARA *has succeeded with her plan;* CRISTIANO's *hands tighten around* PIETRO's *throat.* PIETRO *struggles furiously, choking, unable to free himself.*]

CHIARA [*Hysterically.*]: For me, Cristiano, for me . . . do it for me, for me, for me . . . [*She repeats these words over and over with frenzy, exultation, until* PIETRO's *body falls lifeless at her feet.*]

CRISTIANO [*Contemplating his hands.*]: My hands . . . they're strong, my hands . . . [*The following dialogue should be slow and sustained.* CHIARA's *true character is now revealed through what she says and through the changes of expression in her face: She is numbed by her newly born freedom, physically exalted by the reality of having it; then she pities* CRISTIANO *rationally, and finally she screams, "pretending" a great grief.*]

CHIARA [*Ecstatically.*]: I'm free . . . free . . . free . . .

CRISTIANO: Open, Chiara, open . . .

CHIARA [*Running her hands over her body.*]: I'm free, free to escape, to live . . . to start living . . .

CRISTIANO: Yes, Chiara, open . . . Open . . . We're both free . . . to escape, to start living . . .

[*A silence. Now* CHIARA *just "tells"* CRISTIANO.]

CHIARA [*Looking at* CRISTIANO *with pity, slowly.*]: Thank you, Cristiano . . . they won't do anything to you . . . you're crazy.

CRISTIANO [*Paralyzed with shock.*]: The cage, the cage . . . [*He shakes it feebly.*]

CHIARA [*Very slowly, word by word.*]: We all live in a cage . . . And we haven't the strength to get out . . . We need someone to open it for us—paying . . . You'll pay little, Cristiano . . . You're crazy.

[CRISTIANO, *dazed, stares at her speechless. A long pause.* CHIARA *looks at the body as if she's seen it for the first time. But there is no horror in her eyes. She has been waiting for this moment a long time. She must face the world in her new role of the grief-stricken widow. She pulls herself together in a deliberate manner. She must put on an act for the outside world. She "orders" herself to feel the horror of this murder until it is an overwhelming reality. She goes out screaming with a conviction that is chilling.*]

CHIARA: Murderer! Murderer!

[CRISTIANO *is paralyzed with shock. He stands motionless, his hands holding on to the bars for support. Only his eyes follow* CHIARA's *devastating betrayal. He must project tragedy and grief.*

CURTAIN

THE SUICIDE

A One Act Play

Mario Fratti

Translated by
Marguerita Carra *and* Louise Warner

Characters

The Husband
The Wife
The Mother

The present. In Italy.

SCENE: *A modest kitchen. Two lamps are lighted: a bright one in the center of the room, hanging from the ceiling, and a very dim one over the sink. The* WIFE, *extremely nervous, weeps softly while putting things in order. The* HUSBAND *is seated reading an Italian magazine.**

From a small radio we hear jazz.

HUSBAND [*To his* WIFE, *who annoys him with her crying.*]: Stop that crying! [*He turns up the volume of the radio to shut out the sound of her crying.*]

WIFE [*After a moment.*]: What time is it?

HUSBAND [*Without looking at his wristwatch, which he has checked many times.*]: It's ten past eleven.

[*His* WIFE *turns her back to him, still sobbing. Noticing this and unable to read, he walks over to the radio to turn up the volume; finding that it was all the way up, he turns it off in a rage. His* WIFE *looks at him with gratitude.*]

WIFE [*Timidly.*]: What time was it the night you . . . ?

HUSBAND: When I threw the plate at her? Around ten.
[*Long pause. Both pretend to be busy; she at the sink, he with his magazine; however they are both extremely nervous and upset.*]

HUSBAND [*Aggressively, noticing the look she has given him from the corner of her eye.*]: Why look at *me*? Why? ! [*Gesturing.*] I suppose it's my fault if she's late! [*Pause.*] Why don't you

* Such as *Oggi, Epoca, Europeo.*

answer? Answer me! What do you want to tell me? What are
you reproaching me for? I suppose it's that business with the
olive oil?

WIFE [*Turns toward him angrily; stares at him. A tense pause.
Slowly.*]: Then you knew it too, you knew that she was hurt,
that . . .

HUSBAND [*Gesturing.*]: "Hurt"? ! What's she got to be hurt about?
Why? For taking the bottle away? I'm the boss here, I hope,
and can use a little oil since the guests—and she is a guest,
here, you know—just pour it on. [*There is a tense irony in his
words.*]

WIFE: She was in tears at the table. Later she cried in the other
room.

HUSBAND: That one? She can cry at the drop of a hat! Remember
the story of the pears? She was pretending to cry. I watched her.
She was embarrassed. That's why she shut herself up in her room;
to avoid being put on the spot. You don't cry because the boss
of the house—I—hands out the portions. Haven't I the right?
Let's not forget it's I who carry the loads, pay the bills. [*He rises;
paces nervously. To himself.*] Only three pears to a kilo! How
would you manage? Do I find the money lying on the ground?
I earn it myself, with these two hands! [*He beats his calloused
hands.*] . . . I divide the food equally—equally I say—and I
mean four equal portions. Even my son gets an equal portion,
my own son, my own flesh and blood. But she . . . [*His expression
of scorn is weakened by the severe glance from his* WIFE. *Pause.
He still walks about nervously, looking at his watch. Then,
almost to himself.*] You can be sure she's not about to . . . [*He
stops as his* WIFE *looks at him with tears in her eyes.*]

WIFE: To . . . ? Go on.

HUSBAND [*Cautiously.*]: . . . to do something crazy. No normal
person would, just because she had a bottle of oil taken away . . .
[*His* WIFE's *gaze is so painful that he does not have the courage
to continue.*]

WIFE: You started to say something else. You were thinking . . .
[*Pause.*]

HUSBAND [*Admitting it.*]: I was "thinking," maybe. She could
do anything. She's crazy. At least, I think she's crazy. I know
you don't think so. You're her daughter and you know her
better—you're the one who brought her here, under my nose.

[*Without conviction.*] She's stubborn, that one. She does all right for herself in this world. [*Aware of his* WIFE's *suffering, he controls himself. Pause.*] Is it my fault? Is it my fault? Tell me . . . I do my best. I try to be kind. What can I do with the little I earn? The fruit, for example. Is it my fault if there isn't any? She wouldn't touch it, she refused. She was being stubborn not to eat any. We've saved by not buying it, by getting along without it. A saving . . . a saving that lets all of us—and that means her, too—a saving that lets all of us have more meat and some vegetables. And always equal portions. You dish them out . . . Actually, you favor your mother—sometimes . . . And I keep quiet. She uses my shoe polish for her shoes . . . And I keep quiet; my toothpaste . . . and I keep quiet. What more do you want? What do you expect? [*Plaintively.*] And the little gift for her birthday, and the new shawl, and the little bit of cream in her coffee—she's the only one who takes it . . . [*Flinging his arms.*] More than that! . . . [*Trying to justify himself; fearing the worst, he often glances at his watch; impatiently.*] Have I ever laid a hand on her? . . . After all, I've a right too, you know! I'm the boss here! . . . [*Ironically.*] "The boss." I can't even walk around in my shorts if I want to. Only two rooms and she's always underfoot. I don't know how she manages to be everywhere. Even "there," always when I have to . . . [*Alarmed by his* WIFE's *sobs.*] Months ago, when I threw the plate . . . do you remember? It was during the time when they were threatening to lay us off. I was furious—the boy was in bed, sick, we needed her to go to the drugstore, and where was she? . . . She was out—who knows where!—I could have killed her! On top of everything, I should have to worry about her too? ! If she breaks her leg, or ends up in jail . . . or in hell! I've my son to think about; I have my wife! [*He is worried; goes toward his* WIFE *who avoids him.*] Even our life has changed, thanks to her . . . We've no privacy. We're like strangers, you and I. If we quarrel, it's because of her. Because I've counted the rolls, measured the wine, given her share to the boy. [*Shouting.*] Don't I have the right to? Do I have the right, yes or no? [*Calming himself; he wants a word from his* WIFE, *who avoids him; she fears, as he does, perhaps more than he, the irreparable; long tense pause.*] She's probably with one of her friends . . . gossiping about us . . . even about you . . . because she's jealous . . . [WIFE *looks at him with surprise; she does not understand; he explains.*] . . . that I give you money, that you can buy things, make your own decisions. I've seen how she watches you in the evening when you're working on your budget. And it wouldn't surprise me if . . . [*The* WIFE *looks at him with reproof. He changes his mind and the accusation of theft is avoided. Pause.*] It's no use. Let's forget it. [*Pause.*] But if you think she appreciates your care . . . [*His* WIFE *looks at him with eyes filled with tears; he drops the argument. Trying to justify himself.*] In any case . . . [*Gesture of "washing his hands."*] I deserve, if nothing else, the credit for giving her a roof and for feeding her. [*Firmly.*] No, it's not my fault and I hope you agree with me on this. [*Long pause. No reply from the completely dejected* WIFE, *who is upset by words that confirm her own fears.*] You must speak. You must admit that I've always tried to do my best. I'm not to blame. No blame if . . .

WIFE [*Looking at him sadly*]: If . . . ?

HUSBAND [*After a pause.*]: . . . she decides to do something crazy . . . [*Weakly.*] If she goes complaining to someone . . .

WIFE: That's not what you're really thinking! You know that she's never complained. She wouldn't ask sympathy from anyone.

HUSBAND: Sympathy, why? Why should she? What have I done to her?

WIFE [*Insistent, severe.*]: That's not what you're thinking.

HUSBAND [*After a pause; with false irony in his voice.*]: You don't mean "suicide"!? Not that one! [*Pause while the* WIFE *stares at him.*] All right she's . . . [*Gesture indicating insanity.*] You know her better than I. You know that . . .

WIFE [*Exploding.*]: We've tortured her . . . You and I. You—I, all of us . . . even the little one, copying us . . . over petty, miserable trifles . . .

HUSBAND: Tortured her? We? Who's taken the bread out of his mouth for her? Who? Your sister? Did your sister want her? Oh no. She's clever [*Seized by a sudden thought.*] And now . . . She'll have the nerve, yes, she'll have the nerve to accuse us . . .

WIFE [*Sadly, at this final confirmation.*]: You're even thinking that! . . . thinking that . . . Oh, it's my fault, all my fault! I'm her daughter!—I!—It was my duty to take care of her, to help her . . .

HUSBAND [*Trying to convince her.*]: It's not your fault. It's the sad fate of old people . . . to live badly . . . The time comes in their lives when they realize they're a burden and . . .

WIFE [*Decisively.*]: I'm going! I'm going to see . . . You're thinking the same, the same thing . . . You believe it, too.

HUSBAND [*Holding her back.*]: It's useless . . . Whatever has happened to her . . . It's useless. It's better to wait here. At least, let's convince ourselves of this, that it's not our fault. It's better to prepare . . .

WIFE [*Alarmed.*]: What? Prepare what?

HUSBAND: . . . what to say . . . to your sister . . . to others . . .

WIFE [*Convulsively.*]: What time is it?

HUSBAND [*Delaying her.*]: It's late. She's never stayed out this late. Maybe she's complaining and trying to get some sympathy . . . or maybe she's begging to be put up for the night . . . No. It's impossible. We'd been told by now . . . And you know by whom? She herself . . . out of guilt . . . She's a good woman . . . I realize that I've been brusque with her at times . . . [*With regret, sincerely.*] It's the work, the worries; even the air here costs money. Everything falls on my shoulders. One needs peace of mind to be kind; one needs to have money not to count the drops of oil or the sections of an orange. I've always liked her, poor thing . . . Do you realize that even my mother lives this way? She's being fed crumbs . . . enduring every humiliation . . . It's not my fault, I swear it . . . I've always had veneration and respect for the old. I remember . . . many years ago, when I was child, an old woman asked me to help her down some steps. I even gave her two pennies—it was all I had. She didn't want it. She was rich . . . I didn't understand, then, the difference between a rich person and a poor one. To me old age went hand in hand with misery . . . I thought it was a rule of life. And that even my mother must, some day, stretch out her hand . . . [*He is greatly moved and tender.*]

[*At this moment the* WIFE'S MOTHER *appears in the doorway. She is very humble. The* HUSBAND *jumps to his feet in great surprise, transformed. The daughter is surprised but does not dare to show her relief fearing her* HUSBAND, *who is tense, ready to attack. The old woman timidly moves toward the table but does not have the courage to sit down.*]

HUSBAND [*Irritated; sarcastic; making a deep bow*]: Won't you sit down, duchess? [*He gets the plate with the old woman's supper and almost throws it on the table.*] Buon appetito! [*Very sarcastic.*] Or would you like me to warm it up for you? [*It is evident that he has no intention of doing so; rather, he would like to strike her. The old woman does not dare to eat.*]

HUSBAND [*With anger, very aggressive.*]: Where have you been, old woman? Where? Where? Where? You're driving us crazy, you . . .

WIFE [*With some gentleness.*]: He's right, Mamma . . .

MOTHER [*Looking only at her daughter; with humility.*]: I fell asleep . . . at the cemetery . . .

HUSBAND: At the cemetery? [*With his hands to his face.*] Oh, my God, what next?

MOTHER [*Timidly.*]: It's a year today . . . since your little daughter . . . I bought a few flowers and . . . [*Long pause. The two had forgotten the date.*]

HUSBAND [*Embarrassed.*] Flowers . . . Flowers [*Suddenly, to his* WIFE.] Where did she get the money? Did *you* give it to her?

[*A reproving look from the* WIFE *makes him regret this. He goes out slamming the door, turns back and turns off the central light; leaves, muttering to himself. Only the dim light lamp at right remains. The daughter is moved, but does not have the courage to show her any affection. She puts things in order for a bit, then follows her* HUSBAND *out. The old* MOTHER, *alone, bent by the weight of living, nibbles the food without desire.*]

Curtain